ENSEMBLE LEARNING
Pattern Classification Using Ensemble Methods

Second Edition

SERIES IN MACHINE PERCEPTION AND ARTIFICIAL INTELLIGENCE*

ISSN: 1793-0839

Editors: **H. Bunke** (University of Bern, Switzerland)
P. S. P. Wang (Northeastern University, USA)
Joseph Lladós (Autonomous University of Barcelona, Spain)

This book series addresses all aspects of machine perception and artificial intelligence. Of particular interest are the areas of pattern recognition, image processing, computer vision, natural language understanding, speech processing, neural computing, machine learning, hardware architectures, software tools, and others. The series includes publications of various types, for example, textbooks, monographs, edited volumes, conference and workshop proceedings, PhD theses with significant impact, and special issues of the International Journal of Pattern Recognition and Artificial Intelligence.

Published

*The complete list of the published volumes in the series can be found at
http://www.worldscientific.com/series/smpai

Series in Machine Perception and Artificial Intelligence – Vol. 85

ENSEMBLE LEARNING

Pattern Classification Using Ensemble Methods

Second Edition

Lior Rokach

Ben-Gurion University of the Negev, Israel

 **World Scientific**

NEW JERSEY · LONDON · SINGAPORE · BEIJING · SHANGHAI · HONG KONG · TAIPEI · CHENNAI

Published by

World Scientific Publishing Co. Pte. Ltd.

5 Toh Tuck Link, Singapore 596224

USA office: 27 Warren Street, Suite 401-402, Hackensack, NJ 07601

UK office: 57 Shelton Street, Covent Garden, London WC2H 9HE

British Library Cataloguing-in-Publication Data
A catalogue record for this book is available from the British Library.

Series in Machine Perception and Artificial Intelligence — Volume 85
ENSEMBLE LEARNING
Pattern Classification Using Ensemble Methods
Second Edition

ISBN 978-981-120-195-0

For any available supplementary material, please visit
https://www.worldscientific.com/worldscibooks/10.1142/11325#t=suppl

Printed in Singapore

In memory of my parents,
Ines and Avraham Rokach,
who taught me the value of education and hard work

———————

L.R.

Preface

Machine learning provides computational systems the ability to perform various tasks, such as filtering spam emails, without being explicitly programmed. Instead, these systems improve their performance on a task by learning from data that represents previous experience. Machine learning is also used for automatically discovering useful patterns in large and complex bodies of data. Given the vast amount of data collected today, it is not surprising that machine learning has become the fastest growing sub-area of artificial intelligence, with a wide range of applications, such as autonomous cars and intelligent personal assistants.

A large body of research in the field of machine learning suggests that two approaches are currently dominating this field: deep learning and ensemble learning. Deep learning is known for its ability to automatically discover a useful representation from raw data such as images and audio. Ensemble learning is known to excel in inducing models from tabular data that is already represented using meaningful features. This book is dedicated entirely to ensemble learning and covers all aspects of this important and fascinating approach.

Ensemble learning imitates our second nature to seek several opinions before making a crucial decision. The core principle is to weigh the outcomes of several individual models and combine them in order to reach an outcome that is more accurate than the one obtained by each individual model.

Researchers from various disciplines, such as machine learning, data science, statistics, and pattern recognition, have explored the use of ensemble methods since the late nineteen seventies. Given the growing interest in the field, it is not surprising that researchers and practitioners have a wide variety of methods at their disposal. *Ensemble Learning: Pattern Classification*

Using Ensemble Methods aims to provide a methodic and well-structured introduction to this world by presenting a coherent and unified repository of ensemble methods, theories, trends, challenges, and applications.

The first edition of the book was published a decade ago. The book was well-received by the machine learning and data science communities and was translated into Chinese. The positive reception, along with the fast pace of research in the fields of machine learning and data science, motivated me to update the first edition. I received many requests to include new methods, as well as new applications and software tools that have become available in recent years, in the second edition of the book. The second edition aims to update the previously presented material on the fundamental areas, and to present new findings in the field; more than a third of this edition is comprised of new material.

Its informative pages will provide researchers, students, and practitioners in industry with a comprehensive, yet concise and convenient, resource on ensemble learning methods. The book provides detailed descriptions of the classic methods, as well as extensions and novel approaches that have recently been introduced. Along with algorithmic descriptions of each method, the reader is provided with a description of the settings in which each method is applicable and the consequences and tradeoffs incurred by using the method.

The book consists of nine chapters. Chapter 1 presents the machine learning foundations that are required for reading the book. Chapter 2 provides an in depth introduction to the notion of classification and regression trees, and the algorithms used for learning a tree from data. Chapter 3 introduces the basic algorithmic framework for building an ensemble of models. Specific building blocks for designing and implementing ensemble methods are presented in Chapter 4. Chapter 5 is dedicated to Gradient Boosting Machines which currently dominate applied machine learning and are popular due to their ubiquity in many of the winning solutions of data science challenges. Chapter 6 discusses the important aspect of ensemble diversity. Ensemble selection methods for improving the computational and predictive performance of ensemble models are presented in Chapter 7. Chapter 8 presents the idea of Error-Correcting Output Codes and their usefulness in addressing multi-task and multi-label tasks. Finally, Chapter 9 discusses how ensembles should be evaluated. Several selection criteria are proposed, all of which are presented from a practitioner's standpoint, for choosing the most effective ensemble method.

Throughout the book, special emphasis was placed on the use of illustrative examples. Accordingly, in addition to ensemble theory, the reader is also provided with an abundance of real-world applications from a wide range of fields. The data referred to in this book, as well as most of the R implementations of the presented algorithms, can be obtained via the World Wide Web.

One of the key goals of this book is to provide researchers in the fields of machine learning, data science, computer science, statistics, and management with a critical resource on the topic of ensemble techniques. In addition, the book will prove to be highly beneficial to those engaged in research in the social sciences, psychology, medicine, genetics, and other fields that confront complex data processing problems.

The material in this book serves as optional reading in the "Machine Learning" graduate course taught at the Ben-Gurion University of the Negev. In addition, I am using it as the main textbook for the short course in "ensemble learning" to be held at the 5th International Winter School on Big Data in Cambridge, United Kingdom. This book can also serve as an excellent reference book for graduate, as well as advanced undergraduate, courses in data science. Descriptions of applications that utilize ensemble learning may be of particular interest to the practitioners among the readers. The book is rigorous and requires comprehension of problems and solutions via their mathematical descriptions. Nevertheless, I tried to keep the book as self-contained as possible and assume only basic background knowledge of basic probability theory and computer science (algorithms).

Acknowledgments

Many thanks are owed to Ms. Robin Levy-Stevenson. She has been most helpful in proofreading the new edition and improving the manuscript. Many colleagues generously provided comments on drafts. Many graduate students have also read parts of the manuscript and offered helpful suggestions, and I thank them for that. I am grateful to the readers who have found errors in the first edition; I apologize for those errors, and I have done my best to avoid errors in the new edition.

I would also like to thank to Prof. Horst Bunke and Prof. Patrick Shen-Pei Wang for including my book in their important series in machine perception and artificial intelligence. I also extend my thanks to Mr. Steven Patt, editor, and staff members of World Scientific Publishing for their kind cooperation throughout the writing process of this book.

Last, but certainly not least, I owe special gratitude to my wife and four sons for their patience, time, support, and encouragement.

Lior Rokach
Ben-Gurion University of the Negev
Beer-Sheva, Israel
Hanukkah, December 2018

Contents

Chapter 1

Introduction to Machine Learning

Artificial intelligence (AI) is a scientific discipline that aims to create intelligent machines. Machine learning is a popular and practical AI subfield that aims to automatically improve the performance of computer programs through experience. In particular, machine learning enables computers to perform various tasks by learning from past experience rather than being explicitly programmed.

Various domains such as commerce, biology, medicine, engineering, and cyber-security apply machine learning in order to gain new insights regarding the task in question. Google search engine is an excellent example of a service that applies machine learning on a regular basis. It is well-known that Google tracks users clicks in an attempt to improve the relevance of its search engine results and its advertising capabilities. Moreover, users queries can be analyzed over time for shedding light on the publics interests. Specifically, the Google Trends service enables anyone to view search trends for a topic across regions of the world, including comparative trends of two or more topics. Entrepreneurs use this service to identify new business opportunities and economists are using it to predict market movements [Ball (2013)]. In particular, this service can help in epidemiological studies by aggregating certain search terms that are found to be good indicators of an investigated disease. For example, Ginsberg *et al.* (2008) used search engine query data to detect influenza epidemics. They observed that a pattern forms when all the flu-related phrases are accumulated. An analysis of these various searches reveals that many search terms associated with flu tend to be popular exactly when its flu season.

One of the main goals of machine learning is to be able to make accurate predictions about specific phenomena. However, prediction is not an easy task. As the famous quote says, "It is difficult to make predictions, especially about the future" (attributed to Mark Twain and others). Yet, we rely on prediction all the time, and it guides our behavior and the decisions and choices we make. For example, the popular YouTube website (also owned by Google) analyzes our viewing habits in order to predict other videos we might like. Based on this prediction, YouTube presents us with personalized recommendations which are largely on target. In order to get a rough idea of YouTubes capabilities in this regard you could simply ask yourself how often watching a video on YouTube leads you to watch other similar videos that were recommended to you by the service? Similarly, online social networks (OSNs), such as Facebook and LinkedIn, make predictions in order to automatically suggest friends and acquaintances that we might want to connect with.

Most machine learning techniques are based on inductive learning [Mitchell (1997)], where a model is constructed explicitly or implicitly by generalizing from a sufficient number of training examples. The underlying assumption of the inductive approach is that the trained model is applicable to future unseen examples. In other words, any machine learning method based on inductive learning relies on the training set and assumes that future data shares its characteristics.

Strictly speaking, any form of inference in which the conclusions are not deductively implied by the premises can be thought of as an induction. More formally Mitchell defines machine learning as a computer program that improves at task (T) with respect to performance measure (P) based on experience (E).

Traditionally, data collection was regarded as one of the most important stages in data analysis. An analyst (e.g., a statistician or data scientist) would use the available domain knowledge to select the variables to be collected. The number of variables selected was usually limited, and the collection of their values could be done manually (e.g., utilizing handwritten records or oral interviews). In the case of computer-aided analysis, the analyst had to enter the collected data into a statistical computer package or an electronic spreadsheet. Due to the high cost of data collection, people learned to make decisions based on limited information.

Since the dawn of the big data age, accumulating and storing data has become easier and inexpensive. It has been estimated that the amount of stored information doubles every twenty months [Frawley *et al.* (1991)]. Unfortunately, as the amount of machine-readable information increases, the ability to understand and make use of it does not keep pace with its growth.

1.1 Supervised Learning

1.1.1 *Overview*

In the machine learning community, prediction methods are commonly referred to as supervised learning. In contrast, unsupervised learning refers to modeling the distribution of instances in a typical, high-dimensional input space. According to [Kohavi and Provost (1998)], the term "unsupervised learning" refers to "learning techniques that group instances without a prespecified dependent attribute." .

Supervised methods are methods that attempt to discover the relationship between input attributes (sometimes called independent variables) and a target attribute (sometimes referred to as a dependent variable). The relationship that is discovered is represented in a structure referred to as a *Model*. Usually, models describe and explain phenomena which are hidden in the dataset, and they can be used for predicting the value of the target attribute whenever the values of the input attributes are known.

Supervised learning methods can be implemented in a variety of domains such as marketing, finance, and manufacturing. It is useful to distinguish between two main supervised learning models: *Classification Models (Classifiers)* and *Regression Models*. Regression models map the input space into a real-valued domain. For instance, a regression model can predict the demand for a certain product given its characteristics. Classifiers map the input space into predefined classes. For example, classifiers can be used to classify mortgage consumers as good and bad. There are many alternatives for representing classifiers, including support vector machines, decision trees, probabilistic summaries, algebraic function, etc.

1.1.2 *The Classification Task*

This book deals mainly with classification problems. Along with regression and probability estimation, classification is one of the most studied supervised learning tasks, and possibly the one with the greatest practical relevance to real-world applications.

For example, we may wish to classify flowers from the Iris genus into their subgeni (such as Iris Setosa, Iris Versicolour, and Iris Virginica). In this case, the input vector will consist of the flowers features, such as the length and width of the sepal and petal. The label of each instance will be one of the strings *Iris Setosa*, *Iris Versicolour* and *Iris Virginica*, or alternatively, the labels can take a value from 1,2,3, a,b,c or any other set of three distinct values.

Another common example of classification task is optical character recognition (OCR). These applications convert scanned documents into machine-readable text in order to simplify their storage and retrieval. Each document undergoes three steps. First, an operator scans the document. This converts the document into a bitmap image. Next, the scanned document is segmented such that each character is isolated from the others. Then, a *feature extractor* measures certain features of each character such as open areas, closed shapes, diagonal lines, and line intersections. Finally, the scanned characters are associated with their corresponding alphanumeric character. The association is made by applying a machine learning algorithm to the features of the scanned characters. In this case, the set of labels/categories/classes are the set of all letters, numbers, punctuation marks, etc.

In order to better understand the notion of classification, consider the problem of email spam. We all suffer from email spam in which spammers exploit electronic mail systems to send unsolicited bulk messages. A spam message is any message that the user does not want to receive and did not ask to receive. In order to address the problem of spam email, machine learning is used to train a classification model for detecting spam email messages.

The spam detection model can be trained using past emails that were manually labeled as either spam or not spam. Each training example is usually represented as a set of attributes or features that characterize it. In the case of spam detection, the words in the email's content can be used as the features. The machine learning algorithm aims to generalize from these examples and automatically classify future emails. In particular, the model, which has been trained by analyzing the text of spam emails, looks for incriminating content in a users new unlabeled emails. The more training data the system has, the more accurate it becomes.

Recall that machine learning aims to improve performance for some task with experience. Note that we have the following three components:

(1) Task T that we would like to improve with learning
(2) Experience E to be used for learning
(3) Performance measure P that is used to measure the improvement

In the spam detection case, the task T is to identify spam emails. The performance measures P are the ratio of spam emails that were correctly filtered and the ratio of non-spam emails that were incorrectly filtered out. Finally, the experience E is a database of emails that were received by the user. All emails that were reported by the user as spam are considered as positive examples, while the remaining emails are assumed to be non-spam emails (negative examples).

In order to automatically filter spam messages we need to train a classification model. Obviously, data is very crucial for training the classifier or, as Prof. Deming puts it: "In God we trust; all others must bring data."

The data that is used to train the model is called the "training set." In the spam filtering example, a training set in the form of a database of previous emails. Possible attributes that can be used as indicators of spam activity are: number of recipients, size of message, number of attachments, number of times the string "re" appears in the subject line, country from which the email is sent, etc.

The training set is usually represented as a table. Each row represents a single email instance that was delivered via the mail server. Each column corresponds to an attribute that characterizes the email instance (such as the number of recipients). In any supervised learning task and particularly in classification tasks, one column corresponds to the target attribute that we are trying to predict. In our example the target attribute indicates if the email is spam or ham (non-spam). All other columns contain the input attributes that are used for making the predicted classification. There are three main types of input attributes:

(1) Numeric - such as in the case of the attribute "number of recipients."
(2) Ordinal - provides an order by which the data can be sorted, but unlike the numeric attribute type, there is no notion of distance. For example, the medal awarded in a competition (gold, silver, and bronze) can serve as an ordinal attribute.
(3) Nominal - in which the values are merely distinct names or labels with no meaningful order by which one can sort the data. For example, the gender attribute can be considered a nominal value.

Note that the term categorical attribute refers to any variable that can get two or more categorical values. Categorical attribute can be divided into two subtypes: nominal and ordinal.

Since in many machine learning algorithms, the training set size and the predictive performance are positively correlated, it is usually preferable to use the largest possible training set. In practice, however, we might want to limit the training set size due to resource constraints. Having a large training set implies that the training time will be long as well; therefore, we might select a subset of the data that fits our computational resources. Moreover, data collection and particularly labeling the instances may come with a price tag in terms of human effort. In our email filtering example, labeling the training emails as either "spam" or "ham" is done manually by the users, and therefore it might be too expensive to label all of the emails in the training set.

1.1.3   *Mathematical Notation for Supervised Learning*

In a typical supervised learning setting, a set of instances S, also referred to as a *training set* is provided. The labels of the instances in S are known, and the goal is to construct a classification model (or simply classifier) in order to label new instances.

A learning algorithm aims to train the classifier by generalizing from training examples. For example, a decision tree learning algorithm builds a decision tree model that predicts the value of a class based on several input attributes.

The training set can be described in a variety of ways. Most frequently, each pattern is described by a vector of *feature* values. Each vector belongs to a single class and is associated with the class label. In this case, the training set is stored in a table in which each row consists of a different pattern. Let A and y denote the set of n features: $A = \{a_1, \ldots, a_i, \ldots, a_n\}$ and the class label, respectively.

Features, which are also referred to as attributes, typically fall into one of the following two categories:

Nominal the values are members of an unordered set. In this case, it is useful to denote the attributes domain values by $dom(a_i) = \{v_{i,1}, v_{i,2}, \ldots, v_{i,|dom(a_i)|}\}$, where $|dom(a_i)|$ is the finite cardinality of the domain.

Numeric the values are real numbers. Numeric features have infinite cardinalities.

In a similar way, $dom(y) = \{c_1, c_2, \ldots, c_k\}$ constitutes the set of labels. Table 1.1 illustrates a segment of the Iris dataset. This is one of the best known datasets in the pattern recognition literature. It was first introduced by R. A. Fisher (1936). The goal in this case is to classify flowers into the Iris subgeni according to their characteristic features.

The dataset contains three classes that correspond to three types of Iris flowers: $dom(y) = \{IrisSetosa, IrisVersicolor, IrisVirginica\}$. Each pattern is characterized by four numeric features (measured in centimeters): $A = \{sepallength, sepalwidth, petallength, petalwidth\}$.

Table 1.1: The Iris dataset consisting of four numeric features and three possible classes.

Sepal Length	Sepal Width	Petal Length	Petal Width	Class (Iris Type)
5.1	3.5	1.4	0.2	Iris-setosa
4.9	3.0	1.4	0.2	Iris-setosa
6.0	2.7	5.1	1.6	Iris-versicolor
5.8	2.7	5.1	1.9	Iris-virginica
5.0	3.3	1.4	0.2	Iris-setosa
5.7	2.8	4.5	1.3	Iris-versicolor
5.1	3.8	1.6	0.2	Iris-setosa
$\vdots$				

The instance space (the set of all possible examples) is defined as a Cartesian product of all of the input attribute domains: $X = dom(a_1) \times dom(a_2) \times \ldots \times dom(a_n)$. The universal instance space (or the *labeled instance space*) U is defined as a Cartesian product of all of input attribute domains and the target attribute domain, i.e.: $U = X \times dom(y)$.

The training set is denoted by $S(B)$, and it is composed of m tuples.

$$S(B) = (\langle x_1, y_1 \rangle, \ldots, \langle x_m, y_m \rangle) \tag{1.1}$$

where $x_q \in X$ and $y_q \in dom(y), q = 1, \ldots, m$.

Usually, it is assumed that the training set tuples are randomly generated and independently distributed according to some fixed and unknown joint probability distribution D over U. Note that this is a generalization of the deterministic case in which a supervisor classifies a tuple using a function $y = f(x)$.

As mentioned above, the goal of an inducer is to train classifiers. In general, a classifier partitions the instance space according to the labels of the patterns in the training set. The borders separating the regions are called *frontiers*, and inducers construct frontiers such that new patterns will be classified into the correct region. Specifically, given a training set S with input attribute set $A = \{a_1, a_2, \ldots, a_n\}$ and a nominal target attribute y

from an unknown fixed distribution D, as defined above, the objective is to induce an optimal classifier with minimum generalization error.

Generalization error is defined as the misclassification rate for the distribution D. Formally, let I be an inducer. By $I(S)$ we denote the classifier that is generated by I for the training set S. The classification that is produced by $I(S)$ when it is applied to a pattern x is denoted by $I(S)(x)$. In the case of nominal attributes, the generalization error can be expressed as:

$$\varepsilon(I(S), D) = \sum_{\langle x,y \rangle \in U} D(x, y) \cdot L_{0-1}(y, I(S)(x)) \qquad (1.2)$$

where $L_{0-1}(y, I(S)(x))$ is the zero-one loss function defined as:

$$L_{0-1}(y, I(S)(x)) = \begin{cases} 0 \; if \; y = I(S)(x) \\ 1 \; if \; y \neq I(S)(x) \end{cases} \qquad (1.3)$$

In the case of numeric attributes, the sum operator is replaced with the integration operator.

Loss functions are used to evaluate how well a model fit the data. The loss value represents the price paid for inaccuracy of predictions made by the model. While the zero-one loss presented in Eq. 1.3 is intuitively appealing, it is not always useful, since it is non-convex and non-differentiable.

As a result, it is better to use other differentiable loss functions that are tractable for commonly used learning algorithms. These functions are called surrogate loss functions because they serve as a proxy to the natural loss function (zero-one loss function in this case). Such functions are presented in Figure 1.1.

The hinge loss that is defined as:

$$L_{Hinge}(y, I(S)(x)) = \max(0, 1 - y \times I(S)(x)) \qquad (1.4)$$

Here we assume that the binary labels (the value of y) are encoded with +1 and -1, and the classifier can output any numeric value (positive or negative). The term $y \times I(S)(x)$ is called the margin. When the classifier misclassifies an instance, the margin has a negative value (since the signs disagree). The hinge loss provides a relatively tight, convex upper bound on the zero-loss function.

The square loss is defined:

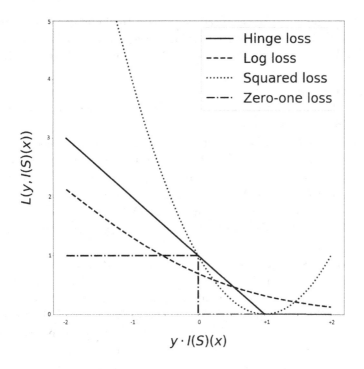

Fig. 1.1: Various loss functions.

$$L_{Squared}\left(y, I\left(S\right)\left(x\right)\right) = \left(y - I\left(S\right)\left(x\right)\right)^2 \tag{1.5}$$

The logistic loss function is defined as:

$$L_{Logisticloss}\left(y, I\left(S\right)\left(x\right)\right) = \frac{1}{\ln 2} \ln(1 + e^{-y \times I(S)(x)}) \tag{1.6}$$

Similarly to the logistic loss, the cross entropy loss (also known as the log loss) is defined as:

$$L_{Logisticloss}\left(t, I\left(S\right)\left(x\right)\right) = -t\ln(I\left(S\right)\left(x\right)) - (1 - t)\ln(1 - I\left(S\right)\left(x\right)) \tag{1.7}$$

Here we are using the alternative label convention $t = (1+y)/2 \in \{0, 1\}$.

1.2 Induction Algorithms

An *induction algorithm*, or more concisely an *inducer* (also known as learner), is an algorithm that gets a training set as an input and constructs a model that generalizes the connection between the input attributes and the target attribute. For example, an inducer may take specific training patterns with their corresponding class labels as input and produce a *classifier*.

Given ongoing productive research and recent advances in the field of pattern classification, there are several established approaches to induction available to practitioners.

An essential component of most classifiers is a model which specifies how a new pattern is classified. The model's representation varies by inducer. For example, C4.5 [Quinlan (1993)] represents the model as a decision tree, while the Naïve Bayes [Duda and Hart (1973)] inducer represents a model in the form of probabilistic summaries. Furthermore, inducers can be deterministic (as in the case of C4.5) or stochastic (as in the case of back propagation).

There two ways in which a new pattern can be classified. The classifier can either explicitly assign a certain class to the pattern (Crisp classifier) or, alternatively, the classifier can produce a vector of the conditional probability that the given pattern belongs to each class (Probabilistic classifier). In this case it is possible to estimate the conditional probability $\hat{P}_{I(S)}(y = c_j | a_i = x_{q,i} ; i = 1, \ldots, n)$ for an observation x_q. Note that the addition of the "hat" to the conditional probability estimation is used for distinguishing it from the actual conditional probability. Inducers that can construct probabilistic classifiers are known as *Probabilistic inducers*.

The following sections briefly review some of the common approaches to supervised learning: decision tree induction, neural networks, genetic algorithms, instance-based learning, statistical methods, Bayesian methods, and support vector machines. This review focuses on methods that are described in further detail later in this book.

1.3   Rule Induction

Rule induction algorithms generate a set of *if-then* rules that describes the classification process. The main advantage of this approach is its high comprehensibility. The rules, which are easy to employ, can be written as a collection of consecutive conditional statements in plain English. Most rule induction algorithms are based on the divide and conquer paradigm [Michalski (1983)]. Consequently, these algorithms: (a) are capable of finding axis-parallel hyperplanes in the attribute space; (b) are well-suited for symbolic domains; and (c) can often easily dispose of irrelevant attributes.

However, rule induction algorithms can experience difficulty when non-axis-parallel frontiers are required to correctly classify the data. Furthermore, they suffer from the *fragmentation problem*, i.e., the available data dwindles as induction progresses [Pagallo and Huassler (1990)]. Another pitfall that should be avoided is the small disjuncts problem. This problem is characterized by rules that cover a very small number of training patterns. Thus, the model fits the training data very well, however, it fails to classify new patterns, resulting in a high generalization error rate [Holte *et al.* (1989)]. This phenomena is usually called *overfitting*.

1.4 Decision Trees

A decision tree is a classifier whose model forms a recursive partition of the instance space. In a decision tree, each internal node splits the instance space into two or more subspaces according to a certain test. In the simplest and most frequent case, each test considers a single attribute, such that the instance space is partitioned according to the attributes value. In the case of numeric attributes, the condition refers to a range. Each leaf is assigned to one class corresponding to the most appropriate target value. Figure 1.2 presents an example of a decision tree that solves the Iris recognition task presented in Table 1.1.

Internal nodes are represented as circles, whereas leaves are denoted by triangles. Each internal node (not a leaf) may have two or more outgoing branches. Each node corresponds to a certain property, and the branches correspond to a range of values. These value ranges must partition the set of values of the given property.

Instances are classified by traversing the tree, starting from the root and continuing down to a leaf, where the path is determined according to the outcome of the partitioning condition at each node. Specifically, we start at the root of a tree and consider the attribute that corresponds to the root. We then determine which outgoing branch the observed value of the given attribute corresponds to. The next node in our path is the one at the end of the chosen branch. We repeat this process and traverse the tree until we reach a leaf.

Note that decision trees can incorporate both nominal and numeric attributes. In the case of numeric attributes, decision trees can be geometrically interpreted as a collection of hyperplanes, each orthogonal to one of the axes.

Naturally, practitioners and decision-makers prefer a less complex deci-

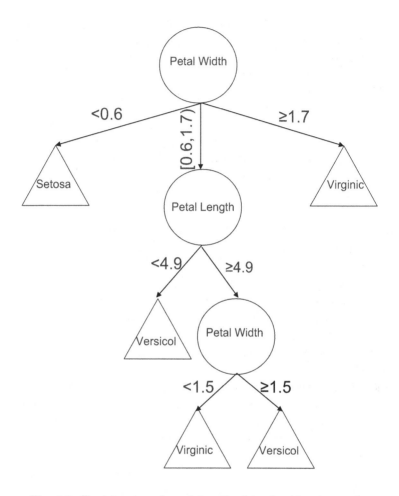

Fig. 1.2: Decision tree for solving the Iris classification task.

sion tree, as it is considered more comprehensible. Furthermore, according to [Breiman *et al.* (1984)], the tree complexity has a crucial effect on its performance accuracy. Usually, large trees are obtained by overfitting the data and hence exhibit poor generalization ability (a pitfall they share with Rule Classifiers). Nevertheless, a large decision tree can generalize well to new patterns, if it was induced without overfitting the data. The tree complexity is explicitly controlled by the stopping criteria used for the construction of the tree and the pruning method that is employed. Common measures for the tree complexity include the following metrics: (a) total number of nodes; (b) total number of leaves; (c) tree depth; and (d) number of attributes used.

Decision tree inducers are algorithms that automatically construct a decision tree from a given dataset. Typically, the goal is to find the optimal decision tree by minimizing the generalization error. However, other target functions can also be defined, for instance, minimizing the number of nodes or minimizing the average depth of the tree.

Construction of an *optimal* decision tree based on a given dataset is considered a difficult task. [Hancock *et al.* (1996)] have shown that finding a *minimal* decision tree for a given training set is NP-hard, while [Hyafil and Rivest (1976)] have proved that constructing a minimal binary tree with respect to the expected number of tests required for classifying an unseen instance is NP-complete. Even finding the minimal equivalent decision tree for a given decision tree [Zantema and Bodlaender (2000)] or building the optimal decision tree from decision tables is known to be NP-hard [Naumov (1991)].

These results indicate that optimal decision tree algorithms are only suitable for very small datasets and a very small number of attributes. Consequently, heuristic methods are required for finding a good enough decision tree. Roughly speaking, these methods can be divided into two groups: methods that employ a top-down approach and methods that follow a bottom-up methodology, with clear preference in the literature to the first group.

There are various top-down decision tree inducers such as ID3 [Quinlan (1986)], C4.5 [Quinlan (1993)], CART [Breiman *et al.* (1984)]. Some inducers consist of two conceptual phases: *Growing* and *Pruning* (C4.5 and CART). Other inducers perform only the growing phase. In the next chapter we will discuss this matter in further detail.

1.5 Bayesian Methods

1.5.1 *Overview*

Bayesian approaches employ probabilistic concept modeling and range from the Naïve Bayes [Domingos and Pazzani (1997)] to Bayesian networks. The basic assumption of Bayesian reasoning is that the attributes are connected via a probability. Moreover, when the problem at hand is supervised, the objective is to find the conditional distribution of the target attribute given the input attribute.

1.5.2   Naïve Bayes

1.5.2.1   The Basic Naïve Bayes Classifier

The most straightforward Bayesian learning method is the Naïve Bayesian inducer [Duda and Hart (1973)]. This method uses a set of discriminant functions for estimating the probability that a given instance belongs to a certain class. Specifically, given an instance, this method uses Bayes rule to compute the probability of each possible value of the target attribute, assuming the input attributes are conditionally independent.

Due to the fact that this method is based on the simplistic, and rather unrealistic, assumption that the causes are conditionally independent given the effect, this method is well known as Naïve Bayes.

The class of the instance is determined according to value of the target attribute which maximizes the following calculated probability:

$$v_{MAP}(x_q) = \underset{c_j \in dom(y)}{\text{argmax}} \ \hat{P}(y = c_j) \cdot \prod_{i=1}^{n} \hat{P}(a_i = x_{q,i} \,|\, y = c_j) \qquad (1.8)$$

where $\hat{P}(y = c_j)$ denotes the estimation of the *a-priori* probability of the target attribute to obtain the value c_j. Similarly, $\hat{P}(a_i = x_{q,i} \,|\, y = c_j)$ denotes the conditional probability of the input attribute a_i to obtain the value $x_{q,i}$ given that the target attribute obtains the value c_j. Note that the above mentioned $\hat{P}$ distinguishes the probability estimation from the actual conditional probability.

A simple estimation for the above probabilities can be obtained using the corresponding frequencies in the training set, namely:

$$\hat{P}(y = c_j) = \frac{|\sigma_{y=c_j} S|}{|S|} \quad ; \quad \hat{P}(a_i = x_{q,i} \,|\, y = c_j) = \frac{|\sigma_{y=c_j \, AND \, a_i = x_{q,i}} S|}{|\sigma_{y=c_j} S|}$$

where $|\sigma_{y=c_j} S|$ denotes the number of instances in S for which $y = c_j$. Using Bayes rule, these equations can be rewritten as:

$$v_{MAP}(x_q) = \underset{c_j \in dom(y)}{\text{argmax}} \ \frac{\prod_{i=1}^{n} \hat{P}(y=c_j \,|\, a_i = x_{q,i})}{\hat{P}(y=c_j)^{n-1}} \qquad (1.9)$$

or, alternatively, after applying the log function as:

$$v_{MAP}(x_q) = \underset{c_j \in dom(y)}{\text{argmax}} \ \log\left(\hat{P}(y = c_j)\right)$$
$$+ \sum_{i=1}^{n} \left(\log\left(\hat{P}(y = c_j \,|\, a_i = x_{q,i})\right) - \log\left(\hat{P}(y = c_j)\right) \right)$$

If the "naive" assumption is true, by the direct application of Bayes' Theorem, this classifier can easily be shown to be optimal (i.e., minimizing the generalization error rate), in the sense of minimizing the misclassification rate or zero-one loss (misclassification rate). In [Domingos and Pazzani (1997)] it was shown that the Naïve Bayes inducer can be optimal under zero-one loss even when the independence assumption is violated by a wide margin. This implies that the Bayesian classifier has a much greater range of applicability than originally assumed, for instance, it can be used for learning conjunctions and disjunctions. Moreover, surprisingly, numerous empirical results show that this method can perform quite well compared to other methods, even in domains where clear attribute dependencies exist.

The computational complexity of the Naïve Bayes classifier is considered very low compared to other methods like decision trees, since no explicit enumeration of possible interactions of various causes is required. More specifically, since the Naïve Bayesian classifier combines simple functions of univariate densities, the complexity of this procedure is $O\,(nm)$. Furthermore, Naïve Bayes classifiers are also very simple and easy to understand [Kononenko (1990)]. Other advantages of the classifier include easy adaptation of the model to incremental learning environments and robustness to irrelevant attributes. The main disadvantage of the Naïve Bayes inducer is that it is limited to simplified models, which in some cases are incapable of representing the complicated nature of a problem. To understand this weakness, consider a target attribute that cannot be explained by a single attribute, for instance, the Boolean exclusive or function (XOR).

The Naïve Bayesian classifier uses all of the available attributes, unless a feature selection procedure is applied as a preprocessing step.

1.5.2.2 *Naïve Bayes Induction for Numeric Attributes*

Originally, the Naïve Bayes classifier assumes that all input attributes are nominal. If this is not the case, there are some options for bypassing the nominal values assumption:

(1) Preprocessing: The numeric attributes are discretized before using the Naïve Bayes approach. [Domingos and Pazzani (1997)] suggested constructing ten equi-length intervals for each numeric attribute (or one per observed value, whichever produces the least number of possible values). Each attribute value is assigned an interval number. There are many other more context-aware discretization methods that can be applied here and probably obtain better results at the cost of high

computational complexity.

(2) Revising the Naïve Bayes: [John and Langley (1995)] suggests using kernel estimation or single variable normal distribution as part of the conditional probability calculation.

1.5.2.3   *Correction to the Probability Estimation*

Using the probability estimation described above as is will typically over-estimate (similar to overfitting in decision trees) the probability. This can be problematic, particularly when a given class and attribute value never co-occur in the training set. This case leads to a zero probability that wipes out the information in all of the other probabilities terms when they are multiplied according to the original Naïve Bayes equation.

There are two known corrections (described below) for the simple probability estimation which circumvent this phenomenon.

1.5.2.4   *Laplace Correction*

According to Laplace's law of succession [Niblett (1987)], the probability of the event $y = c_i$ (y is a random variable, and c_i is a possible outcome of y) which is observed m_i times out of m observations is:

$$\frac{m_i + k p_a}{m + k}$$

where p_a is an *a-priori* probability estimation of the event, and k is the equivalent sample size that determines the weight of the *a-priori* estimation relative to the data observed. According to [Mitchell (1997)], k is referred to as the "equivalent sample size," because it represents an augmentation of the actual observations of m by an additional k virtual samples distributed according to p_a. The ratio above can be rewritten as the weighted average of the *a-priori* probability and the posteriori probability (denoted as p_p):

$$\begin{aligned}
&\frac{m_i + k \cdot p_a}{m + k} \\
&= \frac{m_i}{m} \cdot \frac{m}{m+k} + p_a \cdot \frac{k}{m+k} \\
&= p_p \cdot \frac{m}{m+k} + p_a \cdot \frac{k}{m+k} = \\
&= p_p \cdot w_1 + p_a \cdot w_2
\end{aligned}$$

In the case discussed here the following correction is used:

$$\hat{P}_{Laplace}\left(a_i = x_{q,i} \,|\, y = c_j\right) = \frac{\left|\sigma_{y=c_j \; AND \; a_i = x_{q,i}} S\right| + k \cdot p}{\left|\sigma_{y=c_j} S\right| + k} \tag{1.10}$$

In order to use the correction above, the values of p and k should be determined. There are several possibilities for determining their values. It is possible to use $p = 1/|dom(y)|$ and $k = |dom(y)|$. [Ali and Pazzani (1996)] suggested using $k = 2$ and $p = 1/2$ in any case, even if $|dom(y)| > 2$, in order to emphasize the fact that the estimated event is always compared to the opposite event. Another option is to use $k = |dom(y)|/|S|$ and $p = 1/|dom(y)|$ [Kohavi *et al.* (1997)].

1.5.2.5 *No Match*

According to [Clark and Niblett (1989)], only zero probabilities should be corrected and replaced by the following value: $p_a/|S|$, whereas [Kohavi *et al.* (1997)] suggests using $p_a = 0.5$. An empirical comparison of the Laplace correction and the no-match correction indicates that there is no significant difference between them. However, both of them are significantly better than not performing any correction at all.

1.5.3 *Other Bayesian Methods*

A Bayesian belief network [Pearl (1988)] is a more sophisticated Bayesian-based model that can be used. Usually each node in a Bayesian network represents a certain attribute. The immediate predecessors of a node represent the attributes on which the node depends. By knowing their values, it is possible to determine the conditional distribution of this node. Bayesian networks have the benefit of clearer semantics than more ad hoc methods, and they provide a natural platform for combining domain knowledge (in the initial network structure) and empirical learning (of the probabilities, and possibly of a new structure). However, time complexity of inference in Bayesian networks can be high, and as tools for classification learning they are not yet as developed or well-tested as other approaches. More generally, as [Buntine (1990)] notes, the Bayesian paradigm extends beyond any single representation and forms a framework in which many learning tasks can be usefully studied.

1.6 Other Induction Methods

1.6.1 *Neural Networks*

Neural network methods construct a model using a network of interconnected units called neurons[Anderson and Rosenfeld (2000)]. The neurons are connected in an input/output manner, i.e., the output of one neuron (antecedent) is the input of another (descendant). A neuron may have several antecedents and descendants (including itself in some settings). Every unit performs a simple data processing task by generating an output from the received inputs. The task is usually obtained via a nonlinear function. The most frequently used type of unit incorporating Sigmoidal nonlinearity can be seen as a generalization of a propositional rule, where numeric weights are assigned to antecedents, and the output is graded, rather than binary [Towell and Shavlik (1994)].

The multilayer feedforward neural network is the most widely studied neural network, because it is suitable for representing functional relationships between a set of input attributes and one or more target attributes. In a multilayer feedforward neural network the neurons are organized in layers. Figure 1.3 illustrates a typical feedforward neural network. This network consists of neurons (also referred to as nodes) organized in three layers: an input layer, a hidden layer, and an output layer. The neurons in the input layer correspond to the input attributes and the neurons in the output layer correspond to the target attribute. The neurons in the hidden layer are connected to both the input and the output neurons, and they are the key to the induction of the classifier. Note that the signal flow is directed from the input layer to the output layer, and there are no loops.

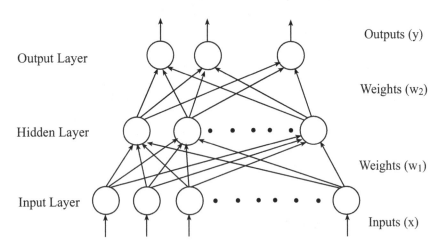

Fig. 1.3: Three-layer feedforward neural network.

In order to construct a classifier from a neural network inducer, a *train-*

ing step must be employed. The training step calculates the connection weights which optimize a given evaluation function of the training data. Various search methods can be used to train these networks, of which the most widely applied is back propagation [Rumelhart *et al.* (1986)]. This method efficiently propagates values of the output evaluation function backward to the input, allowing the network weights to be adapted so as to obtain a better evaluation score. Radial basis function (RBF) networks employ Gaussian nonlinearity in the neurons [Moody and Darken (1989)] and can be viewed as a generalization of nearest neighbor methods with an exponential distance function [Poggio and Girosi (1990)].

Most neural networks are based on a unit called a *perceptron*. A perceptron performs the following: (a) it calculates a linear combination of its inputs, and (b) it invokes an activation function which transforms the weighted sum into a binary output. Figure 1.4 illustrates a perceptron.

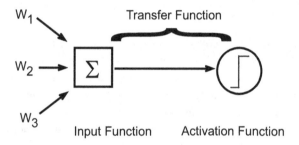

Fig. 1.4: The perceptron.

Using a single perceptron, it is possible to realize any binary decision function (two-class classification) that can be modeled as a hyperplane in the inputs attribute space. Any instance on one side of the hyperplane is assigned to one class, and instances on the other side are assigned to the other class. The equation for this hyperplane is:

$$\sum_{i=1}^{n} w_i \cdot x_i = 0$$

where each w_i is a real-valued weight that determines the contribution of each input signal x_i to the perceptron output.

Neural networks are remarkable for their learning efficiency and tend to outperform other methods (like decision trees) when the information required for the classification is not concentrated in a small subset of the attributes but rather is spread across many of the attributes. Furthermore, neural networks can be trained incrementally, i.e., they can easily be adjusted as new training examples become available.

However, according to [Lu *et al.* (1996)], the drawbacks of applying neural networks to data mining include: difficulty in interpreting the model, difficulty in incorporating prior knowledge about the application domain, and long training time, both in terms of CPU time and the time it takes to manually find parameter settings that will enable successful learning, i.e., optimize the evaluation function. The rule extraction algorithm described in [Lu *et al.* (1996)] uses the neural network structure effectively. The algorithm extracts the (Boolean) rules in a deterministic manner without using the connection weights. The network is then pruned by removal of redundant links and units, with the exception of attributes (Feature selection) whose removal is not considered.

1.6.2   *Genetic Algorithms*

Genetic algorithms are a collection of search methods that can be used to train a wide variety of models, of which the most frequently used is likely *rule sets* [Booker *et al.* (1989)]. Genetic algorithms maintain a population of classifiers during the training, as opposed to just the one classifier used in other search methods. They employ an iterative process that strives to find an optimal classifier by improving the evaluation performance of the classifier population. In order to achieve this, pairs of classifiers that achieve better performance are chosen. Random mutations are applied to the classifier pair and some of them are exchanged between them. This process has a lower chance of reaching a local minima than the simple greedy search employed in most learners does. However, this process may incur a high computational cost. Furthermore, there is a higher risk of producing poor classifiers that accidentally perform well on the training data.

1.6.3   *Instancebased Learning*

Instancebased learning algorithms [Aha *et al.* (1991)] are non-parametric general classification algorithms that classify a new unlabeled instance according to the labels of similar instances in the training set. At the core of these algorithms there is a simple search procedure. These techniques are able to induce complex classifiers from a relatively small number of examples and are naturally suited to numeric domains. However, they can be very sensitive to irrelevant attributes and are unable to select different attributes in different regions of the instance space. Furthermore, although (or more accurately *because*) the time complexity to train these models is low, it is relatively time-consuming to classify a new instance.

The most basic and simplest instance-based method is the nearest neighbor (NN) inducer, which was first examined by [Fix and Hodges (1957)]. A NN inducer can be represented by the following rule: to classify an unknown pattern, choose the class of the nearest example in the training set as measured by a given distance metric. A common extension is to choose the most common class in the k *nearest neighbors* (kNN).

Despite its simplicity, the nearest neighbor classifier has many advantages over other methods. For instance, it can generalize from a relatively small training set. Namely, compared to other methods, such as decision trees or neural networks, the nearest neighbor classifier requires fewer training examples to achieve the same classification performance. Moreover, new information can be incrementally incorporated at runtime a property it shares with neural networks. Consequently, the nearest neighbor classifier can achieve performance that is competitive to more modern and complex methods such as decision trees or neural networks.

1.6.4 *Support Vector Machines*

Support vector machines [Vapnik (1995)] map the input space into a high-dimensional feature space through nonlinear mapping that is chosen *a-priori*. An optimal separating hyperplane is then constructed in the new feature space. The method searches for a hyperplane that is optimal according the VC Dimension theory.

1.6.5 *Ensemble Learning*

The main idea of an ensemble methodology is to combine a set of models, each of which solves the same original task, in order to obtain a better composite global model with more accurate and reliable estimates or decisions than can be obtained from using a single model. The idea of building a predictive model by integrating multiple models has been under investigation for quite some time. In fact, ensemble methodology imitates our tendency to seek a second opinion before making any crucial decision. We weigh the individual opinions, and combine them to reach our final decision [Polikar (2006)].

It is well-known that ensemble methods can be used for improving prediction performance. Researchers from various disciplines such as statistics, machine learning, pattern recognition, and data mining have investigated the use of ensemble methodology.

There are several ways to train an ensemble model to reach a desired outcome, however some key principles should be considered when generating an ensemble model:

Diversity: The superior performance of ensemble models is achieved mainly due to the use of various inductive biases. Therefore, the participating inducers should be sufficiently diverse in order to obtain the desired predictive performance.

Predictive performance: The individual inducer's predictive performance should be as high as possible and at least as good as a random model. These two principles may seem to contradict each other at first glance; furthermore, ensembles with diverse inducers do not always improve the predictive performance. The main idea in combining these two principles is to combine predictive inducers with uncorrelated errors in an ensemble, since it has been empirically and theoretically shown that the predictive performance of the entire ensemble has a positive correlation with the degree to which the errors made by individual inducers are uncorrelated.

Recently, several excellent reviews on ensemble learning have been published in the literature. Some of the reviews [Verikas *et al.* (2011); Kulkarni and Sinha (2013)] focus solely on random forest and its variants. Other reviews do not specifically focus on the decision forest, but rather discuss ensemble learning in general [Kuncheva (2014); Wozniak *et al.* (2014)]. A recent book edited by Criminisi and Shotton [Criminisi and Shotton (2013)] presents a unified model of decision forests for addressing various learning tasks. This excellent and highly recommended book covers theoretical foundations, practical implementation, and application of decision forests.

In the next chapters we will describe various methods for building an ensemble.

Chapter 2

Classification and Regression Trees

In this book we concentrate mainly on decision tree models, because of all the existing models, they benefit most from ensemble methods. Ensemble learning combines many models; thus, fast algorithms that need a relatively short training time, such as decision trees, are considered a perfect match. For this reason decision trees are frequently used as the building blocks of many ensemble models. Slower algorithms can also benefit from ensemble techniques but are less used in practice.

In operations research decision trees refer to a hierarchical model of decisions and their consequences. Decision-makers employ decision trees to identify the strategy which will most likely enable them to reach their goal. In the machine learning community a decision tree refers to a predictive model which can be used to represent both classifiers and regression models. When a decision tree is used for classification tasks, it is most commonly referred to as a classification tree. When it is used for regression tasks, it is called a regression tree.

Classification trees are used to classify an object or instance (such as an insured) into a predefined set of classes (such as risky/non-risky) based on its attributes (such as age or gender). Classification trees are frequently used in applied fields such as finance, marketing, engineering, and medicine. The classification tree is useful as an exploratory technique. However, it does not attempt to replace existing traditional statistical methods, and there are many other techniques that can be used to more accurately classify or predict the affiliation of instances with a predefined set of classes, including artificial neural networks and support vector machines. Figure 2.1 presents a typical decision tree classifier. This decision tree is used to facilitate a banks mortgage underwriting process. As part of this process the applicant completes an application form that requests the following information: number of dependents (DEPEND), loan-to-value ratio (LTV), marital status (MARST), payment-to-income ratio (PAYINC), interest rate (RATE), years at current address (YRSADD), and years at current job (YRSJOB).

This information is used by the underwriter to determine whether the mortgage application should be approved. More specifically, this decision tree classifies mortgage applications into one of the following two classes:

- Approved (denoted as "A") The application should be approved.
- Denied (denoted as "D") The application should be denied.
- Manual underwriting (denoted as "M") An underwriter should manually examine the application and decide if it should be approved (in some cases after requesting additional information from the applicant). The decision tree is based on the fields that typically appear on mortgage application forms.

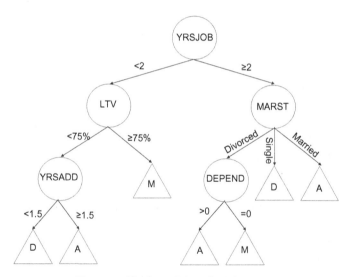

Fig. 2.1: Underwriting decision tree.

This example illustrates how a decision tree can be used to represent a classification model. In fact, it can be seen as an expert system which partially automates the underwriting process. The decision tree can also be regarded as an expert system that was built manually by a knowledge engineer after interrogating an experienced underwriter at a mortgage company. This sort of expert interrogation is called knowledge elicitation, namely, obtaining knowledge from a human expert (or human experts) to be used by an intelligent system. Knowledge elicitation is usually difficult, because it can be challenging to find an expert that is both available and willing to provide the information the knowledge engineer needs to design a reliable expert system. This results in a knowledge elicitation bottleneck, a major obstacle in the development of intelligent systems.

A decision tree can be also used in order to analyze the payment ethics of customers that have received mortgages. In this case there are two classes:

- Paid (denoted as "P") The recipient has fully paid off his or her mortgage.
- Not Paid (denoted as "N") The recipient has not fully paid off his or her mortgage.

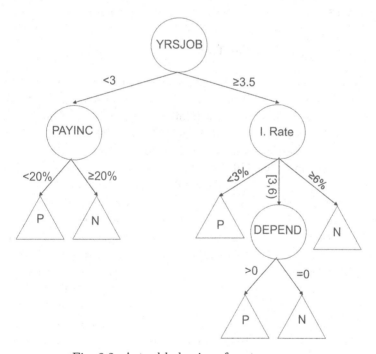

Fig. 2.2: Actual behavior of customer.

This new decision tree can be used to improve the underwriting decision model presented in Figure 2.2. The decision tree shows that there are relatively many customers that pass the underwriting process but that they have not yet fully paid back the loan. In contrast to the decision tree presented in Figure 2.1, the new decision tree is constructed based on data that has accumulated in the database; thus, in this case there is no need to manually elicit knowledge, and in fact, the tree can be built automatically. This type of knowledge acquisition is referred to as knowledge discovery in databases .

The decision tree is a very popular technique in data mining. Many researchers argue that decision trees are widely used due to their simplicity and transparency. Decision trees are self-explanatory; there is no need to be a data mining expert in order to use a specific decision tree. Usually, classification trees are graphically represented as hierarchical structures, which makes them easier to interpret than other techniques. If the classification tree becomes complicated (i.e., has many nodes), its straightforward graphical representation becomes irrelevant. For complex trees, other graphical procedures should be developed to simplify interpretation.

2.1   Training a Decision Tree

Recall from Chapter 1 that decision tree inducers are algorithms that automatically construct a decision tree from a given dataset. Typically the goal is to find a decision tree that minimizes the generalization error. However, other target functions can be also defined, for instance, minimizing the number of nodes or minimizing the average depth of the tree.

As already mentioned above, the induction of an optimal decision tree from a given dataset is considered a difficult task [Hyafil and Rivest (1976)]. An optimal decision tree is one, which is consistent with the training set and minimizes the expected number of tests required for classifying an unseen instance. Finding an optimal decision tree is known to be NP-hard [Hancock *et al.* (1996)]. Even finding the minimal equivalent decision tree for a given decision tree [Zantema and Bodlaender (2000)] or building the optimal decision tree from decision tables is known to be NP-hard [Naumov (1991)].

These findings indicate that the use of optimal decision tree learning algorithms is only feasible for small dataset or simple problems. Consequently, heuristic methods are required for training a decision tree. As indicated in Chapter 1, these heuristic methods can be divided into two groups: top-down and bottom-up, with clear preference given to the first group in the literature.

Figure 2.3 presents typical pseudocode for a top-down decision tree inducing algorithm that uses growing and pruning. Note that these algorithms are greedy by nature and construct the decision tree in a top-down, recursive manner (also known as divide and conquer). In each iteration, the algorithm considers the partition of the training set using the outcome of discrete input attributes. The selection of the most appropriate attribute is made according to specified splitting measures. After the selection of an appropriate split, each node further subdivides the training set into smaller subsets until a stopping criterion is satisfied.

Tree Growing

Input: S - Training Set, A - Input Feature Set, y - Target Feature, *SplitCriterion* - the method for evaluating a specified split, *StoppingCriterion* - the criteria for stopping the growing process

1: Create a new tree T with a single root node.
2: **if** *StoppingCriterion(S)* **then**
3:     Set T as a leaf with the most common value of y in S as a label.
4: **else**
5:     $\forall a_i \in A$ find a that obtain the best *SplitCriterion*(a_i, S).
6:     Label t with a
7:     **for** each outcome v_i of a **do**
8:         Set *Subtree*$_i$= TreeGrowing $(\sigma_{a=v_i} S, A, y)$.
9:         Connect the root node of t_T to *Subtree*$_i$ with an edge that is labeled as v_i
10:     **end for**
11: **end if**
12: **return** TreePruning (S, T, y)

Fig. 2.3: Top-Down algorithmic framework for decision trees induction.

2.2 Illustrative Example

Recall the email spam detection task that has been presented in Chapter 1. Machine learning techniques can be used to automatically detect such spam messages.

In this example, the training set is a table of previous emails. The target attribute indicates if the email is spam or ham (non-spam). All other columns contain the input attributes that can be used as indicators for spam activity, such as: Number of recipients, Size of message, Number

Tree Pruning

Input: S - Training Set, y - Target Feature, T - The tree to be pruned
1: **repeat**
2:    Select a node t in T such that pruning it maximally improves some evaluation criteria.
3:    **if** $t \neq \emptyset$ **then**
4:        $T = pruned(T, t)$
5:    **end if**
6: **until** $t = \emptyset$
7: **return** T

Fig. 2.4: Pruning decision trees.

of attachments, Number of times the string "re" appears in the subject line, the country from which the email is sent, etc.

For the sake of simplicity, let us simplify the spam filtering task and assume that there are only two numeric input attributes. This allows us to project the training set onto a two-dimensional graph as illustrated in Figure 2.5. The x-axis corresponds to the "New Recipients" attribute and the y-axis corresponds to the "Email Length". Each email instance is represented as a circle. More specifically, ham emails are indicated by a filled circle; spam emails are marked by an empty circle.

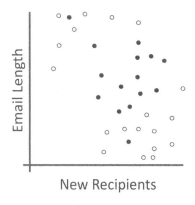

Fig. 2.5: The training set projected onto a two-dimensional graph.

A decision tree divides the space into axis-parallel boxes and associates each box with the most frequent label in it. It begins by finding the best horizontal split and the best vertical split (best in the sense of yielding the lowest misclassification rate). Figure 2.6 presents the best horizontal split and its corresponding decision tree. Similarly, Figure 2.7 presents the best vertical split and its corresponding decision tree. A single node decision tree as presented in Figures 2.6 and 2.7 is sometimes called a Decision Stump.

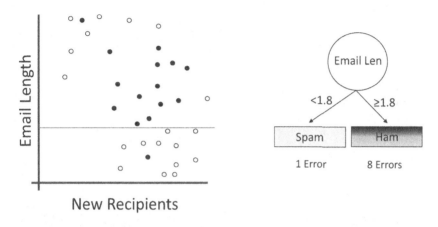

Fig. 2.6: A decision tree (decision stump) based on a horizontal split.

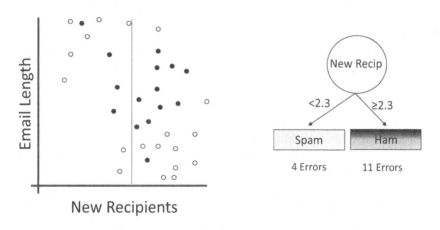

Fig. 2.7: A decision tree (decision stump) based on a vertical split.

Comparing the two trees reveals that the horizontal split leads to 9 misclassification errors (1 misclassification in the left leaf and 8 misclassifications in the right leaf), while the vertical split yields 15 misclassifications.

Therefore, by adopting a greedy strategy, we select the former tree and move on to develop the tree's branches. The procedure is recursively applied to each of the resulting branches. Namely, for each branch we try to split the corresponding subsample even further as illustrated in Figure 2.8.

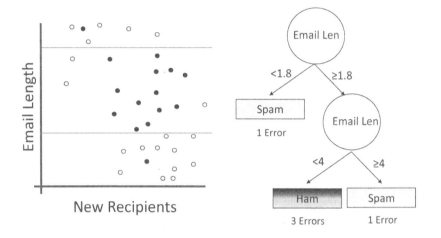

Fig. 2.8: A decision tree obtained after two splits.

Note that the number of classification regions in the graph is equal to the number of leaves in the tree. Moreover, since we are dealing with a binary tree, the amount of internal nodes (i.e. non-leaf nodes) equals the number of leaves minus1.

Each node continues to branch out until we reach a subsample that contains only instances from the same label, or until no further splitting is possible. In the above spam filtering example, the process continues until the graph in Figure 2.9 is reached. Note that there are 9 regions in this graph. Each region consists of instances of only one label. Namely, there are no misclassification errors in regard to the training set. However, the corresponding tree is relatively bushy with 9 leaves and 8 internal nodes.

Complicated decision trees might have limited generalization capabilities, i.e. although it seems to correctly classify all training instances, it fails to do so in new and unseen instances. As we will see later in Section 2.5 in many cases we should prefer simple trees over complicated ones even if the latter seems to outperform the former in the training set.

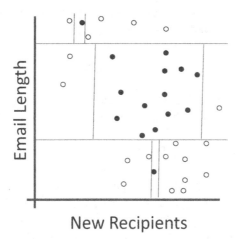

Fig. 2.9: A graph divided into regions with a single label.

2.3 Stopping Criteria

The growing phase continues until a stopping criterion is triggered. The following conditions are common stopping criteria:

(1) All instances in the training set belong to a single value of y.
(2) The maximum tree depth has been reached.
(3) The number of cases in the terminal node is less than the minimum number of cases for parent nodes.
(4) If the node were split, the number of cases in one or more child nodes would be less than the minimum number of cases for child nodes.
(5) The best splitting criterion is not greater than a certain threshold.

In this section, we focused on greedy top-down induction of decision trees given their simplicity and popularity. The lookahead strategy aims to improve the predictive performance of the greedy strategy by exploring the space of all of the possible decision trees up to a specified depth. This more extensive search can improve accuracy, but it becomes intolerable in terms of time very quickly. Limited lookahead search (e.g. two steps ahead) is not time-consuming, but unfortunately, it does not produce significantly better decision trees either. Another approach for improving greedy decision tree induction is to generate decision trees through genetic algorithms (GA) or genetic programming (GP). Barros [Barros *et al.* (2015)] describe approaches for automating the design of decision tree induction algorithms. In particular, they show how a grammar-based GP algorithm can be used for building and evolving individual trees.

2.4   Characteristics of Classification Trees

As already mentioned in Chapter 1, a decision tree is a classifier expressed as a recursive partition of the instance space. The decision tree consists of nodes that form a *rooted tree*. A rooted tree is a tree in which one node has been designated as the root. The "root" node that has no incoming edges. All other nodes have exactly one incoming edge. A node with outgoing edges is referred to as an "internal" node or a "test" node. All other nodes are called "leaves" (also known as "terminal" nodes or "decision" nodes). In a decision tree, each internal node splits the instance space into two or more subspaces according to a certain discrete function of the values of the input attributes. In the simplest and most frequent case, each test considers a single attribute, such that the instance space is partitioned according to the attributes value. In the case of numeric attributes, the test in the node refers to a value range.

Each leaf is assigned to one class representing the most appropriate target value. Additionally, the leaf may hold a probability vector (affinity vector) indicating the probability of the target attribute having a certain value. Figure 2.10 presents another example of a decision tree; in this case the decision tree predicts whether or not a potential customer will respond to a direct mail piece. Recall that internal nodes are represented as circles, whereas leaves are denoted as triangles. Two or more branches may grow from each internal node. Each node corresponds with a certain characteristic, and the branches correspond with a range of values. The value ranges must be mutually exclusive and complete. These two properties of *disjointness* and *completeness* are important, since they ensure that each data instance is mapped to one instance.

Instances are classified by navigating from the root of the tree down to a leaf based on the outcome of the tests performed along the path. We start at the root of a tree; we consider the attribute that corresponds to the root and identify which branch the observed value of the given attribute corresponds to. Then, we consider the next node, which appears in the selected branch. We test the attribute that corresponds to this node and select the next branch accordingly. This process continues until we reach a leaf.

Given this classifier, the analyst can predict the response of a potential customer and understand the behavioral characteristics of the entire population of potential customers regarding the direct mail piece. Each node is labeled with the attribute it tests, and its branches are labeled with its corresponding values.

It is well known that the error of a prediction model can be broken down into three additive components: the intrinsic error, the bias error, and the variance error. The intrinsic error, also known as the irreducible error, is the component that is generated due to noise. This quantity is the lower bound of any prediction model. The bias error of an inducer is the persistent or systematic error that the inducer is expected to make. Variance is a concept closely related to bias. The variance captures random variation in the algorithm from one training set to another. More specifically, it measures the sensitivity of the algorithm to the actual training set, or the error that is due to the training set's finite size.

Dietterich and Kong [Dietterich and Kong (1995)] examined the trade-off between variance and bias errors in decision trees. In a simple decision tree (i.e., a tree with a small number of nodes), the bias component of the error tends to be high, and the variance component of the error tends to be small. As the complexity of the tree increases, the variance component of the error becomes larger, and the bias error component becomes smaller.

The role of the bias-variance tradeoff becomes even more important when we deal with a decision forest. A decision forest consists of several decision trees that their outputs are combined into a final output. Empirical and theoretical evidence show that some decision forest techniques act as variance reduction mechanisms, i.e., they reduce the variance component of the error. Other decision forest techniques reduce both the bias and the variance parts of the error. In particular, we will later describe various boosting algorithms for building decision forests. In these methods, the bias error seems to be reduced in the early iterations, while the variance error decreases in later iterations.

In the case of numeric attributes, decision trees can be geometrically interpreted as a collection of hyperplanes, each orthogonal to one of the axes.

2.4.1 *Tree Size*

Naturally, decision-makers prefer a decision tree that is not complex, since it such trees are apt to be more comprehensible. Furthermore, tree complexity has a significant effect on a decision trees accuracy [Breiman *et al.* (1984)].

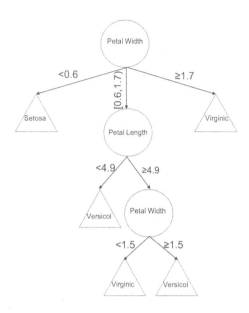

Fig. 2.10: Decision tree presenting response to direct mailing.

Typically, the tree complexity is measured by one of the following metrics: the total number of nodes, total number of leaves, tree depth, or number of attributes used. Tree complexity is explicitly controlled by the stopping criteria and the pruning method that are employed.

2.4.2 *The Hierarchical Nature of Decision Trees*

Another characteristic of decision trees is their hierarchical nature. Imagine that you want to develop a medical system for diagnosing patients according to the results of several medical tests. Based on the results of one test, the physician can perform or order additional laboratory tests. Figure 2.11 illustrates the diagnosis process using decision trees of patients that suffer from a specific respiratory problem. The decision tree employs the following attributes: CT findings (CTF), X-ray findings (XRF), chest pain type (CPT), and blood test findings (BTF). The physician will order an X-ray if the chest pain type is "1". However, if the chest pain type is "2" the physician will order a blood test instead of an X-ray. Using this medical system, medical tests are performed only when needed, thereby reducing the total cost of medical tests.

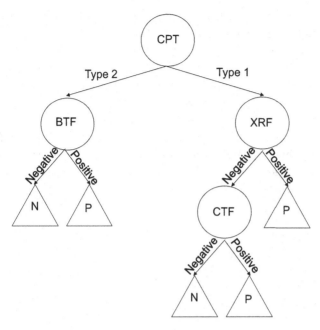

Fig. 2.11: Decision tree for medical applications.

2.5 Overfitting and Underfitting

The concept of overfitting is very important in machine learning. It refers to the situation in which the induction algorithm generates a classifier which perfectly fits the training data but has lost the capability of generalizing to instances not presented during training. In other words, instead of learning, the classifier just memorizes the training instances. Overfitting is generally recognized to be a violation of a fundamental principle in science, known as the Occam's razor : when searching for the explanation of any phenomenon, one should make as few assumptions as possible, and eliminating those that make no difference in the observable predictions of the explanatory hypothesis. The implication in regard to decision trees is that the tree which can be defined as the smallest decision tree that is consistent with the training set is the one that is most likely to classify unseen instances correctly. However, this is only a rule of thumb; in some pathologic cases a large and unbalanced tree can still be easily interpreted [Buja and Lee (2001)].

In decision trees overfitting usually occurs when the tree has too many nodes relative to the amount of training data available. By increasing the number of nodes, the training error usually decreases while at some point the generalization error becomes worse.

Figure 2.12 illustrates the overfitting process. The figure presents the training error and the generalization error of a decision tree as a function of the number of nodes for a fixed training set. The training error continues to decline as the tree become bigger. On the other hand, the generalization error declines at first then at some point starts to increase due to overfitting. The optimal point for the generalization error is obtained for a tree with 130 nodes. In bigger trees the classifier is overfitted. In smaller trees the classifier is underfitted.

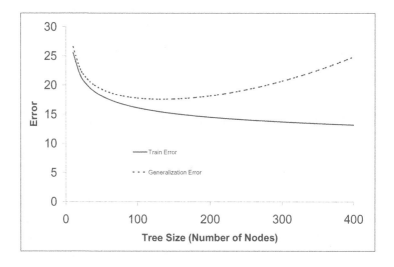

Fig. 2.12: Overfitting in decision trees while increasing the number of nodes for a fixed training set.

Another aspect of overfitting is presented in Figure 2.13. This graph presents the generalization error for increasing training set sizes. The generalization error decreases with the training set size. This can be explained by the fact that for a small training set, it is relatively hard to generalize, and the classifier memorizes all instances.

It was found that overfitting decreases prediction accuracy in decision trees either in the presence of significant noise or when the input attributes are irrelevant to the classification problem [Schaffer (1991)].

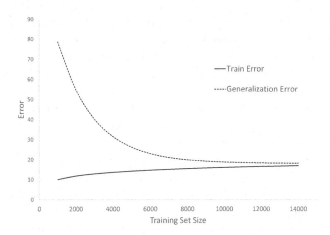

Fig. 2.13: Overfitting in decision trees while increasing training set sizes.

In order to avoid overfitting, it is necessary to estimate when further training will not result in a better generalization. In decision trees there are two mechanisms that help to avoid overfitting. The first is to avoid splitting the tree if the split is not useful (for instance by approving only statistically significant splits). The second approach is to use pruning; after growing the tree, we prune unnecessary nodes.

2.6 Beyond Classification Tasks

While decision trees are most commonly used for classification tasks, they have been found to be useful for many other predictive tasks.

- Regression tree: A regression tree is a decision tree that deals with a continuous (numeric) target attribute. The basic idea is to combine decision trees and linear regression in order to predict a numerical target attribute based on a set of input attributes. These methods perform induction by means of an efficient recursive partitioning algorithm. The choice of the best split at each node of the tree is usually guided by a least squares error criterion.
- Clustering tree [Blockeel *et al.* (1998); Moosmann *et al.* (2008); Dror *et al.* (2014)]: The aim of clustering is to group instances into subsets in such a manner that similar instances are grouped together,

while different instances belong to different clusters. A clustering tree is a decision tree where each node of the tree corresponds to a cluster; thus, the tree as a whole represents a kind of taxonomy.

- Sequence analysis using a hidden Markov model tree [Antwarg *et al.* (2012)]: The Markov model is a method for sequence learning which is capable of estimating the probability of sequences by training from data. In the Markov model tree, each node in the tree is a Markov model which uses the same states of a higher level, or uses just some of these states but with different transition probabilities.

- Recommendation tree [Gershman *et al.* (2010); Rokach and Kisilevich (2012)]: Typically, a recommender system attempts to recommend a set of items to users based on their past reactions to other items in the system and the reactions of other (similar) users. In a recommender tree, the terminal nodes hold a weighted list of recommended items. The internal nodes test properties that are known about the user (e.g., a reaction to a certain item) or demographic characteristics (e.g., age).

- Survival tree: A survival tree [Bou-Hamad *et al.* (2011); Eyal *et al.* (2014)] is a decision tree that aims to predict the amount of time that will elapse until an event of interest occurs. The event can vary from the death of a patient to an occasion when a machine ceases to function. Instead of assuming that the entire population has the same survival pattern, the survival tree splits the population according to its characteristics. In this case, the leaves of the tree hold the hazard functions. The hazard function is the probability that an individual will experience an event (for example, death) within a small time interval, given that the individual has survived up until the beginning of the interval.

- Ranking tree [Xia *et al.* (2008); Svore and Burges (2011); Freund *et al.* (2003)]: Ranking aims to predict instances of ordinal scale. Decision trees can be extended to address ranking tasks by replacing the splitting criterion with impurity measures that take ranking into consideration.

2.7 Advantages of Decision Trees

Decision trees have become popular, because of the many benefits they offer, including [Rokach (2016)]:

- They provide high predictive performance with a relatively small amount of computational effort.

- Decision trees are able to process datasets that may have errors or missing values.
- As we have seen above, decision trees are useful for various tasks, such as classification, regression, clustering, and feature selection.
- Decision trees are self-explanatory models and easy to follow when compacted. That is to say, if the decision tree has a reasonable number of leaves, it can be grasped by non-professional users. Furthermore, since decision trees can be easily converted to a set of if-then rules, this sort of representation is considered comprehensible. In addition, decision trees provide implicit feature selection, i.e., by looking at the tree one can easily determine which feature is important.
- Decision trees are considered a non-parametric method, i.e., decision trees do not hold any assumptions about the space distribution.
- Compared to other methods, decision trees scale well to big data.
- They are able to handle a variety of input data: nominal, numeric, and textual.
- Decision trees are available on many open-source data mining packages and a variety of platforms.
- Decision trees can be combined with other prediction techniques, for example, certain decision tree use neural network models or logistic regression models in the terminal nodes.
- When sensor cost is high, decision trees may be attractive in that they only need the sensors values used along one path, from the root to a leaf. The sensor values can be acquired on demand as we traverse the tree.
- While decision tree algorithms might have several controlling parameters, in many cases the default values yield adequate predictive performance. If tuning is still required, often just a short tuning session is needed.

2.8   Disadvantages of Decision Trees

Decision trees also have several known drawbacks [Rokach   (2016)]. The main drawbacks are listed below.

- Greediness : The myopic nature of most decision tree induction algorithms is supported by the fact that the learning algorithms consider only one level ahead. Specifically, the splitting criterion ranks possible attributes based on their immediate descendants and thus can be trapped in a local minima. This strategy prefers tests that score high in isolation and may overlook combinations of attributes. This is well illustrated in a case in which the tree tries to learn a Boolean function such as y=(A1 xor A2). In this case, knowing the values of both attributes determines the value of y. However, knowing the value of either attribute does not help at all in predicating the value of y. Thus, a myopic algorithm might assume that neither attribute is useful and therefore disregard them both. The use of deeper lookahead strategies is considered computationally expensive and has not consistently been proven.

- Instability: The greedy characteristic of decision trees leads to another disadvantage that should be noted: oversensitivity. Decision trees are unstable due to their oversensitivity to the training set, irrelevant attributes, and noise, in that a minor change in one split close to the root will change the whole subtree below. Small variations in the training set may result in different splits and hence a different decision tree altogether.

- Fragmentation problem: This usually happens if many attributes are tested along a path from the root to the leaf. In this case, the fragmentation problem causes partitioning of the data into smaller fragments. Each fragment consists of a relatively small number of instances, and therefore the prediction confidence of this fragment is limited. Note that replication always implies fragmentation, but fragmentation may happen without any replication.

- Insufficient data and the curse of dimensionality: If the data splits equally (or approximately equally) in every split, a univariate decision tree cannot be deeper than a $O(logn)$ levels (where n is the dataset size). This puts decision trees at a disadvantage for tasks with many relevant features (greater than $O(logn)$).

- Replication problem: Decision trees use a divide and conquer strategy for training the model. Thus, they tend to perform well if a few highly relevant attributes exist, performing less well if many complex interactions among the attributes are present. This phenomenon can be simply illustrated by the decision tree replication problem. Since most decision trees divide the instance space into mutually exclusive regions to represent a concept, in certain cases the tree may contain several copies of the same subtree in order to represent the classifier. For instance, if a tree tries to learn the following Boolean function: y

= (A1 and A2) or (A3 and A4), the minimal univariate decision tree that represents this function has two copies of the subtree that corresponds to the first term (A1 and A2) or two copies of the subtree that corresponds to the second term (A3 and A4).

- Limited representation: The decision boundaries of decision trees are parallel to the axis, and therefore if the patterns in the training set cannot be expressed using axis-parallel hyperplanes, the decision tree may have difficulty representing it.

- Prediction plateau: Two similar samples can have very different predictions if they are assigned to two different paths. Consider a case where the root node branches to the left if a certain attribute, say a_4, is greater than a certain threshold value, say 6.5, and branches to the right if a_4 is less or equal to 6.5. Due to the fact that there might be a very big difference in the outcome between being on the left side of a boundary or the right side, very different predictions can be obtained for two almost identical samples just because in the first case the value is $a_4 = 6.6$, and in the second case the value is $a_4 = 6.4$.

2.9 Decision Forest for Mitigating Learning Challenges

Some of the drawbacks of the single tree described above can be mitigated by growing a decision forest. In fact, the full potential of decision trees is realized when they are used to form a forest. A study published in 2014, provocatively entitled "Do we need hundreds of classifiers to solve real world classification problems?" [Fernandez-Delgado *et al.* (2014)], empirically compared 179 classification algorithms from 17 learning families; this comprehensive study involving 121 datasets concluded that decision forests, and in particular random forests, tend to outperform other learning methods. The key to the improved predictive performance is that the mistakes made by an individual decision tree are compensated for by other decision trees included in the forest. Moreover, although several decision trees are required to create a decision forest, such a forest is still considered very attractive in terms of computational cost due to the low computational cost of the base tree induction algorithm.

In this section we discuss several learning settings that are known to pose a challenge to machine learning algorithms in general, and to decision trees in particular. As described below, decision forests have been used to mitigate these challenges:

(1) Class Imbalance - Class imbalance usually occurs when, in a classification problem, there are many more examples of a certain class than there are of another class. In such cases, standard machine learning techniques may be overwhelmed by the majority class and ignore the minority class. One way to deal with this challenge is to adjust the base induction algorithm of the individual trees. In particular, Cieslak and Chawla [Cieslak and Chawla (2008)] suggest replacing the splitting criterion in the decision tree with a skew insensitive measure such as the Hellinger distance. In addition to modifying the base tree induction algorithm, a decision forest can be used to mitigate the class imbalance. One easy approach is to create a forest where each individual tree is trained using a balanced subsample in which all minority classes are included and the majority class is undersampled randomly [Nikulin *et al.* (2009)]. Galar [Galar *et al.* (2012)] introduce a taxonomy for ensemble-based methods to address the class imbalance. Their detailed experimental comparison of state of the art methods showed that excellent results can be obtained by combining random undersampling techniques with ensemble techniques such as bagging or boosting. The predictive performance can be further enhanced using the EUSBoost method [Galar *et al.* (2013)] which combines boosting and evolutionary undersampling that is adjusted to promote diversity among the individual trees.

(2) Concept Drift - In many online learning scenarios, the underlying distribution of the target attribute tends to evolve over time. This results in predictions that become less accurate over time. To prevent this phenomenon, learning algorithms need to adapt quickly and appropriately to the changes. Gama [Gama *et al.* (2006)] extended existing tree induction algorithms in response to the concept drift issue by continuously comparing the class distribution of the last tree built with the class distribution within the time window of the most recent examples. Another possible solution is to build a forest of trees. Kolter and Maloof [Kolter and Maloof (2003)] develop a dynamic weighted majority (DWM) forest model that dynamically creates and deletes individual trees in response to changes in performance. Minku [Minku *et al.* (2010)] show that different diversity levels in a forest are required in order to maintain high generalization to both old and new concepts. Moreover, diversity alone can help to reduce the initial increase in error caused by concept drift. Consequently, Minku and Yao [Minku and Yao. (2012)] suggest an online ensemble learning approach called diver-

sity for dealing with drifts (DDD) that maintains two forests: one with a low diversity level and the second with a high diversity level. The diversity in a forest can be controlled directly by using a modified version of online bagging [Minku *et al.* (2010)]. Prior to drift detection, only the low diversity forest is used for predictions. Once a concept drift is detected, new low diversity and high diversity forests are trained, and classification of new instances is provided by the weighted majority vote of the output of 1) the old high diversity forest, 2) the new low diversity forest, and 3) the old low diversity forest.

(3) Curse of Dimensionality - High dimensionality of the input (i.e., the number of attributes) increases the size of the search space exponentially and thus increases the chance that the inducer will find spurious classifiers that are not valid. It has been estimated that as the number of dimensions increases, the sample size required to train a decision tree should increase exponentially in order to obtain an effective estimate of multivariate densities. Some ensemble learning methods can be used to lessen the impact of the curse of dimensionality. For example, Bryll [Bryll *et al.* (2003)] introduce a method called attribute bagging (AB) where each tree is trained on a small randomly selected subset of attributes. AB also searches for the appropriate size of the attribute subset by testing the prediction performance of random subsets of attributes of various sizes. Huang [Huang *et al.* (2010)] introduce the improved decision forest (IDF) algorithm that encompasses a feature selection mechanism and therefore is capable of addressing high dimensional datasets, particularly gene expression data that is comprised of thousands of genes. Rokach [Rokach (2008a)] presents a genetic algorithm (GA) based on building a forest for a dataset with many features. Instead of randomly sampling the feature set, the algorithm searches for the best mutually exclusive partitioning of the feature set, such that the individual decision trees are trained on disjoint subsets [Maimon and Rokach (2001)]. This method was found to be particularly useful for datasets with thousands of input features.

2.10 Relation to Rule Induction

Decision tree induction is closely related to if-then rule induction. Ifthen rule consists of two parts: the antecedent part (if-part) and the consequence part (then-part). The antecedent part contains values of the input variables, and the consequence part contains the value of the target attribute.

Each path from the root of a decision tree to one of its leaves can be transformed into a rule simply by conjoining the tests along the path in order to form the antecedent part of the rule and taking the leaf's class prediction as the class value. For example, one of the paths in Figure 2.10 can be transformed into the rule: "If customer age is less than or equal to 30, and the gender of the customer is male, the customer will respond to the mail." The resulting rule set can then be simplified to improve its comprehensibility to a human user, and possibly its accuracy [Quinlan (1987)].

2.11   Using Decision Trees in R

Probably the most popular decision tree induction algorithms are C4.5 [Quinlan (1993)] and CART [Breiman *et al.* (1984)]. Both algorithms are top-down induction algorithms that use splitting criterion and pruning methods as described above. There are several open-source implementations of these two popular algorithms. For example rpart package [Therneau and Atkinson (1997)] is an R package implementation of the CART algorithm. While these implementations are expected to perform similarly, a comparative study indicates that this is not always the case [Moore *et al.* (2009)]. In this section we will review some of the most popular open-source packages in R that are freely available.

For illustrative purposes we will use the Iris dataset which was first introduced by R.A. Fisher in 1936. As was mentioned previously in the first chapter, this is one of the best known datasets in the pattern recognition literature. The goal in this case is to classify flowers into the Iris subgeni (such as Iris Setosa, Iris Versicolour, and Iris Virginica) based on their characteristics. The dataset consists of 150 instances. Each instance refers to one of the flowers. A flower is characterized by its features, such as the length and width of the sepal and petal. The label of every instance is one of the strings *Iris Setosa*, *Iris Versicolour*, and *Iris Virginica*. The task is to induce a classifier which will be able to predict the class to which a flower belongs using its four attributes: sepal length, sepal width, petal length, and petal width (all in centimeters).

Table 2.1 illustrates a segment of the Iris dataset. This table is identical to Table 1.1 and it is presented here again for convenience. The dataset contains three classes that correspond to three types of iris flowers: $dom\,(y) \,=\, \{IrisSetosa, IrisVersicolor, andIrisVirginica\}$. Each instance is characterized by four numeric features (measured in centimeters):

$A = \{sepallength, sepalwidth, petallength, and petalwidth\}.$

Table 2.1: The Iris dataset consists of four numeric features and three possible classes.

Sepal Length	Sepal Width	Petal Length	Petal Width	Class (Iris Type)
5.1	3.5	1.4	0.2	Iris-setosa
4.9	3.0	1.4	0.2	Iris-setosa
6.0	2.7	5.1	1.6	Iris-versicolor
5.8	2.7	5.1	1.9	Iris-virginica
5.0	3.3	1.4	0.2	Iris-setosa
5.7	2.8	4.5	1.3	Iris-versicolor
5.1	3.8	1.6	0.2	Iris-setosa
⋮				

R is a free software programming language that is widely used among data scientists to develop data mining algorithms. Most of a data scientist's tasks can be accomplished in R with a short script code thanks to the diversity and richness of the contributed packages in CRAN (comprehensive R archive network). In this section we review the packages: **party**, **rpart**, and **randomForest** which are used to train decision trees and decision forests.

2.11.1 *Party Package*

The party package provides a set of tools for training classification and regression trees [Hothorn *et al.* (2006)]. At the core of the party package is the `ctree()` function which implements a conditional inference procedure to train the tree. The following R script illustrates the use of the ctree function for training a classification tree.

```
1 library("party")
2
3 IrisClassifcationTree<-ctree(Species  .,data = iris)
4
5 plot(irisct)
```

First, the R script shown above loads the party package assuming it has been already installed (see user guide for instructions on how to install a package). It then trains a classification tree for the Iris dataset where species is the target attribute, and all other attributes are used as input attributes. Then, in the third line the plot function is used to represent the tree as illustrated in Figure 2.14. The tree nodes are numbered. Each leaf node contains a histogram that shows the probability of an instance to be labeled with each of the classes.

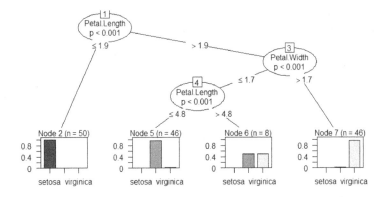

Fig. 2.14: The classifier tree obtained for the Iris dataset.

The tree induction algorithm can be configured using the `ctree_control()` function. In particular, the following parameters can be set:

(1) mincriterion - the threshold value of the splitting criterion, which must be exceeded in order to implement a split.
(2) minsplit - the minimum number of instances in a node in order to be considered for splitting.
(3) minbucket - the minimum number of instances in a terminal node.
(4) stump - a Boolean parameter that indicates whether a decision stump should be built.
(5) maxdepth - the maximum depth of the tree.

The following script illustrates a more complicated learning process. The script begins by splitting the Iris data into training set (2/3 of the instances) and test set (the remaining instances). Then, it trains a classification tree using only the training set, with the following input attributes: Sepal.Length, Petal.Length, and Sepal.Width. The training algorithm's parameters are set to the following values: `minsplit=3` and `maxdepth=3`.

After training the tree, we plot it using a simple graph (instead of showing the histogram, it shows the class distribution). Finally, we classify the instances in the test data and evaluate the predictive performance of the tree by presenting the confusion matrix.

```
1  library("party")
2
3  # split the data into train and test
4  trainIndex<-sample(nrow(iris), 2/3*nrow(iris))
5  trainData <- iris[trainIndex,]
6  testData <- iris[-trainIndex,]
7
8  # train the classification tree
9  irisClassifcationTree <- ctree(Species  Sepal.Length+
10                                 Petal.Length + Sepal.Width,
11                                 data = trainData, control =
12                                 ctree_control(minsplit=3,
13                                               maxdepth=3))
14 # plot a simple tree
15 plot(irisClassifcationTree,type="simple")
16
17 # predict on test data
18 testPrediction <- predict(irisClassifcationTree,
19                                 newdata= testData)
20
21 # show the confusion matrix
22 table(testPrediction, testData$Species)
```

With party package, it is possible to train different types of trees other than classification trees using the model-based recursive partitioning functionality. The mob() function provides a specific implementation of recursive partitioning based on parametric models for building linear regression trees, logistic regression trees, or survival trees.

With the mob() function [Zeileis *et al.* (2008)] some input attributes are used for fitting the model, while others are used for partitioning. For example, the following script trains a tree using the attributes Sepal.Width, Species, and Petal.Width as partitioning attributes. Each leaf tries to predict the value of Sepal.Length by fitting a simple linear regression with Petal.Length serving as an explanatory variable. Figure 2.15 presents the resulting regression tree. The regression coefficients for each leaf node can be obtained by the function coef(SepalLengthRegression).

```
1  SepalLengthRegression<-mob(Sepal.Length~Petal.Length|
2                             Sepal.Width+Species+
3                             Petal.Width, control =
4                             mob_control(minsplit = 10),
5                             data=trainData,
6                             model = linearModel)
7
8  plot(SepalLengthRegression)
```

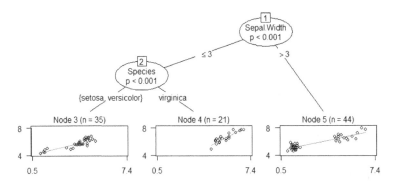

Fig. 2.15: Regression tree.

In addition to linear regression, it is possible to train other parametric models such as logistic regression models (model = glinearModel,family = binomial()) and survival regression models (model=survReg).

2.11.2   *The Rpart Package*

The rpart package [Therneau and Atkinson (1997)] is another implementation for training classification and regression trees using recursive partitioning and a two-stage procedure. In the first stage the tree is built recursively until no sufficient data is left or no improvement can be seen. The second stage of the procedure consists of using cross-validation to prune the tree.

The following script trains a classification tree for the Iris dataset using the rpart package and plots the resulting model which is presented in Figure 2.16. Note that the leaf nodes include the class frequency and the most frequent class.

```
1 library(rpart)
2 fit <- rpart(Species ., data = iris)
3 plot(fit)
4 text(fit, use.n = TRUE))
```

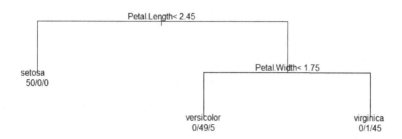

Fig. 2.16: RPart output.

The function **rpart()** is capable of inducing not only classification trees but also regression trees, survival trees, and Poisson trees. This is done by setting the method argument to the following values: **anova** (for regression tree), **class** (for classification tree), **exp** (for survival tree), or **poisson** (for Poisson Regression tree). If the method argument is not set, the function makes an intelligent guess. Note that Poisson regression is a type of regression that aims to model the event rate, which follows a Poisson distribution. For example, in a manufacturing scenario the target attribute may refer to the defective rate. Poisson regression assumes that the logarithm of the target attribute's expected value can be represented as a linear combination of the input attributes.

The function **rpart()** lets the user select the splitting criterion: Gini index or information gain. This is done by setting the split parameter to either **split = "information"** or **split="gini"**. In addition, similarly to ctree(), a control object can be included to set various parameters such as **minsplit**, **minbucket**, and **maxdepth**. The following script illustrates this tuning capability by indicating that the splitting criterion is information gain and the number of instances should exceed five in order to consider splitting a certain node.

```
1 fit <- rpart(Species ., data = iris,
2              split="information",
3              control = rpart.control(minsplit = 5)
```

Chapter 3

Introduction to Ensemble Learning

The main idea behind the ensemble methodology is to weigh several individual pattern classifiers and combine them, in order to obtain a classifier that outperforms all of them. The ensemble methodology imitates our second nature to seek several opinions before making any crucial decision. We weigh the individual opinions and combine them to reach our final decision [Polikar (2006)]. In the literature, the term "ensemble methods" is usually reserved for collections of models that are minor variants of the same basic model. In this book we also cover hybridization of models that are not from the same family. The latter is referred to as "multiple classifier systems" in the literature.

The idea of building a predictive model that integrates multiple models has been investigated for quite some time. The history of ensemble methods dates back to as early as 1977 with Tukeys twicing [Tukey (1977)]: an ensemble of two linear regression models. Tukey suggested fitting the first linear regression model to the original data and the second linear model to the residuals. Two years later, Dasarathy and Sheela (1979) proposed partitioning the input space using two or more classifiers. Major progress in the field was achieved during the 1990s. Hansen and Salamon (1990) presented an ensemble of similarly configured neural networks to improve the predictive performance of a single network. At the same time, Schapire (1990) laid the foundation for the award winning AdaBoost [Freund and Schapire (1996)] algorithm by showing that a strong classifier in the *probably approximately correct* (PAC) sense can be generated by combining "weak" classifiers (that is, simple classifiers whose classification performance is only slightly better than random classification). Ensemble methods can also be used for improving the quality and robustness of other supervised learning tasks (e.g. regression) as well as of unsupervised tasks. In this book we focus on classifier ensembles.

In the past few years, experimental studies conducted by the machine learning community show that combining the outputs of multiple classifiers reduces the generalization error [Domingos (1996); Quinlan (1996); Bauer and Kohavi (1999); Opitz and Maclin (1999)] of the individual classifiers. Ensemble methods are very effective, mainly because different types of classifiers have different "inductive biases" [Mitchell (1997)]. Ensemble methods can effectively make use of such diversity to reduce the variance error [Tumer and Ghosh (1996); Ali and Pazzani (1996)] without increasing the bias error. In certain situations, an ensemble method can also reduce bias error, as shown by the theory of large margin classifiers [Bartlett and Shawe-Taylor (1998)]. In this chapter, we will discuss some of the basic concepts of ensemble learning and examine how these concepts can be used to train accurate supervised learning models.

3.1   Back to the Roots

Marie Jean Antoine Nicolas de Caritat, Marquis de Condorcet (1743-1794) was a French mathematician who wrote the Essay on the Application of Analysis to the Probability of Majority Decisions in 1785. This work presented the well-known Condorcet Jury Theorem which refers to a jury of voters who need to make a decision regarding a binary outcome (for example whether to convict or acquit a defendant). Originally, the Condorcet Jury Theorem was used to provide a theoretical basis for democracy, however the same principle can be applied in ensemble learning. Specifically, if each voter has a probability p of being correct, and the probability of a majority of voters being correct is M, then:

- $p > 0.5$ implies $M > p$
- M approaches 1, for all $p > 0.5$, as the number of voters approaches infinity.

This theorem has two major limitations: the assumption that the votes are independent and the assumption that there are only two possible outcomes. Nevertheless, if these two preconditions are met, a correct decision can be obtained by simply combining the votes of a large enough jury which is composed of voters whose judgments are slightly better than a random vote. In pattern recognition and machine learning, an inducer that is given a training set consisting of labeled data and produces a classifier which can be arbitrarily accurate is considered a strong learner. A weak learner produces a classifier that is only slightly more accurate than random classification. The formal definitions of weak and strong learners are beyond the scope of this book, and the reader is referred to [Schapire (1990)] for their definition with regard to the PAC theory. A decision stump inducer is an example of a weak learner. A decision stump is a one level decision tree with a categorical or numerical class label. Figure 3.1 presents a decision stump for the Iris dataset specified in Table 1.1. The classifier distinguishes between three cases: petal length greater or equal to 2.45, petal length smaller than 2.45, and unknown petal length. The classifier predicts a different class distribution for each case.

Fig. 3.1: A decision stump classifier for solving the Iris classification task.

One of the basic issues that has been investigated in ensemble learning is whether a collection of weak classifiers can create a single strong one. The application of the Condorcet Jury Theorem insinuates that this goal could be achieved. Namely, by constructing an ensemble that consists of independent classifiers, each of which correctly classifies a case with a probability of $p > 0.5$, we can jointly classify a case to its correct class with a probability of $M > p$.

3.2 The Wisdom of Crowds

Sir Francis Galton (1822-1911) was an English philosopher and statistician who conceived the basic concepts of standard deviation and correlation. While visiting a livestock fair held at Plymouth, Galton was intrigued by a simple weight guessing contest in which visitors were requested to guess the weight of an ox [Galton (1907)]. Hundreds of people participated in this contest, but no one succeeded in guessing the exact weight of 1,198 pounds, however, Galton found that the average of all of the guesses came quite close to the exact weight: 1,197 pounds. Similar to the Condorcet Jury Theorem, Galton revealed the power of combining many simplistic predictions in order to obtain an accurate prediction. Lior Zoref has recently recreated Galtons original experiment during his TED talk. He brought a real ox onstage and let the TED crowd guess its weight. The average guess was 1,792 pounds, while the oxs real weight was 1,795 pounds.

James Michael Surowiecki, an American financial journalist, published the book, The Wisdom of Crowds: Why the Many Are Smarter Than the Few and How Collective Wisdom Shapes Business, Economies, Societies and Nations, in 2004. Surowiecki argues that under certain controlled conditions, the aggregation of information from several sources results in decisions that are often superior to those that could have been made by any single individual - even experts.

Naturally, not all crowds are wise (for example, greedy investors during a stock market bubble). Surowiecki indicates that in order to become wise, the crowd should comply with the following criteria:

- **Diversity of opinion** – Each member should have private information, even if it is just an eccentric interpretation of the known facts.
- **Independence** – Members' opinions are not determined by the opinions of those around them.
- **Decentralization** – Members are able to specialize and draw conclusions based on local knowledge.
- **Aggregation** – Some mechanism exists for turning private judgments into a collective decision.

In the following subsections, we review some popular ensemble learning methods. We begin with the simplest method for building an ensemble of classifiers that utilizes bootstrapping for injecting randomness and encouraging diversity among the ensembles members.

3.3 The Bagging Algorithm

Bagging (bootstrap aggregating) is a simple yet effective method for generating an ensemble of classifiers. The ensemble classifier that is created by this method consolidates the outputs of various learned classifiers into a single classification. This results in a classifier whose accuracy is greater than the accuracy of each individual classifier. Specifically, each classifier in the ensemble is trained on a sample of instances taken with replacement (allowing repetitions) from the training set. All classifiers are trained using the same learning algorithm.

To ensure that there is a sufficient number of training instances in every sample, it is common to set the size of each sample to the size of the original training set. Figure 3.2 presents the pseudocode for building an ensemble of classifiers using the bagging algorithm [Breiman (1996a)]. The algorithm receives an induction algorithm I which is used for training all members of the ensemble. The stopping criterion in line six terminates the training when the ensemble size reaches T. One of the main advantages of bagging is that it can be implemented easily in a parallel mode by training the various ensemble classifiers on different processors.

Bagging Training

Input: I (a base inducer), T (the number of iterations), S (the original training set), μ (the sample size).

1: $t \leftarrow 1$
2: **repeat**
3:     $S_t \leftarrow$ a sample of μ instances from S with replacement.
4:     Construct classifier M_t using I, with S_t as the training set
5:     $t \leftarrow t + 1$
6: **until** $t > T$

Fig. 3.2: Bagging algorithm.

Note that since sampling with replacement is used, some of the original instances of S may appear more than once in S_t, and some may not be included at all. Furthermore, using a large sample size causes individual samples to overlap significantly, with many of the same instances appearing in most samples. So while the training sets in S_t may be different from one another, they are certainly not independent from a statistical standpoint. In order to ensure diversity among the ensemble members, a relatively unstable inducer should be used. This will result is an ensemble of sufficiently different classifiers which can be acquired by applying small perturbations to the training set. If a stable inducer is used, the ensemble will be composed of a set of classifiers that produce nearly similar classifications and thus are unlikely to improve the accuracy of a single classifier.

In order to classify a new instance, each classifier returns the class prediction for the unknown instance. The ensemble returns the class with the highest number of predictions. This is known as majority voting. It is simple yet effective in aggregating individual classifications and turning them into a collective classification. Majority voting is considered the most common approach for classification tasks. Majority voting is replaced with arithmetic mean for regression tasks.

Bagging Classification

Input: x (an instance to be classified).
Output: C (predicted class)
  1: $Counter_1, \ldots, Counter_{|dom(y)|} \leftarrow 0$ {initializes class vote counters}
  2: **for** $i = 1$ to T **do**
  3:   $vote_i \leftarrow M_i(x)$ {get predicted class from member i}
  4:   $Counter_{vote_i} \leftarrow Counter_{vote_i} + 1$ {increase the counter of the corresponding class by 1}
  5: **end for**
  6: $C \leftarrow$ the class with the largest number of votes
  7: Return C

Fig. 3.3: Bagging classification.

We demonstrate the bagging procedure by applying it to the Labor dataset presented in Table 3.1. Each instance in the table represents a collective agreement reached in the business or personal services sector (such as teachers and nurses) in Canada during the years 1987-1988. The aim of the learning task is to distinguish between acceptable and unacceptable agreements (as classified by experts in the field). The last column represents the target binary class as determined by the experts. The first eight columns represent the characteristics of the agreement that can be used as input features. Missing values are indicated by a question mark. The input features selected that characterize the agreement are:

- Dur – the duration of the agreement
- Wage – the wage increase in the first year of the contract
- Stat – the number of statutory holidays
- Vac – the number of paid vacation days
- Dis – the employer's help during employees long-term disability
- Dental – the contribution of the employer to a dental plan
- Ber – the employer's financial contribution to the costs of bereavement
- Health – the employer's contribution to the cost of the health plan

Table 3.1: Labor dataset.

Dur	Wage	Stat	Vac	Dis	Dental	Ber	Health	Class
1	5	11	average	?	?	yes	?	good
2	4.5	11	below	?	full	?	full	good
?	?	11	generous	yes	half	yes	half	good
3	3.7	?	?	?	?	yes	?	good
3	4.5	12	average	?	half	yes	half	good
2	2	12	average	?	?	?	?	good
3	4	12	generous	yes	none	yes	half	good
3	6.9	12	below	?	?	?	?	good
2	3	11	below	yes	half	yes	?	good
1	5.7	11	generous	yes	full	?	?	good
3	3.5	13	generous	?	?	yes	full	good
2	6.4	15	?	?	full	?	?	good
2	3.5	10	below	no	half	?	half	bad
3	3.5	13	generous	?	full	yes	full	good
1	3	11	generous	?	?	?	?	good
2	4.5	11	average	?	full	yes	?	good
1	2.8	12	below	?	?	?	?	good
1	2.1	9	below	yes	half	?	none	bad
1	2	11	average	no	none	no	none	bad
2	4	15	generous	?	?	?	?	good
2	4.3	12	generous	?	full	?	full	good
2	2.5	11	below	?	?	?	?	bad
3	3.5	?	?	?	?	?	?	good
2	4.5	10	generous	?	half	?	full	good
1	6	9	generous	?	?	?	?	good
3	2	10	below	?	half	yes	full	bad
2	4.5	10	below	yes	none	?	half	good
2	3	12	generous	?	?	yes	full	good
2	5	11	below	yes	full	yes	full	good
3	2	10	average	?	?	yes	full	bad
3	4.5	11	average	?	half	?	?	good
3	3	10	below	yes	half	yes	full	bad
2	2.5	10	average	?	?	?	?	bad
2	4	10	below	no	none	?	none	bad
3	2	10	below	no	half	yes	full	bad
2	2	11	average	yes	none	yes	full	bad
1	2	11	generous	no	none	no	none	bad
1	2.8	9	below	yes	half	?	none	bad
3	2	10	average	?	?	yes	none	bad
2	4.5	12	average	yes	full	yes	half	good
1	4	11	average	no	none	no	none	bad
2	2	12	generous	yes	none	yes	full	bad
2	2.5	12	average	?	?	yes	?	bad
2	2.5	11	below	?	?	yes	?	bad
2	4	10	below	no	none	?	none	bad
2	4.5	10	below	no	half	?	half	bad
2	4.5	11	average	?	full	yes	full	good
2	4.6	?	?	yes	half	?	half	good
2	5	11	below	yes	?	?	full	good
2	5.7	11	average	yes	full	yes	full	good
2	7	11	?	yes	full	?	?	good
3	2	?	?	yes	half	yes	?	good
3	3.5	13	generous	?	?	yes	full	good
3	4	11	average	yes	full	?	full	good
3	5	11	generous	yes	?	?	full	good
3	5	12	average	?	half	yes	half	good
3	6	9	generous	yes	full	yes	full	good

Applying a decision stump inducer on the Labor dataset results in the model that is depicted in Figure 3.4. Using ten-fold cross-validation, the estimated generalized accuracy of this model is 59.64%.

Next, we execute the bagging algorithm using decision stump as the base inducer ($I = DecisionStump$), four iterations ($T = 4$), and a sample size that is equal to the original training set ($\mu = |S| = 57$). Recall that the sampling is performed with replacement. Consequently, in each iteration some of the original instances from S may appear more than once, and

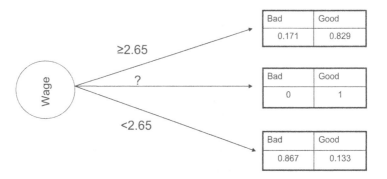

Fig. 3.4: Decision stump classifier for solving the Labor dataset classification task.

others may not be included at all. Table 3.2 indicates the number of times each instance was sampled in each iteration.

Figure 3.5 presents the four classifiers that were built. The estimated generalized accuracy of the ensemble classifier that uses them increases to 77.19%.

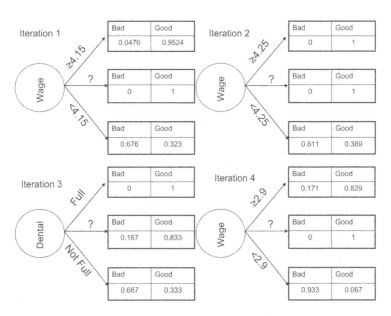

Fig. 3.5: Decision stump classifiers for solving the Labor classification task.

Table 3.2: Bagging sample sizes for the labor dataset.

Instance	Iteration 1	Iteration 2	Iteration 3	Iteration 4
1			1	1
2	1	1	1	1
3	2	1	1	1
4	1	1		
5		1	2	1
6	2	1		1
7		1	1	1
8	1		1	1
9		2		
10	1	1	2	
11		1		1
12	1	1	1	
13		1	1	2
14	1	1		2
15	1		1	1
16	2	3	2	1
17	1			
18	1	2	2	1
19	1			2
20		1	3	
21	2		1	1
22	2	1	1	
23		1	2	1
24	1	1		1
25	2	2	1	2
26	1	1	1	1
27		1		
28	2	1	1	1
29	1		1	1
30	1	1		
31		1	1	3
32	2	1	2	
33	1			1
34	2	2	1	
35				2
36	1	1	1	1
37		2	1	
38	2	1		1
39	2	1	1	
40	1	1	1	2
41	1	2	2	2
42		3	2	1
43	2			1
44	1	2	1	3
45	3	1	2	1
46	1		1	2
47	1	1	2	1
48		1	1	1
49	1	2	1	2
50	2		1	1
51	1	1	1	1
52	1	1	1	
53	1	2	2	2
54	1	1		
55			2	2
56	1	1	1	1
57	1	1	2	1
Total	57	57	57	57

Bagging often produces a combined model that outperforms the model that is built using a single instance of the original data. Breiman (1996) notes that this is particularly true for unstable inducers, since bagging can eliminate their instability. In this context, an inducer is considered unstable if perturbations in the learning set can produce significant changes in the classifier constructed.

3.4   The Boosting Algorithm

Boosting is a general method for improving the performance of a weak learner. This method works by iteratively invoking a weak learner on training data that is taken from various distributions. Similar to bagging, the classifiers are generated by resampling the training set. The classifiers are then combined into a single strong composite classifier. In contrast to bagging, the resampling mechanism in boosting improves the sample in order to provide the most useful sample for each consecutive iteration. Breiman [Breiman (1996a)] refers to the concept of boosting as the most significant development in classifier design of the 1990s.

The boosting algorithm is described in Figure 3.6. The algorithm generates three classifiers. The sample S_1, which is used to train the first classifier M_1, is randomly selected from the original training set. The second classifier M_2 is trained on a sample M_2, half of which consists of instances that are incorrectly classified by M_1, and the other half is composed of instances that are correctly classified by M_2. The last classifier M_3 is trained with instances that the two previous classifiers disagree on. In order to classify a new instance, each classifier produces the predicted class of the instance. The ensemble classifier returns the class that has the majority of the votes.

Boosting Training

Input: I (a weak inducer), S. (a training set), and k (the sample size for the first classifier)

Output: M_1, M_2, M_3

1: $S_1 \leftarrow$ Randomly selected $k < m$ instances from S without replacement;

2: $M_1 \leftarrow I(S_1)$

3: $S_2 \leftarrow$ Randomly selected instances (without replacement) from $S - S_1$ such that half of them are correctly classified by M_1.

4: $M_2 \leftarrow I(S_2)$

5: $S_3 \leftarrow$ any instances in $S - S_1 - S_2$ that are classified differently by M_1 and M_2.

Fig. 3.6: Boosting algorithm.

3.5 The AdaBoost Algorithm

First introduced in [Freund and Schapire (1996)], AdaBoost (adaptive boosting) is a popular ensemble algorithm that improves the simple boosting algorithm via an iterative process. The main idea behind this algorithm is to give more focus to patterns that are harder to classify. The amount of focus is quantified by a weight that is assigned to every pattern in the training set. Initially, the same weight is assigned to all of the patterns. In each iteration the weight of each misclassified Instance is increased, while the weight of correctly classified instances is decreased. As a result, a weak learner is forced to focus on the difficult instances of the training set by performing additional iterations and creating more classifiers. Furthermore, a weight is assigned to each individual classifier. This weight measures the *overall accuracy* of the classifier and is a function of the total weight of the correctly classified patterns. Thus, higher weights are given to more accurate classifiers. These weights are used for the classification of new cases.

This iterative procedure provides a series of classifiers that complement one another. In particular, it has been shown that AdaBoost approximates a large margin classifier such as the SVM [Rudin *et al.* (2004)].

The pseudocode of the AdaBoost algorithm is described in Figure 3.7. This algorithm assumes that the training set consists of m instances which are either labeled as -1 or $+1$. The classification of a new instance is obtained by voting on all classifiers $\{M_t\}$, each having an overall accuracy of α_t. Mathematically, it can be written as:

$$H(x) = sign(\sum_{t=1}^{T} \alpha_t \cdot M_t(x)) \tag{3.1}$$

Breiman [Breiman (1998)] explores a simpler algorithm called Arc-x4 whose purpose it is to demonstrate whether AdaBoost works because of the adaptive resampling or the specific form of weighing function used. In Arc-x4, a new pattern is classified according to unweighted voting, and the updated $t + 1$ iteration probabilities are defined by:

$$D_{t+1}(i) = 1 + m_{t_i}^4 \tag{3.2}$$

where m_{t_i} is the number of misclassifications of the i-th instance by the first t classifiers.

AdaBoost assumes that the weak inducers that are used to train the classifiers can handle weighted instances. For example, most decision tree

AdaBoost Training

Input: I (a weak inducer), T (the number of iterations), and S (a training set).

Output: $M_t, \alpha_t; t = 1, \ldots, T$

1: $t \leftarrow 1$
2: $D_1(i) \leftarrow 1/m; i = 1, \ldots, m$
3: **repeat**
4:    Build Classifier M_t using I and distribution D_t
5:    $\varepsilon_t \leftarrow \sum\limits_{i:M_t(x_i) \neq y_i} D_t(i)$
6:    **if** $\varepsilon_t > 0.5$ **then**
7:        $T \leftarrow t - 1$
8:        exit Loop.
9:    **end if**
10:    $\alpha_t \leftarrow \frac{1}{2} \ln\left(\frac{1-\varepsilon_t}{\varepsilon_t}\right)$
11:    $D_{t+1}(i) = D_t(i) \cdot e^{-\alpha_t y_t M_t(x_i)}$
12:    Normalize D_{t+1} to be a proper distribution.
13:    $t \leftarrow t + 1$
14: **until** $t > T$

Fig. 3.7: AdaBoost algorithm.

algorithms can handle weighted instances. However, if this is not the case, an unweighted dataset is generated from the weighted data via resampling. Namely, instances are chosen with a probability according to their weights (until the dataset becomes as large as the original training set).

In order to demonstrate how the AdaBoost algorithm works, we apply it to the Labor dataset using decision stump as the base inducer. For the sake of simplicity we use a feature reduced version of the Labor dataset which is composed of two input attributes: wage and statutory. Figure 3.8 presents the dataset that is projected into two dimensions; the plus symbol represents the "good" class, and the minus sign represents the "bad" class.

The initial distribution D_1 is set to be uniform. Consequently, it is not surprising that the first classifier is identical to the decision stump classifier that was presented in Figure 3.4. Figure 3.9 depicts the decision bound of the first classifier. The training misclassification rate of the first classifier is $\varepsilon_1 = 23.19\%$, therefore the overall accuracy weight of the first classifier is $\alpha_1 = 0.835$.

The weights of the instances are updated according to the misclassifica-

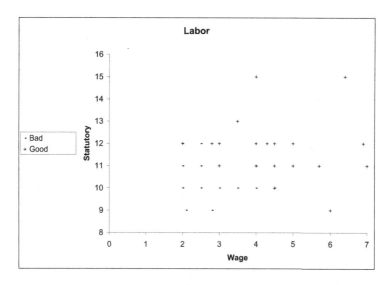

Fig. 3.8: Labor dataset.

tion rates as described in lines 11-12 of the algorithm. Figure 3.10 illustrates the new weights; instances whose weights were increased are depicted by larger symbols. Table 3.3 summarizes the exact weights after each iteration.

Applying the decision stump algorithm once more produces the classifier shown in Figure 3.11. The training misclassification rate of the second classifier is $\varepsilon_1 = 25.94\%$, and therefore the overall accuracy weight of the second classifier is $\alpha_1 = 0.79$. The new decision boundary, which is derived from the second classifier, is shown in Figure 3.12.

The subsequent iterations create the additional classifiers presented in Figure 3.11. Using the ten-fold cross-validation procedure, AdaBoost increased the estimated generalized accuracy from 59.64% to 87.71% after only four iterations. This improvement appears to be better than the improvement resulting from bagging (77.19%). AdaBoost was given a reduced version of the Labor dataset with only two input attributes. These two attributes were not selected arbitrarily, and in fact, the attributes were selected based on prior knowledge, so that AdaBoost would focus on the most relevant attributes. If AdaBoost is provided with the same dataset that was given to the bagging algorithm, it obtains the same accuracy as bagging. However, by increasing the ensemble size, AdaBoost continues to improve the accuracy while the Bagging algorithm shows very little im-

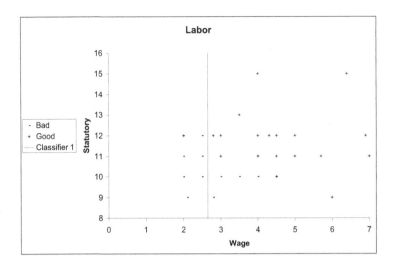

Fig. 3.9: The labor dataset with the decision bound of the first classifier.

provement. For example, in a case in which ten classifiers are trained over the entire Labor dataset, AdaBoost obtains an accuracy of 82.45%, while bagging obtains an accuracy of only 78.94%. AdaBoost seems to improve the accuracy for two main reasons:

(1) When using the training set it generates a final classifier whose error is small by combining many hypotheses whose error may be large.
(2) It produces a combined classifier whose variance is significantly lower than the variances produced by the weak base learner.

However, AdaBoost sometimes fails to improve the performance of the base inducer. According to Quinlan [Quinlan (1996)], the main reason for AdaBoost's failure is overfitting. The objective of boosting is to construct a composite classifier that performs well on the data by iteratively improving the classification accuracy, although a large number of iterations may result in an overly complex ensemble which is significantly less accurate than a single classifier. One possible way of avoiding overfitting is to keep the number of iterations as small as possible.

Bagging, like boosting, is a technique that improves the accuracy of a classifier by generating a composite model that combines multiple classifiers, all of which are derived from the same inducer. Both methods follow a voting approach, which is implemented differently in each method, in

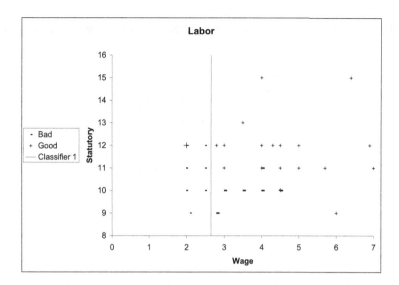

Fig. 3.10: Labor instance weights after the first iteration. Instances whose weights were increased are depicted by larger symbols. The vertical line depicts the decision boundary derived by the first classifier.

order to combine the outputs of the various classifiers. Unlike bagging, in boosting each classifier is influenced by the performance of the classifiers that were built prior to its construction. Specifically, the new classifier pays more attention to classification errors of the previously built classifiers, where the amount of attention was determined by their performance. In bagging each instance is chosen with equal probability, while in boosting instances are chosen with a probability that is proportional to their weight. Furthermore, as mentioned above (Quinlan, 1996), bagging requires an unstable learner as the base inducer; although boosting does not rely upon inducer instability, it does require that the error rate of each classifier be kept below 0.5.

Meir and Ratsch (2003) provide an overview of theoretical aspects of AdaBoost and its variants. They also suggest a generic scheme called leveraging, and many boosting algorithms have been derived from this scheme. The generic scheme is presented in Figure 3.13. Different algorithms use different loss functions G.

Table 3.3: The weights of the instances in the Labor dataset after each iteration.

				Weights		
Wage	Statutory	Class	Iteration 1	Iteration 2	Iteration 3	Iteration 4
5	11	good	1	0.59375	0.357740586	0.217005076
4.5	11	good	1	0.59375	0.357740586	0.217005076
?	11	good	1	0.59375	0.357740586	0.217005076
3.7	?	good	1	0.59375	0.357740586	1.017857143
4.5	12	good	1	0.59375	0.357740586	0.217005076
2	12	good	1	3.166666667	1.907949791	5.428571429
4	12	good	1	0.59375	0.357740586	1.017857143
6.9	12	good	1	0.59375	0.357740586	0.217005076
3	11	good	1	0.59375	0.357740586	1.017857143
5.7	11	good	1	0.59375	0.357740586	0.217005076
3.5	13	good	1	0.59375	0.357740586	1.017857143
6.4	15	good	1	0.59375	0.357740586	0.217005076
3.5	10	bad	1	3.166666667	1.907949791	1.157360406
3.5	13	good	1	0.59375	0.357740586	1.017857143
3	11	good	1	0.59375	0.357740586	1.017857143
4.5	11	good	1	0.59375	0.357740586	0.217005076
2.8	12	good	1	0.59375	0.357740586	1.017857143
2.1	9	bad	1	0.59375	0.357740586	0.217005076
2	11	bad	1	0.59375	1.744897959	1.058453331
4	15	good	1	0.59375	0.357740586	1.017857143
4.3	12	good	1	0.59375	0.357740586	0.217005076
2.5	11	bad	1	0.59375	1.744897959	1.058453331
3.5	?	good	1	0.59375	0.357740586	1.017857143
4.5	10	good	1	0.59375	1.744897959	1.058453331
6	9	good	1	0.59375	1.744897959	1.058453331
2	10	bad	1	0.59375	0.357740586	0.217005076
4.5	10	good	1	0.59375	1.744897959	1.058453331
3	12	good	1	0.59375	0.357740586	1.017857143
5	11	good	1	0.59375	0.357740586	0.217005076
2	10	bad	1	0.59375	0.357740586	0.217005076
4.5	11	good	1	0.59375	0.357740586	0.217005076
3	10	bad	1	3.166666667	1.907949791	1.157360406
2.5	10	bad	1	0.59375	0.357740586	0.217005076
4	10	bad	1	3.166666667	1.907949791	1.157360406
2	10	bad	1	0.59375	0.357740586	0.217005076
2	11	bad	1	0.59375	1.744897959	1.058453331
2	11	bad	1	0.59375	1.744897959	1.058453331
2.8	9	bad	1	3.166666667	1.907949791	1.157360406
2	10	bad	1	0.59375	0.357740586	0.217005076
4.5	12	good	1	0.59375	0.357740586	0.217005076
4	11	bad	1	3.166666667	9.306122449	5.64508443
2	12	bad	1	0.59375	1.744897959	1.058453331
2.5	12	bad	1	0.59375	1.744897959	1.058453331
2.5	11	bad	1	0.59375	1.744897959	1.058453331
4	10	bad	1	3.166666667	1.907949791	1.157360406
4.5	10	bad	1	3.166666667	1.907949791	5.428571429
4.5	11	good	1	0.59375	0.357740586	0.217005076
4.6	?	good	1	0.59375	0.357740586	0.217005076
5	11	good	1	0.59375	0.357740586	0.217005076
5.7	11	good	1	0.59375	0.357740586	0.217005076
7	11	good	1	0.59375	0.357740586	0.217005076
2	?	good	1	3.166666667	1.907949791	5.428571429
3.5	13	good	1	0.59375	0.357740586	1.017857143
4	11	good	1	0.59375	0.357740586	1.017857143
5	11	good	1	0.59375	0.357740586	0.217005076
5	12	good	1	0.59375	0.357740586	0.217005076
6	9	good	1	0.59375	1.744897959	1.058453331

3.6   Occam's Razor and AdaBoost's Training and Generalization Error

Freund and Schapire (1997) present an upper bound for the training error of AdaBoost ensemble. If AdaBoost calls a weak learning algorithm several time and generates classifiers with weighted training errors $\epsilon_1 \ldots \epsilon_T$ then the ensemble's training error is bounded above by:

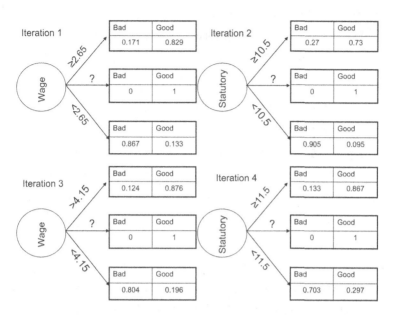

Fig. 3.11: Classifiers obtained by the first four iterations of AdaBoost.

$$\epsilon \leq 2^{T-1} \prod_{t=1}^{T} \sqrt{\epsilon_t(1 - \epsilon_t)} \tag{3.3}$$

Figure 3.14 illustrates Eq. 3.3 for three ϵ_t values: 0.49, 0.475 and 0.45. It can be seen from the figure that if each base classifier is (at least slightly) better than random (i.e. $\epsilon_t < 0.5$), then AdaBoost will converges to zero training error as the number of iterations T goes to infinity.

While Eq. 3.3 presents the training error, generalization error is the main goal. VC (Vapnik-Chervonenkis) theory provides upper bounds for generalization error in the case of binary classification task and zero-one loss function. In particular it characterizes a learning algorithm by its VC-dimension. VC-dimension measures the complexity (capacity) of the functions space that can be learned by a learning algorithm. It is defined as the cardinality of the largest set of points that can be shattered by the algorithm.

Coming back to our case, Freund and Schapire (1997) show that if the base classifiers in AdaBoost has a VC-dimension of d then the VC-dimension of the entire AdaBoost ensemble is at most $2(d + 1)(T + 1)log_2(e(T + 1))$. Thus based on the VC thoery the generalization error

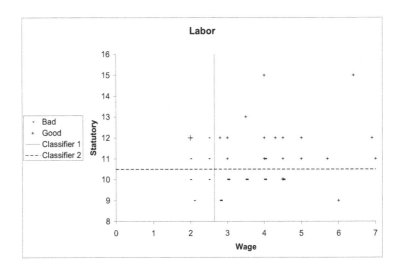

Fig. 3.12: Labor instance weights after the second iteration. Instances whose weights were increased are depicted by larger symbols. The horizontal line depicts the decision boundary that was added by the second classifier.

Input: $S = \langle (\boldsymbol{x}_1, y_1), \ldots, (\boldsymbol{x}_N, y_N) \rangle$, No. of Iterations T
   Loss function $G : \mathbb{R}^N \to \mathbb{R}$
Initialize: $f_0 \equiv 0$, $d_n^1 = g'(f_0(\boldsymbol{x}_n), y_n)$ for all $n = 1 \ldots N$
Do for $t = 1, \ldots, T$,
 (a) Train classifier on $\{S, \mathbf{d}^t\}$ and obtain hypothesis $H \in h_t : \mathbb{X} \to \mathbb{Y}$
 (b) Set $\alpha_t = \mathrm{argmin}_{\alpha \in \mathbb{R}} G[f_t + \alpha h_t]$
 (c) Update $f_{t+1} = f_t + \alpha_t h_t$ and $d_n^{(t+1)} = g'(f_{t+1}(\boldsymbol{x}_n), y_n)$, $n = 1, \ldots, N$
Output: f_T

Fig. 3.13: Leveraging algorithm presented by Meir and Ratsch (2003).

of AdaBoost is bounded by:

$$\epsilon_{generalization} \leq \epsilon_{train} + \mathcal{O}(\sqrt{\frac{Td}{m}}) \tag{3.4}$$

According to Eq. 3.4 one may expect that once the training error reaches zero, there is no point to add additional classifiers to the ensemble because a more complicated ensemble (i.e. bigger T) may perform worse.

This result is closely related to Occam's razor. William of Occam was a 14th century English philosopher who presented an important principle in

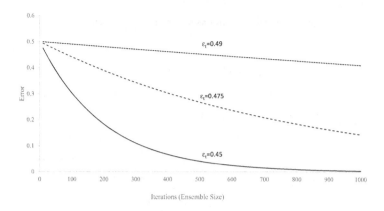

Fig. 3.14: Upper bound of the training error for $\epsilon_t = 0.49$, $\epsilon_t = 0.475$ and $\epsilon_t = 0.45$.

science which bears his name. *Occam's razor* states that the explanation of any phenomenon should make as few assumptions as possible, eliminating those that make no difference in the observable predictions of the explanatory hypothesis or theory.

In contrast to the Occam's razor and Eq. 3.4, it has been empirically observed that often certain ensemble techniques dont overfit the model, even when the ensemble contains thousands of classifiers and occasionally, the generalization error would continue to improve long after the training error reached zero.

Figure 3.15 illustrates this phenomenon. The figure shows the graphs of the training and test error produced by an AdaBoost algorithm as a function of its size. As expected from Eq. 3.3, the training error is a monotonically decreasing function. This curve demonstrates an interesting phenomenon, where the test error is also a monotonically decreasing function despite the fact that as the ensemble become more and more complex, we expect their generalization error eventually to increase.

Moreover, the curve demonstrates another apparent paradox. While the training error reaches zero, the test error which approximates the generalization error continues to decrease. This apparently contradicts the spirit of the Occam's razor. Comparing the performance of the ensemble that contains twenty members to the one that contains thirty members, we can see that they both have the same training error. Thus, according to simple

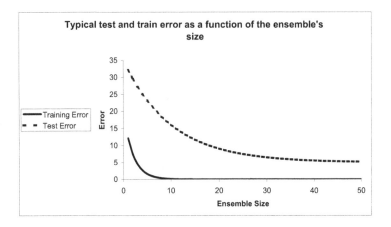

Fig. 3.15: Graphs of the training and test errors produced by an ensemble algorithm as a function of its size.

interpretation of Occams razor, one should prefer the simplest ensemble (in this case twenty members). However, the graph indicates that we should, instead, prefer the largest ensemble, since it obtains a lower test error.

In attempt to explain this paradox, Schapire *et al.* (1998) have shown that if the base-classifier has VC-dimension d, then with probability at least $1 - \delta$ the generalization error is bounded by:

$$\epsilon_{generalization} \leq \mathrm{P}_S[yf(\mathbf{x}) \leq \theta] + O(\frac{1}{\sqrt{m}}(\frac{d\log^2(m/d)}{\theta^2} + \log(1/\delta))^{1/2}) \quad (3.5)$$

where S is a sample of m instances chosen independently at random and θ represents the margin threshold.

Eq. 3.5 can be used to explain the apparent contradiction. The bound is independent of number of iterations T. Moreover, because AdaBoost concentrates on the hardest instances in the training set, the value of $yf(\mathbf{x})$ is expected to increase. As a result more base classifier agree and hence more iterations does not necessarily imply that final AdaBoost classifier is getting less accurate.

Despite the above explanation, it is important to note that AdaBoost can still overfit, if the base classifiers are too complex or predict values that are close to random guessing and hence the value of the term $yf(\mathbf{x})$ is too small.

According to [Domingos (1999)], there are two different interpretations of Occam's razor when it is applied to the machine learning domain:

- First interpretation – Given two classifiers with the same generalization error, the simpler one should be preferred, because simplicity is desirable in itself.
- Second interpretation – Given two classifiers with the same training set error, the simpler one should be preferred, because it is likely to have a lower generalization error.

This apparent contradiction of Occam's razor can be resolved by arguing that the first interpretation of Occams razor is largely agreed upon, while the second one, when taken literally, is false [Domingos (1999)].

Freund (2009) claims that there are two main theories for explaining the phenomena presented in Figure 3.15. The first theory relates ensemble methods such as Adaboost to logistic regression. The decrease in the misclassification rate of the ensemble is seen as a by-product of the likelihood's improvement. The second theory refers to the large margins theory. Like the theory of support vector machines (SVM), the focus of large margin theory is on the task of reducing the classification error rate obtained on the test set.

3.7 No-Free-Lunch Theorem and Ensemble Learning

Empirical comparison of different ensemble approaches and their variants in a wide range of application domains has shown that each performs best in some, but not all, domains. This has been termed the *selective superiority problem* [Brodley (1995a)].

It is also well-known that no existing learning algorithm can produce the best performance in all possible domains. Each algorithm is either explicitly or implicitly biased [Mitchell (1980)], preferring certain generalizations over others, and the algorithm is successful as long as this bias matches the characteristics of the application domain [Brazdil *et al.* (1994)]. Furthermore, other research has demonstrated the existence and correctness of the "conservation law" [Schaffer (1994)] or "No-Free-Lunch Theorem" [Wolpert (1996)].

The No Free Lunch Theorem implies that for a given problem, a certain approach can derive more information than other approaches when applied to the same data: "for any two learning algorithms, there are just as many situations (appropriately weighted) in which algorithm one is superior to algorithm two and vice versa, according to any of the measures of superiority." [Wolpert (2001)]

A distinction should be made between all of the mathematically possible domains and domains that occur in the real world [Rao *et al.* (1995)]. Obviously, there are many domains in the former group that are not in the latter, and the average accuracy in real-world domains can be increased at the expense of accuracy in domains that never occur in practice. Indeed, achieving this is the goal of machine learning research. It is still true that some algorithms will be more suited to certain classes of naturally occurring domains than other algorithms and therefore achieve higher accuracy than the other algorithms. However, this does not preclude an improved algorithm from being as accurate as the best in all domains.

Indeed, in many application domains the generalization error of even the best methods is significantly higher than 0%, and an important outstanding question is whether those methods can be improved, and if so how. In order to answer this question, one must first determine the minimum error achievable by any classifier in the application domain (known as the optimal Bayes error). If existing classifiers do not reach this level, new approaches are needed. Although this problem has received considerable attention (see for instance [Tumer and Ghosh (1996)]), none of the methods proposed in the literature thus far is accurate for a wide range of problem domains.

The no-free-lunch concept presents a dilemma to practitioners who must determine which learning algorithm to use. The quest for inventing the ultimate learning algorithm, or the *master algorithm*, that always provides the best predictive performance, is still in progress. Although the algorithm does not yet exist, Domingos (2015) examines how it will remake our world once it is discovered.

Ensemble methods tackle the no-free-lunch dilemma by combining the outputs of many classifiers, assuming that each classifier performs well in certain domains while being suboptimal in others. Specifically, *multistrategy learning* [Michalski and Tecuci (1994)] attempts to combine two or more different paradigms within a single algorithm. Most research in this area has focused on combining empirical and analytical approaches (see, for instance [Towell and Shavlik (1994)]). Ideally, a multistrategy learning algorithm should always perform as well as the best of its members, thereby alleviating the need to individually employ each one and simplifying the knowledge acquisition task. A more ambitious goal would be to combine different paradigms may produce synergistic effects (for example, by constructing various types of frontiers between different class regions in the instance space), leading to levels of accuracy that no single approach can achieve.

3.8   Bias-Variance Decomposition and Ensemble Learning

It is well-known that error can be decomposed into three additive components [Kohavi and Wolpert (1996)]: intrinsic error, bias error and variance error. Intrinsic error, also known as irreducible error, is the component that is generated due to noise. This quantity is the lower bound of any inducer, i.e., it is the expected error of the Bayes optimal classifier.

The bias error of an inducer is the persistent or systematic error that the inducer is expected to make. The bias error represents the tendency of the learning algorithm to consistently learn the same wrong thing because the hypothesis space considered by the learning algorithm does not include sufficient hypotheses.

Variance is a concept closely related to bias. The variance error captures random variation in the algorithm from one training set to another. It represents the tendency of the learning algorithm to learn random things irrespective of the real signal due to the particular training set used. Namely, it measures the sensitivity of the algorithm to the actual training set, or the error that results from the training set's finite size.

The following equations provide one of the possible mathematical definitions of the various error in the case of a zero-one loss:

$$t(I, S, c_j, x) = \begin{cases} 1 & \hat{P}_{I(S)}(y = c_j \,|x\,) > \hat{P}_{I(S)}(y = c^* \,|x\,) \, \forall c^* \in dom(y), \neq c_j \\ 0 & Otherwise \end{cases}$$

$$bias^2(P(y\,|x\,), \hat{P}_I(y\,|x\,)) =$$

$$\frac{1}{2} \sum_{c_j \in dom(y)} \left[P(y = c_j \,|x\,) - \sum_{\forall S, |S| = m} P(S\,|D) \cdot t(I, S, c_j, x) \right]^2$$

$$var(\hat{P}_I(y\,|x\,)) = \frac{1}{2} \left\{ 1 - \sum_{c_j \in dom(y)} \left[\sum_{\forall S, |S| = m} P(S\,|D) \cdot t(I, S, c_j, x) \right]^2 \right\}$$

$$var(P(y\,|x\,)) = \frac{1}{2} \left\{ 1 - \sum_{c_j \in dom(y)} [P(y = c_j \,|x\,)]^2 \right\}$$

Note that the probability of misclassifying the instance x using inducer I and a training set of size m is:

$$\varepsilon(x) = bias^2(P(y\,|x), \hat{P}_I(y\,|x)) + \text{var}(\hat{P}_I(y\,|x)) + \text{var}(P(y\,|x))$$
$$= 1 - \sum_{c_j \in dom(y)} P(y = c_j\,|x) \cdot \sum_{\forall S,|S|=m} P(S\,|D) \cdot t(I, S, c_j, x)$$

where I is an inducer, S is a training set, c_j is a class label, x is a pattern, and D is the instance domain. It is important to note that in the case of a zero-one loss there are other definitions for the bias and variance components. These definitions are not necessarily consistent. In fact, there is considerable debate in the literature about what the most appropriate definition should be. For a complete list of these definitions please refer to [Hansen (2000)].

Nevertheless, in the regression problem domain a single definition of bias and variance has been adopted by the entire community. Specifically, the bias-variance components are defined by referring to the quadratic loss, as follows:

$$E\left(f(x) - \hat{f}_R(x)^2\right) =$$
$$\text{var}(f(x)) + \text{var}\left(\hat{f}_R(x)\right) + bias^2\left(f(x), \hat{f}_R(x)\right)$$

where $\hat{f}_R(x)$ is the prediction of the regression model, and $f(x)$ is the actual value. The intrinsic variance and bias components are respectively defined as:

$$\text{var}(f(x)) = E((f(x) - E(f(x)))^2)$$
$$\text{var}(\hat{f}_R(x)) = E((\hat{f}_R(x) - E(\hat{f}_R(x)))^2)$$
$$bias^2(f(x), \hat{f}_R(x)) = E((E(\hat{f}_R(x)) - E(f(x)))^2$$

Simpler models tend to have a higher bias error and a smaller variance error than complicated models. Bauer and Kohavi (1999) published experimental results demonstrating how models complexity affect the bias-variance tradeoff in case of Naïve Bayes learning algorithm, while others examined the bias-variance issue in decision trees algorithms [Dietterich and Kong (1995)]. Figure 3.16 illustrates the tradeoff between variance and bias. When the classifier is simple it has a large bias error and a small variance error. As the complexity of the classifier increases, the variance error becomes larger, and the bias error becomes smaller. The minimum generalization error is obtained somewhere in between.

Empirical and theoretical evidence show that some ensemble techniques (such as bagging) act as a variance reduction mechanism, i.e., they reduce

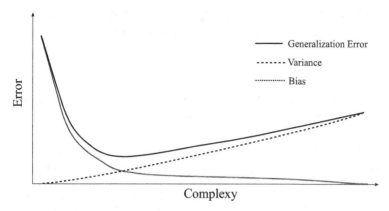

Fig. 3.16: Bias error vs. variance error in the deterministic case (Hansen, 2000).

the variance component of the error. Moreover, empirical results suggest that other ensemble techniques (such as AdaBoost) reduce both the bias and the variance components of the error. In particular, it seems that the bias error is mainly reduced in the early iterations, while the variance error decreases in later ones.

3.9 Classifier Dependency

Ensemble methods can be differentiated based on the extent each classifier affects the other classifiers. This property indicates whether the various classifiers are dependent or independent. In a dependent framework the outcome of a certain classifier affects the creation of the next classifier as it happens in AdaBoost. In an independent framework each classifier is built independently, and their results are combined in some fashion. Some researchers refer to this property as "the relationship between modules" and distinguish between three different types: successive, cooperative, and supervisory [Sharkey (1996)]. Roughly speaking, "successive" refers to "dependent," while "cooperative" refers to "independent." The last type applies to those cases in which one model controls the other model.

3.9.1 *Dependent Methods*

In dependent approaches for learning ensembles there is an interaction between the learning runs. Thus, it is possible to take advantage of knowledge generated in previous iterations to guide the learning in upcoming iterations. We distinguish between two main approaches for dependent learning, as described in the following sections [Provost and Kolluri (1997)].

3.9.1.1   *Model-Guided Instance Selection*

In this dependent approach the classifiers that were constructed in previous iterations are used for manipulating the training set for the next iteration (see Figure 3.17). One can embed this process within the basic learning algorithm. These methods usually ignore all data instances for which their initial classifier is correct and only learn from misclassified instances.

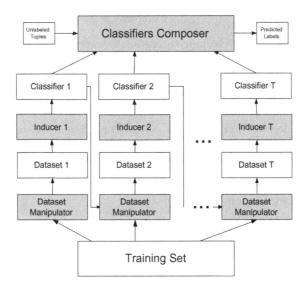

Fig. 3.17: Model-guided instance selection diagram.

3.9.1.2   *Basic Boosting Algorithms*

The most well-known model-guided instance selection method is boosting. Boosting, also known as arcing (adaptive resampling and combining), is a general method for improving the performance of a weak learner. The method works by repeatedly running a weak learner (such as classification rules or decision trees) on various distributed training data. The classifiers produced by the weak learners are then combined into a single composite strong classifier, in order to achieve greater accuracy than the individual classifiers would achieve.

Recall that the main idea of this AdaBoost algorithm is to assign a weight to each instance in the training set. In the beginning, all weights are equal, but in every round the weights of all misclassified instances are increased, while the weights of correctly classified instances are decreased. As a consequence, the weak learner is forced to focus on the difficult instances of the training set. This procedure provides a series of classifiers that complement one another.

The basic AdaBoost algorithm deals with binary classification. Freund and Schapire describe two versions of the AdaBoost algorithm (AdaBoost.M1, AdaBoost.M2), which are equally effective for binary classification but differ in their handling of multiclass classification problems. Figure 3.18 describes the pseudocode of AdaBoost.M1. The classification of a new instance is performed according to the following equation:

$$H(x) = \underset{y \in dom(y)}{\mathrm{argmax}} \left(\sum_{t: M_t(x) = y} \log \frac{1}{\beta_t} \right) \tag{3.6}$$

where β_t is defined in Figure 3.18.

Input: I (a weak inducer), T (the number of iterations), and S (the training set).

Output: $M_t, \beta_t; t = 1, \ldots, T$

1: $t \leftarrow 1$
2: $D_1(i) \leftarrow 1/m; i = 1, \ldots, m$
3: **repeat**
4:     Build classifier M_t using I and distribution D_t
5:     $\varepsilon_t \leftarrow \sum\limits_{i: M_t(x_i) \neq y_i} D_t(i)$
6:     **if** $\varepsilon_t > 0.5$ **then**
7:         $T \leftarrow t - 1$
8:         exit Loop.
9:     **end if**
10:     $\beta_t \leftarrow \frac{\varepsilon_t}{1 - \varepsilon_t}$
11:     $D_{t+1}(i) = D_t(i) \cdot \begin{cases} \beta_t & M_t(x_i) = y_i \\ 1 & Otherwise \end{cases}$
12:     Normalize D_{t+1} to be a proper distribution.
13:     $t++$
14: **until** $t > T$

Fig. 3.18: AdaBoost.M1 algorithm.

AdaBoost.M2 extends the basic AdaBoost algorithm for dealing with multiclass classification tasks. This extension requires more elaborate communication between the boosting algorithm and the weak learning algorithm. AdaBoost.M2 uses the notion of "pseudo-loss" which measures the goodness of the weak hypothesis. The pseudocode of AdaBoost.M2 is presented in Figure 3.19. A different weight $w_{i,y}^t$ is maintained for each instance i and label $y \in Y - \{y_i\}$. The function $q = \{1, \ldots, m\} \times Y \to [0, 1]$, called the *label weighting function*, assigns a probability distribution to each example i in the training set such that for each i: $\sum_{y \neq y_i} q(i, y) = 1$. The inducer gets both a distribution D_t and a label weight function q_t. The inducer's target is to minimize the pseudo-loss ϵ_t for a given distribution D and weighting function q.

AdaBoost.M2

Input: I (a base inducer), T (the number of iterations), $S = (x_1, y_1), \ldots, (x_m, y_m); y_i \in Y$ (the original training set).

1: Initialize the weight vector $D_1(i) \leftarrow 1/m$ for $i = 1, \ldots, m$ and $w_{i,y}^1 = D_1(i)/(k-1)$ for $i = 1, \ldots, m$; $y \in Y - y_i$.

2: **for** $t = 1, 2, \ldots, T$ **do**

3:    Set $W_i^t = \Sigma_{y \neq y_i} w_{i,y}^t$

4:    For $y \neq y_i$ set $q_t(i, y) = \frac{w_{i,y}^t}{W_i^t}$

5:    Set $D_t(i) = \frac{W_i^t}{\sum_{i=1}^m W_i^t}$

6:    Call I, providing it with distribution D_t and label weighting function q_t; get back a hypothesis $M_t : X \times Y \longrightarrow [0, 1]$

7:    Calculate the pseudo-loss of M_t: $\epsilon_t = \frac{1}{2} \sum_{i=1}^m D_t(i)(1 - M_t(x_i, y_i) + \frac{1}{k-1} \sum_{y \neq y_i} q_t(i, y) M_t(x_i, y))$

8:    Set $\beta_t = \epsilon_t/(1 - \epsilon_t)$

9:    Set the weight vector to be: $w_{i,y}^{t+1} = w_{i,y}^t \beta_t^{(1/2)(1+M_t(x_i,y_i)-M_t(x_i,y))}$ for $i = 1, \ldots, m$, $y \in Y - \{y_i\}$.

10: **end for**

Fig. 3.19: The AdaBoost.M2 algorithm.

3.9.1.3   *Advanced Boosting Algorithms*

Friedman *et al.* [Friedman *et al.* (2000)] present a generalized version of AdaBoost, which they call Real AdaBoost. The revised algorithm combines the class probability estimate of the classifiers by fitting an additive logistic regression model in a forward stepwise manner. The revision reduces computation cost and may lead to better performance, especially in decision trees. Moreover, it can provide interpretable descriptions of the aggregate decision rule.

Friedman [Friedman (2002)] developed gradient boosting which builds an ensemble by sequentially fitting base learner parameters to current pseudo-residuals by least squares in each iteration. The pseudo-residuals are the gradient of the loss function being minimized, with respect to the model values at each training data point evaluated in the current step. To improve accuracy, increase robustness, and reduce computational cost, a subsample of the training set is randomly selected (without replacement) and used to fit the base classifier in each iteration.

Phama and Smeuldersb [Phama and Smeuldersb (2008)] present a strategy to improve the AdaBoost algorithm with a quadratic combination of base classifiers. The idea is to construct an intermediate learner operating on the combined linear and quadratic terms.

First, a classifier is trained by randomizing the labels of the training examples. Next, the learning algorithm is called repeatedly, using a systematic update of the labels of the training examples in each round. In contrast to the AdaBoost algorithm, this method reweights training examples. Together they form a powerful combination which makes intensive use of the given base learner by both reweighting and relabeling the original training set. Compared to AdaBoost, quadratic boosting better exploits the instances space; it also compares favorably with AdaBoost on large datasets, however this favorable performance comes at the cost of training speed. Although training the ensemble takes about 10 times more time than AdaBoost, the classification time for both algorithms is equivalent.

Tsao and Chang [Tsao and Chang (2007)] refer to boosting as a stochastic approximation procedure. Based on this viewpoint they developed the SABoost (stochastic approximation) algorithm which is similar to AdaBoost except for the way in which members' weights are calculated.

All of the boosting algorithms presented assume that the weak inducers provided can cope with weighted instances. If this is not the case, an unweighted dataset is generated from the weighted data by a resampling technique. Namely, instances are chosen with a probability according to their weight (until the dataset becomes as large as the original training set).

AdaBoost rarely suffers from overfitting problems. Freund and Schapire (2000) note that "one of the main properties of boosting that has made it interesting to statisticians and others is its relative (but not complete) immunity to overfitting." In addition, Breiman (2000) indicates that "a crucial property of AdaBoost is that it almost never overfits the data no matter how many iterations it is run." Still, in very noisy datasets overfitting does occur.

Another important drawback of boosting is that it is difficult to understand. The resulting ensemble is considered to be less comprehensible, since the user must grasp several classifiers instead of a single classifier. Despite the above disadvantages, Breiman [Breiman (1996a)] refers to the boosting idea as the most significant development in classifier design of the 1990s.

Sun *et al.* [Sun *et al.* (2006)] pursue a strategy which penalizes the data distribution skewness in the learning process to prevent several hard instances from spoiling decision boundaries. They use two smooth convex penalty functions based on Kullback–Leibler divergence (KL) and L2-Norm , in order to derive two new algorithms: AdaBoostKL and AdaBoost-Norm2 . These two AdaBoost variations achieve better performance on noisy datasets.

Induction algorithms have been applied with practical success in many relatively simple and small-scale problems, however most of these algorithms require loading the entire training set to the main memory. The need to induce from large masses of data has caused a number of previously unknown problems, which, if ignored, may turn the task of efficient pattern recognition into mission impossible. Managing and analyzing huge datasets requires special and very expensive hardware and software, which often forces us to exploit only a small portion of the stored data.

Huge databases pose several challenges:

- Computing complexity: Since most induction algorithms have a computational complexity that is greater than linear in the number of attributes or tuples, the execution time needed to process such databases might become an important issue.
- Poor classification accuracy due to difficulties in identifying the correct classifier. Large databases increase the size of the search space, and this in turn increases the chances that the inducer will select an overfitted classifier that is generally not valid.
- Storage problems: In most machine learning algorithms, the entire training set should be read from the secondary storage (such as magnetic storage) into the computer's primary storage (main memory)

before the induction process begins. This causes problems, since the main memory's capacity is much smaller than that of magnetic disks.

Instead of training on a very large data base, Breiman (1999) proposes taking small portions of the data, training a classifier on each small piece, and then combining these predictors together. Because each classifier is grown on a modestly-sized training set, this method can be used on large datasets. Moreover, this method provides accuracy which is comparable to that which would have been obtained if all of the data could have been held in the main memory. Nevertheless, the main disadvantage of this algorithm is that in most cases it requires many iterations to obtain accuracy comparable to AdaBoost.

An online boosting algorithm called IVoting trains the base models using consecutive subsets of training examples of some fixed size [Breiman (1999)]. For the first base classifier the training instances are randomly selected from the training set. To generate a training set for the kth base classifier, IVoting selects a training set in which half the instances have been correctly classified by the ensemble consisting of the previous base classifiers, and half have been misclassified. This algorithm is an improvement on boosting which is less vulnerable to noise and overfitting. Further, since it does not require assigning weights to the base classifiers, IVoting can be used in a parallel fashion, as demonstrated in [Chawla *et al.* (2004)].

Merler *et al.* [Merler *et al.* (2007)] developed the P-AdaBoost algorithm which is a distributed version of AdaBoost. Instead of updating the "weights" associated with instances in a sequential manner, P-AdaBoost works in two phases. In the first phase, the AdaBoost algorithm runs in its standard sequential fashion for a limited number of steps. In the second phase, the classifiers are trained in parallel using weights that are estimated from the first phase. P-AdaBoost yields approximations for the standard AdaBoost models which can be easily and efficiently distributed on a network of computing nodes.

Zhang and Zhang [Zhang and Zhang (2008)] propose an AdaBoost variant called LocalBoost. In this algorithm a local error is calculated for each training instance which is then used to update the probability that this instance is chosen for the training set of the next iteration. After each iteration a global error measure is calculated that refers to all instances. Consequently, noisy instances might affect the global error measure, even if most of the instances can be classified correctly. Local boosting aims to solve this problem by inspecting each iteration locally, per instance. A local error measure is calculated for each instance of each iteration, and the instance receives a score which will be used to measure its significance in classifying new instances. Each instance in the training set also maintains a local weight which controls its chances of being picked in the next iteration. Instead of automatically increasing the weight of a misclassified instance (like in AdaBoost), they first compare the misclassified instance with similar instances in the training set. If these similar instances are classified correctly, the misclassified instance is likely to be a noisy one that cannot contribute to the learning procedure, and thus its weight is decreased. If the instance's neighbors are also misclassified, the instance's weight is increased. As in AdaBoost, if an instance is classified correctly, its weight is decreased. Classifying a new instance is based on its similarity with each training instance.

The advantages of local boosting compared to other ensemble methods are:

(1) The algorithm tackles the problem of noisy instances. It has been empirically shown that the local boosting algorithm is more robust to noise than AdaBoost.
(2) With respect to accuracy, LocalBoost generally outperforms AdaBoost. Moreover, LocalBoost outperforms bagging and random forest when the noise level is low.

The disadvantages of local boosting compared to other ensemble methods are:

(1) When the amount of noise is large, LocalBoost sometimes performs worse than bagging and random forest.
(2) Saving the data for each instance increases storage complexity; this might confine the use of this algorithm to limited training sets.

The AdaBoost.M1 algorithm guarantees an exponential decrease of the upper bound of the training error rate as long as the error rates of the base classifiers are less than 50%. For multiclass classification tasks this condition can be too restrictive for weak classifiers like decision stumps. In order to make AdaBoost.M1 suitable for weak classifiers, the BoostMA algorithm modifies it by using a different function to weight the classifiers [Freund (1995); Eibl and Pfeiffer (2005)]. Specifically, the modified function becomes positive if the error rate is less than the error rate of the default classification. As opposed to AdaBoost.M2, where the weights are increased if the error rate exceeds 50%, in BoostMA the weights are increased for instances for which the classifier performed worse than the default classification (i.e., classification of each instance as the most frequent class). Moreover, in BoostMA the base classifier minimizes the confidence-rated error instead of the pseudo-loss / error rate (as in Adaboost.M1 or AdaBoost.M2) which makes it easier to use with already existing base classifiers.

AdaBoost-R is a variant of AdaBoost which considers not only the last weak classifier, but a classifier formed by the last r selected weak classifiers (r is a parameter of the method). If the weak classifiers are decision stumps, the combination of r weak classifiers is a decision tree. A primary drawback of AdaBoost-R is that it will only be useful if the classification method does not generate strong classifiers.

Figure 3.20 presents the pseudocode of AdaBoost-R. In line one we initialize a distribution on the instances so that the sum of all weights is one, and all instances obtain the same weight. In line three we perform a number of iterations according to the parameter T. In lines 4-8 we define the training set S' on which the base classifier will be trained. We check whether the resampling or reweighting version of the algorithm is required. If resampling is needed, we resample the training set according to distribution D_t. The resampled set S' is the same size as S, however the instances it contains were drawn with replacement from S according to D_t. Otherwise (if reweighting is needed) we simply set S' as the entire original dataset S. In line nine we train a base classifier M_t from the base inducer I on S' while using the values of distribution D_t as instance weights. The major difference from the standard AdaBoost algorithm can be seen in line 10. Each of the instances of the original dataset S is classified with the base classifier M_t. The most recent classification is saved in the sequence of the last R classifications. Since we are dealing with a binary class problem, the class can be represented by a single bit (0 or 1). Therefore, the sequence can be stored as a binary sequence with the most recent classification being appended as the least significant bit. This is how existing base classifiers are combined through the classification sequence. The sequence can be treated as a binary number representing a leaf in the combined classifier M_t^r to which the instance belongs. Each leaf has two buckets (one for each class). When an instance is assigned to a certain leaf, its weight is added to the bucket representing the instance's real class. Afterwards, the final class of each leaf of M_t^r is determined by the heaviest bucket. The combined classifier does not need to be explicitly saved, since it is represented by the final classes of the leaves and the base classifiers M_t, $M_{t-1}, \ldots M_{max(t-r,1)}$. In line 11 the error rate ε_t of M_t^r of the original dataset S is computed by summing the weight of all of the instances the combined classifier misclassified and dividing the sum by the total weight of all of the instances in S. In line 12 we check whether the error rate is over 0.5 which would indicate that the newly combined classifier is even worse than random classifier or the error rate is 0 which indicates overfitting. In cases in which resampling was used and an error rate of 0 was obtained, it could indicate an unfortunate resampling, in which case the recommendation is to return to the resampling section (line 8) and retry (up to a certain number of failed attempts, e.g., 10). Line 15 is executed in cases in which the error rate was under 0.5, and therefore we define α_t to be $\frac{1-\varepsilon_t}{\varepsilon_t}$. In lines 16-20 we iterate over all of the instances in S and update the weights of the instances for the next iteration (D_{t+1}). If the combined classifier misclassified the instance, its weight is multiplied by α_t. In line 21, after the weights have been updated, they are normalized so that D_{t+1} will be a well-defined distribution (i.e., all weights will sum to one). This concludes the iteration, with everything ready for the next iteration.

In order to classify an instance, we traverse each of the combined classifiers, classify the instance with it, and receive either -1 or 1. The class is then multiplied by $\log(\alpha_t)$, which is the weight assigned to the classifier trained in iteration t, and added to a global sum. If the sum is positive, the class "1" is returned; if it is negative, "-1" is returned; and if the sum is 0, the returned class is random. This can also be viewed as summing the weights of the classifiers per class and returning the class with the maximal sum. Since we do not explicitly save the combined classifier M_t^r, we obtain its classification by classifying the instance with the relevant base classifiers and using the binary classification sequence which is given by $(M_t(x), M_{t-1}(x), \ldots M_{\max(t-r,1)}(x))$ as a leaf index into the combined classifier and using the final class of the leaf as the classification result of M_t^r.

AdaBoost.M1 is known to have problems when the base classifiers are weak, i.e., the predictive performance of each base classifier is not much higher than that of random guessing.

AdaBoost.M1W is a revised version of AdaBoost.M1 that aims to improve its accuracy in such cases (Eibl and Pfeiffer, 2002). In this version only one line in the pseudocode of AdaBoost.M1 is adjusted, specifically the new weight of the base classifier is defined as:

AdaBoost-R Algorithm

Input: I (a base inducer), T (the number of iterations), S (the original training set), ρ (whether to perform resampling or reweighting), and r (reuse level).

1: Initiate: $D_1(X_i) = \frac{1}{m}$ for all i's.
2: $T = 1$
3: **repeat**
4:    **if** ρ **then**
5:      $S' = resample(S, D_t)$
6:    **else**
7:      $S' = S$
8:    **end if**
9:    Train base classifier M_t with I on S' with instance weights according to D_t
10:    Combine classifiers $M_t, M_{t-1}, \ldots M_{max(t-r,1)}$ to create M_t^r.
11:    Calculate the error rate ε_t of the combined classifier M_t^r on S
12:    **if** $\varepsilon_t \geq 0.5$ or $\varepsilon_t = 0$ **then**
13:      End;
14:    **end if**
15:    $\alpha_t = \frac{1-\varepsilon_t}{\varepsilon_t}$
16:    **for** $i{=}1$ to m **do**
17:      **if** $M_t^r(X_i) \neq Y_i$ **then**
18:        $D_{t+1}(X_i) = D_t(X_i) \times \alpha_t$
19:      **end if**
20:    **end for**
21:    Renormalize D_{t+1} so it will be a distribution
22:    $t \leftarrow t + 1$
23: **until** $t > T$

Fig. 3.20: The AdaBoost-R algorithm.

$$\alpha_t = \ln\left(\frac{(|dom(y)| - 1)(1 - \varepsilon_t)}{\varepsilon_t}\right) \tag{3.7}$$

where ε_t is the error estimation which is defined in the original AdaBoost.M1, and $|dom(y)|$ represents the number of classes. Note the above equation generalizes AdaBoost.M1 by setting $|dom(y)| = 2$.

3.9.1.4 *Incremental Batch Learning*

In this method the classification produced in one iteration is given as "prior knowledge" to the learning algorithm in the following iteration. The learning algorithm uses the current training set, together with the classification of the former classifier, for building the next classifier. The classifier constructed in the last iteration is chosen as the final classifier.

3.9.2 *Independent Methods*

In independent methods the original dataset is partitioned into several subsets from which multiple classifiers are induced. These independent methods aim either at improving the predictive power of classifiers or decreasing the total execution time. Figure 3.21 illustrates the independent ensemble methodology. The subsets created from the original training set may be disjointed (mutually exclusive) or overlapping. A combining procedure is then applied in order to produce a single classification for a given instance. Since the method for combining the results of induced classifiers is usually independent of the induction algorithms, it can be used with different inducers in each subset. Moreover independent methods are easily parallelized. The following sections describe several algorithms that follow this methodology.

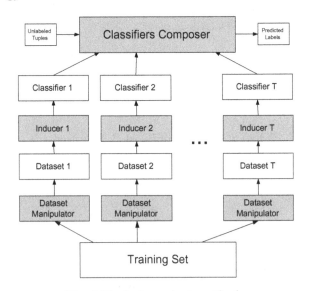

Fig. 3.21: Independent methods.

3.9.2.1 *Bagging*

The most well-known independent method is bagging (Bootstrap Aggregating) [Breiman (1996a)]. The method aims to increase accuracy by creating an improved composite classifier by amalgamating the various outputs of learned classifiers into a single prediction. Each classifier is trained on a sample of instances taken with a replacement from the training set. Each sample size is equal to the size of the original training set. Note that since sampling with replacement is used, some of the original instances may appear in each training set more than once, and some may not be included at all.

So while the training sets may be different from each other, they are certainly not independent from a statistical point of view. To classify a new instance, each classifier returns the class prediction for the unknown instance. The composite bagged classifier, returns the class that has been predicted most often (voting method). The result is that bagging produces a combined model that often performs better than the single model built from the original data. Breiman [Breiman (1996a)] notes that this is true especially for unstable inducers, because bagging can mitigate their instability. In this context, an inducer is considered unstable if perturbing the learning set can cause significant changes in the classifier constructed.

Bagging, like boosting, is a technique for improving the accuracy of a classifier by producing different classifiers and combining multiple models. They both use a kind of voting for classification in order to combine the outputs of different classifiers of the same type. In contrast to bagging, in boosting each classifier is influenced by the performance of those built before it, with the new classifier trying to pay more attention to errors that were made in the previous classifiers and their performance. In bagging, each instance is chosen with equal probability, while in boosting, instances are chosen with a probability proportional to their weight. Furthermore, according to Quinlan [Quinlan (1996)], as mentioned above, bagging requires that the learning system is stable, whereas boosting does not preclude the use of unstable learning systems, provided that their error rate can be kept below 0.5.

3.9.2.2 *Wagging*

Wagging is a variant of bagging [Bauer and Kohavi (1999)] in which each classifier is trained on the entire training set, but each instance is stochastically assigned a weight. Figure 3.22 presents the pseudocode of the wagging algorithm.

In fact bagging can be considered as wagging with an allocation of weights from the Poisson distribution (each instance is represented in the sample a discrete number of times). Alternatively, it is possible to allocate the weights from the exponential distribution, because the exponential distribution is the continuous valued counterpart to the Poisson distribution [Webb (2000)].

Input: I (an inducer), T (the number of iterations), S (the training set), and d (weighting distribution).
Output: $M_t; t = 1, \ldots, T$
   1: $t \leftarrow 1$
   2: **repeat**
   3:    $S_t \leftarrow S$ with random weights drawn from d.
   4:    Build classifier M_t using I on S_t
   5:    $t + +$
   6: **until** $t > T$

Fig. 3.22: Wagging algorithm.

3.9.2.3 *Random Forest and Random Subspace Projection*

A random forest ensemble [Breiman   (2001)] uses a large number of individual, unpruned decision trees. The individual trees are constructed using a simple algorithm presented in Figure 3.23. The IDT in Figure 3.23 represents any top-down decision tree induction algorithm [Rokach and Maimon (2001)] with the following modification: the decision tree is not pruned and at each node, rather than choosing the best split among all attributes, the inducer randomly samples N of the attributes and chooses the best split from among those variables. The classification of an unlabeled instance is performed using majority vote.

Originally, the random forest algorithm applied only to building decision trees and is not applicable to all types of classifiers, because it involves picking a different subset of the attributes in each node of the tree. Nevertheless, the main step of the random forest algorithm can easily be replaced with the broader random subspace method [Ho (1998)], which can be applied to many other inducers, such as nearest neighbor classifiers [Ho (1998)] or linear discriminators [Skurichina and Duin (2002)].

Of all of the random forest hyperparameters, the most crucial hyperpa-

Input: IDT (a decision tree inducer), T (the number of iterations), S (the training set), μ (the subsample size), and N (the number of attributes used in each node).

Output: $M_t; t = 1, \ldots, T$

1: $t \leftarrow 1$
2: **repeat**
3:     $S_t \leftarrow$ Sample μ instances from S with replacement.
4:     Build classifier M_t using $IDT(N)$ on S_t
5:     $t++$
6: **until** $t > T$

Fig. 3.23: Random forest algorithm.

rameter to tune is N - the number of attributes that are randomly selected in each node. One rule of thumb can be to use the square root of the total number of features in the dataset. This works pretty well in most cases.

One important advantage of the random forest method is its ability to handle a very large number of input attributes [Skurichina and Duin (2002)]. Another important feature of the random forest method is that it is fast.

There are other ways to obtain random forests. For example, instead of using all of the instances to determine the best split point for each feature, a subsample of the instances is used [Kamath and Cantu-Paz (2001)]. This subsample varies with the feature. The feature and split value that optimize the splitting criterion are chosen as the decision at that node. Since the split made at a node is likely to vary with the sample selected, this technique results in different trees which can be combined in forests.

Another method for randomization of the decision tree involving the use of histograms was proposed in [Kamath *et al.* (2002)]. Histograms have long been suggested as a means of making the features discrete, while reducing the time consumed handling very large datasets. Typically, a histogram is created for each feature, and the bin boundaries are used as potential split points. The randomization in this process is expressed by selecting the split point randomly in a proximity to the best bin boundary.

Using an extensive simulation study, Archer and Kimes [Archer and Kimes (2008)] examine the effectiveness of random forest variable importance measures in identifying the true predictor among a large number of candidate predictors. They concluded that the random forest technique is useful in domains which require both an accurate classifier and insight regarding the discriminative ability of individual attributes (like in microarray studies).

3.9.3 *Extremely Randomized Trees*

Extremely randomized trees algorithm aims to generate a decision forest while injecting randomness [Geurts *et al.* (2006)]. Recall that random forest selects the best splitting attribute and its best corresponding cut-point among a random subset of features. In contrast, extremely randomized trees randomizes both the splitting feature and its corresponding cut-point.

For selecting the splitting feature, the algorithm randomly chooses a certain number of features, of which the best feature is determined. In addition to numerical features, the algorithm draws a random cut-point uniformly in the feature value domain, i.e., the cut-points are selected totally at random, independently of the target attribute. In the extreme case, the algorithm randomly selects a single attribute and cut-point for each node, and hence a totally randomized tree grows. Moreover, in contrast to random forest, extremely randomized trees does not use the bootstrap instances procedure to construct a set of the training samples for each tree, and the same input training set is used to induce all decision trees. An individual extremely randomized tree tends to have high bias and variance components. However, the variance component can be canceled out by fusing a sufficiently large forest of trees.

3.9.4 *Rotation Forest*

Rotation forest is a method that generates diversity among decision tree inducers by training each inducer on the whole dataset in a rotated feature space [Rodriguez (2006)]. When creating the training data for the base classifier, the features are randomly split into K subsets and principal component analysis (PCA) is applied to each subset. The idea of PCA is to orthogonally transform any possible correlated features into a set of linearly uncorrelated features (called principal components). Each component is a linear combination of the original.

The transformation guarantees that the first principal component has the greatest variance possible. Every subsequent component has the greatest variance possible under the constraint that it is orthogonal to the previous components. This transformation, in the context of ensembles, effectively forms new features for each base learner, as different feature partitions will lead to different sets of transformed features, and thus different classification trees. In addition to encouraging diversity among the trees, rotating trees also alleviates the decision tree constraint of only splitting the input space into hyperplanes that are parallel to the original feature axes. A detailed description of rotation forest is provided in section 6.5.2.5.

3.9.5 *Random Projections*

Despite having been evaluated as outperforming random forest in terms of accuracy, rotation forest has two main drawbacks. First, calculating the PCA in each induction creates computational overhead that does not exist when training random forests. Second, the inducers interpretability is impaired as the nodes of the trees obtained use transformed features rather than the original features.

Schclar and Rokach (2009) suggest using random projections for creating the individual trees rather than using the PCA projection [Schclar and Rokach (2009)]. This reduces the computational complexity burden that stems from the calculation of the principle components. Each derived feature used for training the tree is a random linear combination of the original features. Random projection random discretization ensembles (RPRDE) is a variation of rotation forest that creates discrete features from continuous features and then provides random linear combinations of the discrete features for each of the inducers [Ahmad and Brown (2014)].

3.9.6 *Nonlinear Boosting Projection (NLBP)*

Nonlinear boosting projection (NLBP) combines boosting and subspace methods as follows [Garcia-Pddrajas *et al.* (2007)]:

(1) All of the classifiers receive all of the training instances for learning as input. Since all of the instances are equally weighted, we are not placing more emphasis on misclassified instances as is done in boosting.
(2) Each classifier uses a different nonlinear projection of the original data onto a space of the same dimension.
(3) The nonlinear projection is based on the projection made by the hidden neuron layer of a multilayer perceptron neural network.
(4) Following the basic principles of boosting, each nonlinear projection is constructed in order to make it easier to classify difficult instances.

Figure 3.24 presents the pseudocode of the NLBP algorithm. In lines 1-2 we convert the original dataset (S) to a standard dataset for multilayer perceptron learning (S'). It includes a transformation from nominal attributes to binary attributes (one binary attribute for each nominal value) and a normalization of all numeric (and binary) attributes to the $[-1, 1]$ range. In line three we construct the first classifier M_0 using the base inducer (I) and the converted dataset S'. In lines 4-14 we construct the remaining $T - 1$ classifiers.

Each iteration includes the following steps. In lines 5-9 we try to classify each instance in S' with the previous classifier. S'' stores all of the instances that were misclassified. In lines 10-11 we train a multilayer perceptron neural network using S''. The hidden layer of the network consists of the same number of hidden neurons as input attributes in S''. After training the network we retrieve the input weights of the hidden neurons and store them in a data structure with the iteration index (ProjectionArray). In line 12 we project all of the instances of S' with the projection P to get S'''. In line 13 we construct the current classifier using the converted and projected dataset (S''') and the base inducer (I). In lines 15-16 we convert the instance (nominal to binary and normalization of attributes) as we did with the training dataset. The final classification is a simple majority vote.

The advantages of NLBP compared to other ensemble methods are:

(1) Experiments comparing NLBP to popular ensemble methods (bagging, AdaBoost, LogitBoost, Arc-x4) using different base classifiers (C4.5, ANN, SVM) show very good results for NLBP.

(2) *"Bagging provides diversity but to a lesser degree than boosting. On the other hand, the improvement of diversity associated with boosting is accompanied by the negative side effect of decreased accuracy. NLBP behavior is midway between these two methods. It is able to improve diversity but to a lesser degree than boosting, without damaging accuracy as much as boosting. This behavior suggests that the performance of NLBP in noisy problems can be better than the performance of boosting methods.*

The drawbacks of NLBP compared to other ensemble methods are:

(1)(a) The necessity of training an additional neural network for each iteration increases the computational complexity of the algorithm compared to other approaches.

(b) Using a neural network for projection may increase the dimensionality of the problem. Every nominal attribute is transformed to a set of binary attributes.

(c) The classifiers that are constructed by this approach use a different set of attributes than the original set. Since these new attributes lose the meaning of the original attributes, it is difficult to understand the meaning of the constructed models in terms of the original domain.

NLBP - Building the Ensemble

Input: I (a base inducer), T (the number of iterations), and S (the original training set).

1: $S* = $ A nominal to binary transformation of S
2: $S' = $ A normalization of $S*$
3: $M_1 = I(S')$
4: **for** $t = 2$ to T **do**
5:    $S'' = \emptyset$
6:    **for** each $x_j \in S'$ **do**
7:      **if** $M_{t-1}(x_j) \neq y_j$ **then**
8:        $S'' = S'' \bigcup \{Xj\}$
9:      **end if**
10:   **end for**
11:   Train network H using S'' and get the projection $P(X)$ implemented by a hidden layer of H
12:   $ProjectionArray[t] = P$
13:   $S''' = P(S')$
14:   $M_t = I(S''')$
15: **end for**

Fig. 3.24: NLBP - building the ensemble.

3.9.7 *Cross-Validated Committees*

This procedure creates k classifiers by partitioning the training set into k sets of equal size and training on all but the i-th set. This method, first used by Gams [Gams (1989)], employed 10-fold partitioning. Parmanto *et al.* [Parmanto *et al.* (1996)] also used this idea for creating an ensemble of neural networks. Domingos [Domingos (1996)] used cross-validated committees to speed up his own rule induction algorithm RISE, whose complexity is $O(n^2)$, making it unsuitable for processing large databases. In this case, partitioning is applied by predetermining a maximum number of examples to which the algorithm can be applied at once. The full training set is randomly divided into approximately equal size partitions. RISE is then run on each partition separately. Each set of rules grown from the examples in partition p is tested on the examples in partition $p + 1$, in order to reduce overfitting and improve accuracy.

3.9.8   *Robust Boosting*

A robust classifier is one whose predictive performance is not sensitive to changes in the training data. Freund (1995) proposes a simple robust version of the boosting algorithm which is called the boost by majority (BBM) algorithm. In BBM the number of iterations is set in advance based on two parameters that are specified by the user: the desired accuracy and an error bound such that the induction algorithm is guaranteed to always generate a classifier whose error is smaller than that value. The main idea of BBM is to give less weight to instances with large negative margins. Intuitively, it ignores instances which are unlikely to be classified correctly when the boosting procedure terminates. Contrary to AdaBoost, BBM assigns the weights to the base classifier regardless of their accuracy. Thus, the drawback of BBM is that it is not adaptive. On the other hand, it is less sensitive to noise comparing to the AdaBoost algorithm. Specifically, the accuracy of AdaBoost decreases rapidly when random noise is added to the training set.

In order to avoid these drawbacks, Freund (2001) proposes BrownBoost which is an adaptive version of BBM in which classifiers with a low misclassification rate are assigned a greater weight than base classifiers with a high misclassification rate. BrownBoost has a time variable denoted as t that increases with each iteration. Figure 3.25 specifies the pseudocode of BrownBoost.

Most recently, Freund (2009) proposed an updated version of Brown-Boost called RobustBoost. The main difference is that instead of minimizing the training error, the goal of RobustBoost is to minimize the number of examples whose normalized margins are smaller than some value $\theta > 0$:

$$\frac{1}{N} \sum_{i=1}^{N} 1\left[\bar{m}\left(x_i, y_i\right) \leq \theta\right] \tag{3.8}$$

where $\bar{m}(x, y)$ is the normalized margin defined as:

$$\bar{m}(x, y) = \frac{y \cdot \text{sign}\left(\sum_i \alpha_i C_i\left(x\right)\right)}{\sum_i |\alpha_i|} \tag{3.9}$$

Friedman *et al.* (2000) show that AdaBoost approximates a stepwise additive logistic regression model by optimizing an exponential criterion. Based on this observation, Friedman *et al.* (2000) propose a variant of AdaBoost called LogitBoost, which fits additive models directly. Since it uses Newton-like steps to optimize the binomial log-likelihood criterion, it is significantly better than AdaBoost at tolerating noise. Despite such claims, Mease and Wyner (2008) indicate that when the Bayes error is not zero, LogitBoost often overfits while AdaBoost does not. In fact Mease and Wyner (2008) encourage readers to try the simulation models provided on the following website: http://www.davemease.com/contraryevidence. Other closely related algorithms are the log-loss boost [Collins *et al.* (2002)] and MAdaboost [Domingo and Watanabe (2000)]. The pseudocode of BrownBoost is presented in Figure 3.25.

BrownBoost Training

Input: I (a base inducer), S (the original training set), and T (the number of iterations).
1: Set initial weights as $w_i = 1/N$
2: Set $F(x) = 0$
3: **for** $t = 1$ to T **do**
4:    Fit the function f_t by a weighted least squares regression of Z_i to x_i with weights w_i.
5:    Set $F(x) = F(x) + f_t(x)$
6:    Set $w_i \leftarrow w_i e^{-y_i f_t(x_i)}$
7: **end for**

Fig. 3.25: BrownBoost algorithm.

Zhang's boosting algorithm (Zhang *et al.*, 2009) is an AdaBoost variant with the following differences: (a) instead of using the entire dataset, a subsample of the original training data in each iteration trains the weak classifier, and (b) the sampling distribution is set differently to overcome AdaBoosts sensitivity to noise. Specifically, a parameter introduced into the reweighted scheme proposed in AdaBoost updates the probabilities assigned to training examples. The results of these changes are better prediction accuracy, faster execution time, and robustness to classification noise. Figure 3.26 presents the pseudocode of this variant. The sampling introduces randomness into the procedure. Using the f parameter, one can control the amount of data available to train the weak classifier. The parameter β is used to alleviate AdaBoost's problem in which more and more weight is assigned to noisy examples in later iterations. Thus, the weight increment of inaccurately predicted examples is smaller than that in AdaBoost.

Zhang's Boosting Algorithm

Input: I (a base inducer), T (the number of iterations), S (the original training set), sample fraction f, and positive parameter β.

1: Initialize: set the probability distribution over S as $D_1(i) = 1/N(i = 1, 2, \cdots N)$

2: **for** $t = 1, \cdots T$ **do**

3:    According to the distribution D_t, draw $\overline{N} = \lfloor f \cdot N \rfloor (f \leq 1)$ examples from S with replacement to compose a new training set $S_t = \{(\mathbf{x}_i^{(t)}, y_i^{(t)})\}_{i=1}^{\overline{N}}$ in which $\lfloor A \rfloor$ stands for the largest integer small than A.

4:    Apply I to S_t to train a weak classifier $h_t : X \rightarrow \{-1, +1\}$, and compute the error of h_t as $\epsilon_t = \sum\limits_{i.h_t(\mathbf{x}_l) \neq y_l}^{N} D_t(i)$.

5:    **if** $\epsilon i_t > 0.5$ **then**

6:        set $T = t - 1$ and abort loop.

7:    **end if**

8:    choose $\alpha_t = \dfrac{1}{2} \ln(\dfrac{1 - \epsilon_t}{\epsilon_t})$.

9:    Update the probability distribution over S as $D_{t+1}(i) = \dfrac{D_t(i)}{Z_t} \times$ $\begin{cases} e^{-\alpha_t/\beta}, & \text{if } h_t(\mathbf{x}_i) = y_i \\ e^{\alpha_t/\beta}, & \text{if } h_t(\mathbf{x}_i) \neq y_i \end{cases} = \dfrac{D_t(i) \exp((-\frac{\alpha_t}{\beta}) y_i h_t(\mathbf{x}_i))}{Z_t}$ where Z_t is a normalization factor (it should be chosen so that D_{t+1} is a distribution over S).

10: **end for**

Fig. 3.26: Zhang's boosting algorithm.

3.9.9   *IPGA-Forest*

Martinez-Munoz and Suarez (2004) suggest utilizing the nature of the IPGA decision tree induction algorithm to generate a decision forest. In the base IPGA decision tree induction algorithm the training data is randomly divided into two subsets. In the first iteration the first subset is used to grow the decision tree. The second subset is then used to prune the tree. In the second iteration the roles of the data subsets are reversed. Starting from the tree that was grown in the first iteration, the tree is grown again using the training instances of the second subset. Then the tree is pruned using the first subset. The roles of the data subsets are reversed again, and the two iterations are repeated until the two consecutive pruned trees have the same size. In order to generate a variety of classifiers for the forest, the two subsets are randomly created for each tree in the forest [Martinez-Munoz and Suarez (2004)].

3.9.10 *Switching Classes*

Breiman (2000) presents a decision forest in which each decision tree in the forest is generated using the original training set but with randomized class labels. The class label of each training instance is switched according to a transition matrix that defines the probability that a class i is replaced with class j. The switching probabilities are chosen to maintain the class distribution of the original training set. Martinez-Munoz and Suarez (2005) show that the switching classes method is particularly accurate when the forest is large enough and it is created using high class switching rates that do not necessarily maintain the original class distribution. The relaxation of the original class distribution constraint is crucial for using the switching classes method in an imbalanced dataset. In each iteration a fixed fraction of the original training is randomly selected. The classes of these selected instances are switched at random.

3.10 Ensemble Methods for Advanced Classification Tasks

3.10.1 *Cost-Sensitive Classification*

AdaBoost does not differentiate between the various classes. Thus, a misclassification in the majority class is treated the same as a misclassification of the minority class. However, in certain scenarios it is more desirable to augment the weight of misclassification errors of the minority class. For example, in direct marketing scenarios companies are interested in estimating customer interest in their offer, however positive response rates are usually low. For example, a mail marketing response rate of 2% or a phone marketing response rate of 10% is considered good. Nevertheless, in such cases the minority class is more important than the majority class, because it reflects the companys income. AdaC2 aims to make AdaBoost cost-sensitive. This is done by adapting the weight function to include a cost δ (Yanim *et al.*,

2007). Specifically, for successful classification the distribution update is revised to:

$$D^{t+1}(i) = \frac{D^t(i)\sqrt{\frac{\sum_{[i,M_t(x_i)\neq y_i]}\delta \cdot W_i}{\sum_{[i,M_t(x_i)=y_i]}\delta \cdot W_i}}}{Z_t} \tag{3.10}$$

For unsuccessful classification, the distribution update is revised to:

$$D^{t+1}(i) = \frac{D^t(i)\Big/\sqrt{\frac{\sum_{[i,M_t(x_i)\neq y_i]}\delta \cdot W_i}{\sum_{[i,M_t(x_i)=y_i]}\delta \cdot W_i}}}{Z_t} \tag{3.11}$$

where Z_t is a normalization factor.

Fan *et al.* (1999) presented AdaCost. The purpose of AdaCost is to improve AdaBoosts fixed and variable misclassification costs. It introduces a cost adjustment function which is integrated into the weight updating rule. In addition to assigning high initial weights to costly instances, the weight updating rule takes cost into account and increases the weights of costly misclassification. Figure 3.27 presents AdaCosts pseudocode where $\beta(i) = \beta(\text{sign}(y_i h_t(x_i)), c_i)$ is a cost adjustment function. Z_t is a normalization factor selected so that D_{t+1} will be a distribution. The final classification is: $H(x) = \text{sign}(f(x))$ where $f(x) = (\sum_{t=1}^{T} \alpha_t h_t(x))$

AdaCost

Input: I (a base inducer), T (the number of iterations), and $S = \{(x_1, c_1, y_1), \ldots, (x_m, c_m, y_m)\}$. $x_i \in \mathcal{X}, c_i \in \mathbb{R}^+, y_i \in \{-1, +1\}$

1: Initialize $D_1(i)(T$: such as $D_1(i) = c_i/\sum_j^m c_j)$.

2: **repeat**

3:    Train weak inducer using distribution D_t.

4:    Compute weak classifier h_t: $\mathcal{X} \rightarrow \mathbb{R}$.

5:    Choose $\alpha_t \in \mathbb{R}$ and $\beta(i) \in \mathbb{R}^+$.

6:    Update $D_{t+1}(i) = \frac{D_t(i)\exp(-\alpha_t y_i h_t(x_i)\beta(i))}{Z_t}$

7:    $t \leftarrow t + 1$

8: **until** $t > T$

Fig. 3.27: The AdaCost algorithm.

3.10.2 *Ensemble for Learning Concept Drift*

Concept drift is an online learning task in which concepts change or drift over time. More specifically, concept drift occurs when the class distribution changes over time.

Concept drift exists in many applications that involve models of human behavior, such as recommender systems. Kolter and Maloof (2007) suggested an algorithm that tries to solve this problem by presenting an ensemble method for concept drift that dynamically creates and removes weighted experts according to a change in their performance. The suggested algorithm, known as dynamic weighted majority (DWM), is an extension of the weighted majority algorithm (MWA), but it adds and removes base learners in response to global and local performance. As a result, DWM is better able to respond in non-stationary environments than other algorithms, especially those that rely on an ensemble of unweighted learners. The main disadvantage of DWM is its poor performance in terms of running time, compared to the AdaBoost algorithm.

3.10.3 *Reject Driven Classification*

Reject driven classification[Frelicot and Mascarilla (2001)] is a method of classification that allows a tradeoff between misclassification and ambiguity (assigning more than one class to an instance). Specifically, the algorithm introduces a method for combining reject driven classifiers using belief theory methods. The algorithm adjusts the results of the reject driven classifiers by using the Dempster-Shafer theory. For each classifier, a basic probability assignment (BPA) is calculated to classify unseen instances.

The main strength of this algorithm is its ability to control the tradeoff between ambiguity and rejection. We can decide (with the proper threshold) if we prefer to classify an unseen instance to a single class and might be wrong or give an ambiguity classification. A major drawback of the algorithm is its inability to handle datasets with many classes, since the BPA calculation needs to calculate the probability for any pair of classes.

3.11 Using R for Training a Decision Forest

In the previous chapter we presented how R is used to train a single decision tree. In this section we show how we can extend it to train a decision forest. Specifically, we review the packages: `party` and `randomForest` which are both used to train a decision forest.

3.11.1   *Training a Random Forest with the Party Package*

The party package provides an implementation of the random forest and bagging ensemble algorithms utilizing a CTree algorithm as a base inducer. The following script illustrates the creation and evaluation of a random forest with 10 trees (`ntree=10`). The number of randomly preselected attributes is set by `mtry` parameter.

```
1 irisForest <- cforest(Species~., data=trainData,
2               control = cforest_unbiased(ntree=
3                         10, mtry = 2))
4
5 testPrediction <- predict(irisForest,
6                           newdata = testData)
7
8 table(testPrediction, testData$Species)
```

3.11.2   *RandomForest Package*

In the previous section we saw how the function `cforest()` can be used to build an ensemble of classification trees. An alternative way of building a random forest is to use the RandomForest package [Liaw and Wiener (2002)].

```
1 library("randomForest")
2
3 # split the data into to train and test
4 trainIndex<-sample(nrow(iris), 2/3*nrow(iris))
5 trainData <- iris[trainIndex,]
6 testData <- iris[-trainIndex,]
7
8 # build the forest
9 irisRandomForest <- randomForest(Species ~ .,
10                     data = trainData)
11
12 # predict on test data
13 testPrediction <- predict(irisRandomForest ,
14                           newdata = testData)
15
16 # show the confusion matrix
17 table(testPrediction, testData$Species)
```

The function `randomForest()` has several arguments that control the execution of the algorithm, such as: `ntree` (number of trees to grow), `mtry` (number of attributes randomly sampled as candidates in each split), `replace-` (whether sampling of cases can be done with or without a replacement), `sampsize` (the sizes of the samples to draw), and `nodesize` (minimum size of terminal nodes). Finally, the RandomForest package provides additional useful functions, such as the function `getTree()` for extracting a certain single tree from a forest and the function `grow()` for adding additional trees to an existing forest.

3.12   Scaling Up Decision Forests Methods

With the recent growth in the amount of data collected by information systems, there is a need for decision tree algorithms that can induce from large datasets. While the availability of large amounts of data is ideal for the needs of data scientists, it poses time and memory challenges for many learning algorithms. Big data is a term coined recently to refer to large datasets that are extremely difficult to process using existing methods. For small to medium datasets the computational complexity of decision tree induction algorithms is considered to be relatively low. However, when training a dense forest on large datasets, one can encounter difficulties. Scalability refers to the ability of the method to train the predicative method efficiently given large amounts of data. The greedy nature of the tree induction algorithm does not scale well to a large dataset. For example, to find the best split in the root node, going over all instances in the dataset is required, and when the entire dataset does not fit in the main memory, such a complete scan becomes a major problem. In the prebig data era scalability efforts were focused on relaxing the memory constraint. Several decision tree algorithms were developed that do not require that all of the training data be loaded into the main memory. This category includes the following algorithms: SPRINT [Shafer *et al.* (1996)], SLIQ [Mehta *et al.* (1996)], and FastC4.5 [He *et al.* (2007)]. It should be noted that these algorithms are still limited by the resources of a single machine and the cost of scanning data from secondary storage. Thus, in recent years efforts regarding scalability have focused on parallelization techniques such as MapReduce and MPI which distribute the training effort among many machines. MapReduce is one of the most popular parallel programming frameworks for data mining. In this framework, programmers need to specify a map function which processes key-value pairs to emit a set of intermediate key-value pairs and a reduce function that aggregates all intermediate values associated with the same intermediate key. The MapReduce framework was pioneered by Google and popularized by the open-source Apache Hadoop project. While there are other parallel programming frameworks (such as CUDA and MPI), MapReduce has become the industry standard and is implemented on cloud computing services such as Amazon EC2 and various companies such as Cloudera which provide services to ease Hadoop deployment. PLANET [Panda *et al.* (2009)] is a decision forest algorithm implemented in the MapReduce framework. The basic idea of PLANET is to iteratively grow the decision tree, one layer at a time, until the data partitions are small enough to fit the main memory and the remaining subtree can be grown locally on a single machine. For higher levels, the key idea of PLANET is that the splitting criterion at a certain node does not need the entire dataset but rather a compact data structure of sufficient statistics which in most cases can fit in-memory. These statistics are calculated on the mappers. Bootstrapping-based methods for generating a decision forest (such as random forest) can be easily emulated by replacing the bootstrap sample with local data, i.e., each machine in the cluster is trained on the locally stored data. On the other hand, parallelizing boosting-based methods such as AdaBoost and gradient boosted decision trees is not straightforward due to their inherent sequential nature.

Ye [Ye *et al.* (2009)] present two distributed versions of the stochastic gradient boosted decision trees method: the first is implemented in the MapReduce framework and the second in the MPI framework. The methods produce trees identical to those generated by the corresponding serial version. In order to obtain the exact solution, all nodes in the cluster are required to evaluate the potential split points found by all other nodes.

Palit and Reddy [Palit and Reddy (2012)] utilize the MapReduce framework for developing two parallel boosting algorithms, AdaBoost.PL and LogitBoost.PL, which are competitive with their corresponding serial versions in terms of predicative performance. These algorithms need only one cycle of MapReduce to complete. Each Mapper runs a respective AdaBoost algorithm on its own subset of the data in order to induce the set of weak models. Then the base models are sorted and transmitted (along with their weights) to the reducers. The reducer averages the weights to derive the weights of the final ensemble.

Del Ro [Del Ro *et al.* (2014)] introduce a MapReduce implementation for various common methods that are capable of tackling imbalanced classification tasks using random forest. The results show that in most cases the execution time is reduced when the number of mappers is increased; nevertheless, too many mappers may result in deteriorated performance.

Various distributed implementations of decision forests are available for practitioners. In particular, Mahout, which is an Apache project that provides free implementations of scalable machine learning algorithms, includes an implementation of random forest on top of the Hadoop framework. ML-lib, a distributed machine learning framework, provides implementations for random forest and gradient-boosted trees on top of the Apache Spark framework. Apache Spark was originally developed at the University of California, Berkeley's AMPLab and it is currently considered to be the most popular open-source distributed general-purpose cluster-computing framework.

3.13   Ensemble Methods and Deep Neural Networks

Deep neural networks (DNNs) have become an important force in the machine learning community. In recent years, the use of DNNs has dramatically improved the state of the art in speech recognition, visual object recognition, object detection, and many other domains [LeCun *et al.* (2015)]. DNNs are composed of multiple layers of nonlinear operations. They are able to discover complex structure and learn high-level concepts in large datasets. In recent years there have been a few attempts to combine ensemble and DNN approaches. Most of them center around developing an ensemble of DNNs.

Deep neural decision forests is a learning approach that unifies convolutional neural networks (CNNs) and decision forest techniques [Kontschieder *et al.* (2015)]. It introduces a stochastic backpropagation version of decision trees that are then combined into decision forests. Another example of an ensemble composed of CNNs has recently been developed for facial expression recognition tasks [Wen *et al.* (2017)]. An ensemble of DNNs has been also used for regression and time series forecasting [Qiu *et al.* (2014)]. In this ensemble, the outputs of the DNNs construct the input of a Support Vector Regression (SVR) model that produces the final output. Moreover, Deng and Platt [Deng *et al.* (2014)] stack convolutional, recurrent, and fully connected neural networks to address speech recognition challenges. Experimental results demonstrate a significant increase in phone recognition accuracy.

A novel approach that also combines ensemble methods with DNNs, gcForest [Zhou and Feng (2017)] replaces DNN neurons with random forest models where the output vector of each random forest is fed as the input of the next layers, in contrast to the abovementioned methods. In addition, it supports representational learning by applying multigrained scanning when the inputs are of high dimensionality.

Finally. it is also worth mentioning that the dropout technique, in which some of the neurons are dropped from the DNN in each iteration, can also be viewed as an ensemble method composed of different neural networks, each with different dropped neurons [Srivastava *et al.* (2014)].

Chapter 4

Ensemble Classification

Ensemble classification refers to the process of using the classifiers that make up an ensemble in order to provide a single and unified classification to an unseen instance.

There are two main ways of classifying new instances. In the first approach, the classifications are *fused* in some fashion during the classification phase. In the second approach, the classification of one classifier is *selected* according to some criterion. In this chapter, we discuss both approaches in detail.

4.1 Fusion Methods

Fusing methods aim at providing classification by combining the outputs of several classifiers. We assume that the output of each classifier i is a k-long vector $p_{i,1}, \cdots, p_{i,k}$. The value $p_{i,j}$ represents the support that instance x belongs to class j according to the classifier i. For the sake of simplicity, it is also assumed that $\sum_{j=1}^{k} p_{i,j} = 1$. If we are dealing with a crisp classifier i, which explicitly assigns the instance x to a certain class l, it can still be converted to k-long vector $p_{i,1}, \cdots, p_{i,k}$ such that $p_{i,l} = 1$ and $p_{i,j} = 0; \ \forall j \neq l$.

Fusion methods can be further partitioned into weighting methods and metalearning methods. These techniques are described in the sections that follow.

4.1.1 *Weighting Methods*

The base members classifications are combined using weights that are assigned to each member. The member's weight indicates its effect on the final classification. The assigned weight can be fixed or dynamically determined for the specific instance to be classified.

Weighting methods are best suited for problems where the individual classifiers perform the same task and have comparable success or when we would like to avoid problems associated with added learning (such as overfitting or long training time).

4.1.2 *Majority Voting*

In this combining scheme, a classification of an unlabeled instance is performed according to the class that obtains the highest number of votes (the most frequent vote). This method is also known as the plurality vote (PV) or the basic ensemble method (BEM). This approach has frequently been used as a combining method for comparing newly proposed methods.

For example, we are given an ensemble of ten classifiers which are attempting to classify a certain instance x to one of the classes: A, B or C. Table 4.1 presents the classification vector and the selected label (vote) that each classifier provides to the instance x. Based on these classifications, we create the voting table presented in Table 4.1 which indicates that the majority vote is class B.

Table 4.1: Illustration of majority voting: classifiers output.

Classifier	A score	B score	C score	Selected Label
1	0.2	0.7	0.1	B
2	0.1	0.1	0.8	C
3	0.2	0.3	0.5	C
4	0.1	0.8	0.1	B
5	0.2	0.6	0.2	B
6	0.6	0.3	0.1	A
7	0.25	0.65	0.1	B
8	0.2	0.7	0.1	B
9	0.2	0.2	0.8	C
10	0.4	0.3	0.3	A

Table 4.2: Illustration of majority voting.

	Class A	Class B	Class C
Votes	2	5	3

Mathematically, majority voting can be written as:

$$class(x) = \underset{c_i \in dom(y)}{\arg\max} \left(\sum_k g\left(y_k(x), c_i\right) \right) \qquad (4.1)$$

where $y_k(x)$ is the classification of the k'th classifier, and $g(y, c)$ is an indicator function defined as:

$$g\left(y, c\right) = \begin{cases} 1 & y = c \\ 0 & y \neq c \end{cases} \tag{4.2}$$

Note that in the case of a probabilistic classifier, the crisp classification $y_k(x)$ is usually obtained as follows:

$$y_k(x) = \underset{c_i \in dom(y)}{\arg\max}\, \hat{P}_{M_k}(y = c_i \,|\, x) \tag{4.3}$$

where M_k denotes classifier k, and $\hat{P}_{M_k}(y = c \,|\, x)$ denotes the probability of y obtaining the value c given an instance x.

4.1.3 *Performance Weighting*

The weight of each classifier can be set proportional to its accuracy performance on a validation set [Opitz and Shavlik (1996)]:

$$w_i = \frac{(\alpha_i)}{\sum\limits_{j=1}^{T} (\alpha_j)} \tag{4.4}$$

where α_i is a performance evaluation of classifier i on a validation set (for example, the accuracy). Once the weights for each classifier have been computed, we select the class that received the highest score:

$$class(x) = \underset{c_i \in dom(y)}{\arg\max} \left(\sum_k \alpha_i g\left(y_k(x), c_i\right) \right) \tag{4.5}$$

Since the weights are normalized and summed up to 1, it possible to interpret the sum in the last equation as the probability that x_i is classified to c_j.

Moreno-Seco *et al.* (2006) examined several variations of performance weighting methods:

Re-scaled weighted vote The idea is to weight values proportionally to some given ratio N/M as follows:
$$\alpha_k = \max\left\{1 - \frac{M \cdot e_k}{N \cdot (M-1)}, 0\right\}$$
where e_i is the number of misclassifications made by classifier i.

Best-worst weighted vote The idea is that the best and worst classifiers obtain the weight of 1 and 0 respectively. The rest of classifiers are rated linearly between these extremes:

$$\alpha_i = 1 - \frac{e_i - \min_i(e_i)}{\max_i(e_i) - \min_i(e_i)}$$

Quadratic best-worst weighted vote In order to give additional weight to the classifications provided by the most accurate classifiers, the values obtained by the best-worst weighted vote approach are squared:

$$\alpha_i = \left(\frac{\max_i(e_i) - e_i}{\max_i(e_i) - \min_i(e_i)} \right)^2$$

4.1.4 *Distribution Summation*

The idea of the distribution summation combining method is to add the conditional probability vectors obtained from each classifier [Clark and Boswell (1991)]. The selected class is chosen according to the highest value in the total vector. Mathematically, it can be written as:

$$Class(x) = \underset{c_i \in dom(y)}{\operatorname{argmax}} \sum_k \hat{P}_{M_k}(y = c_i \,|\, x) \tag{4.6}$$

4.1.5 *Bayesian Combination*

In the Bayesian combination method, the weight associated with each classifier is the posterior probability of the classifier given the training set [Buntine (1990)].

$$Class(x) = \underset{c_i \in dom(y)}{\operatorname{argmax}} \sum_k P(M_k \,|\, S) \cdot \hat{P}_{M_k}(y = c_i \,|\, x) \tag{4.7}$$

where $P(M_k \,|\, S)$ denotes the probability that the classifier M_k is correct given the training set S. The estimation of $P(M_k \,|\, S)$ depends on the classifier's representation. To estimate this value for decision trees, the reader is referred to [Buntine (1990)].

4.1.6 *Dempster–Shafer*

The idea of using the Dempster–Shafer theory of evidence [Buchanan and Shortliffe (1984)] for combining classifiers was suggested in [Shilen (1990)]. This method uses the notion of basic probability assignment defined for a certain class c_i given the instance x:

$$bpa(c_i, x) = 1 - \prod_k \left(1 - \hat{P}_{M_k}(y = c_i \,|x)\right) \qquad (4.8)$$

Consequently, the selected class is the one that maximizes the value of the belief function:

$$Bel(c_i, x) = \frac{1}{A} \cdot \frac{bpa(c_i, x)}{1 - bpa(c_i, x)} \qquad (4.9)$$

where A is a normalization factor defined as:

$$A = \sum_{\forall c_i \in dom(y)} \frac{bpa(c_i, x)}{1 - bpa(c_i, x)} + 1 \qquad (4.10)$$

4.1.7 *Vogging*

The idea behind the vogging approach (Variance Optimized Bagging) is to optimize a linear combination of base classifiers so as to aggressively reduce variance while attempting to preserve the accuracy [Derbeko *et al.* (2002)]. For this purpose, Derbeko *et al* implemented the Markowitz mean-variance portfolio theory which is used for generating low variance portfolios of financial assets.

4.1.8 *Naïve Bayes*

Using Bayes' rule, one can extend the Naïve Bayes idea for combining various classifiers:

$$Class(x) = \underset{\substack{c_j \in dom(y) \\ \hat{P}(y=c_j) > 0}}{\text{argmax}} \quad \hat{P}(y = c_j) \cdot \prod_{k=1} \frac{\hat{P}_{M_k}(y = c_j \,|x)}{\hat{P}(y = c_j)} \qquad (4.11)$$

4.1.9 *Entropy Weighting*

In this combining method each classifier is given a weight that is inversely proportional to the entropy of its classification vector.

$$Class(x) = \underset{c_i \in dom(y)}{\text{argmax}} \sum_{k:c_i = \underset{c_j \in dom(y)}{\text{argmax}} \hat{P}_{M_k}(y=c_j|x)} E(M_k, x) \qquad (4.12)$$

where:

$$E(M_k, x) = -\sum_{c_j} \hat{P}_{M_k}(y = c_j \,|x) \log\left(\hat{P}_{M_k}(y = c_j \,|x)\right) \qquad (4.13)$$

4.1.10   *Density-based Weighting*

If the various classifiers were trained using datasets obtained from different regions of the instance space, it might be useful to weight the classifiers according to the probability of sampling x by classifier M_k, namely:

$$Class(x) = \underset{c_i \in dom(y)}{\operatorname{argmax}} \underset{k:c_i = \underset{c_j \in dom(y)}{\operatorname{argmax}} \hat{P}_{M_k}(y=c_j|x)}{\sum} \hat{P}_{M_k}(x) \qquad (4.14)$$

The estimation of $\hat{P}_{M_k}(x)$ depends on the classifier representation and can not always be estimated.

4.1.11   *DEA Weighting Method*

There have been attempts to use the data envelopment analysis (DEA) methodology [Charnes *et al.* (1978)] in order to assign weights to different classifiers [Sohn and Choi (2001)]. DEA is used to empirically measure productive efficiency of decision making units (or DMUs). DEA can be used to find the efficiency score of each DMU and can figure out the set of efficient DMUs based on the set of non-dominated solutions. In our case, the individual classifiers are considered as DMUs while. These studies argue that the weights should be based on several performance measures (e.g. sensitivity, specificity, bias and variance of misclassification rate) rather than according to a single performance measure. Because there is a tradeoff among the various performance measures, the DEA is employed in order to determine the set of efficient classifiers.

4.1.12   *Logarithmic Opinion Pool*

According to the logarithmic opinion pool [Hansen (2000)], the selection of the preferred class is performed according to:

$$Class(x) = \underset{c_j \in dom(y)}{\operatorname{argmax}} e^{\sum_k \alpha_k \cdot \log(\hat{P}_{M_k}(y=c_j|x))} \qquad (4.15)$$

where α_k denotes the weight of the k-th classifier, such that:

$$\alpha_k \geq 0; \sum \alpha_k = 1 \qquad (4.16)$$

4.1.13   *Order Statistics*

Order statistics can be used to combine classifiers [Tumer and Ghosh (2000)]. These combiners offer the simplicity of a simple weighted combination method together with the generality of metacombination methods (see the following section). The robustness of this method is helpful when there are significant variations among classifiers in some part of the instance space.

4.2 Selecting Classifiers

Recall that ensemble classification can be performed by fusing the outputs of all ensemble members or selecting the output of a single member. In this section, we explore the latter. The premise in this approach is that there is a competent authority that nominates the best classifier for a given instance x. The output of the selected classifier is referred to as the output of the ensemble as a whole.

Very often the input space is partitioned into k competence subspaces which can be any shape or size. Then, for each subspace we nominate one classifier to be the predictor.

Clustering and classification are both considered fundamental tasks in data mining. In essence, the difference between clustering and classification lies in the manner in which knowledge is extracted from data: whereas in classification the knowledge is extracted in a supervised manner based on predefined classes, in clustering the knowledge is extracted in an unsupervised way without any guidance from the user.

Decomposition may divide the database horizontally (subsets of rows or tuples) or vertically (subsets of attributes). This section deals with the former, namely tuple decomposition.

Many methods have been developed for partitioning the tuples into subsets. Some of them are aimed at minimizing the space and time needed for the classification of a dataset, whereas others attempt to improve accuracy. These methods can be divided roughly according to the manner in which tuples are divided into subsets:

Sample—based tuple decomposition The training tuples are divided into subsets via sampling. This category includes sampling, a degenerate form of decomposition that decreases complexity as well as accuracy [Catlett (1991)]. The sampling may be sequential, trying to take advantage of knowledge gained in one iteration for use in the next iteration. Such methods include algorithms like windowing [Quinlan (1983)], which try to improve the sample they generate from one iteration to another, and the boosting algorithm [Schapire (1990)] which increases the probability of selecting instances that are misclassified by the current classifier for constructing the next one, in order to improve accuracy.

Sample-based decomposition may also be concurrent, thus enabling parallel learning. Classifiers produced by concurrent methods may be combined using a number of methods, varying from simple voting (e.g., bagging) to more sophisticated metaclassifying methods, such as stacking [Wolpert (1992)], grading [Seewald and Furnkranz (2001)], and arbiter tree [Chan and Stolfo (1993)]. Many multiple model methods have been shown to improve accuracy. This improvement in accuracy may stem from the diversity among the classifiers or from the advantages of the sequential process.

Space—based decomposition The training tuples are divided into subsets according to the part of space they belong to. [Kusiak (2000)] describes the notion of "feature value decomposition" in which objects or instances are partitioned into subsets according to the values of selected input attributes. Kusiak also suggests the notion of "decision value decomposition" in which objects are partitioned according to the value of the decision (or more generally, the target attribute). Kusiak does not describe a method for selecting the set of attributes according to which the partition is performed. In fact, his work deals only with the decision-making process and does not offer an automated procedure for space-based decomposition.

Model Class Selection (MCS) — a system that searches different classification algorithms for different regions in the instance space is proposed by [Brodley (1995a)]. The MCS system, which can be regarded as implementing an instance space decomposition strategy, uses dataset characteristics and expert—rules to select one of three possible classification methods (a decision tree, a discriminant function, or an instance—based method) for each region in the instance space. The expert-rules are based on past empirical comparisons of classifier performance, which can be considered prior knowledge.

In the neural network community, several researchers have examined the decomposition methodology. [Nowlan and Hinton (1991)] examined the mixture–of–experts (ME) methodology which decomposes the input space, such that each expert examines a different part of the space. However the subspaces have soft "boundaries," namely subspaces are allowed to overlap. A gating network is responsible for combining the various experts. [Jordan and Jacobs (1994)] have proposed an extension to the basic mixture of experts, known as hierarchical mixtures of experts (HME). This extension decomposes the space into subspaces and then recursively decomposes each subspace to subspaces.

Variations of the basic mixture–of–experts method have been developed to accommodate specific domain problems. [Hampshire and Waibel (1992)] and [Peng *et al.* (1996)] use a specialized modular network called the Meta–Pi network to solve the vowel—speaker problem. [Weigend *et al.* (1995)] proposed nonlinear gated experts for time—series, while citeOhno–MachadoMusen used a revised modular network for predicting the survival of AIDS patients. [Rahman and Fairhurst (1997)] proposed a new approach for combining multiple experts for improving recognition of handwritten numerals.

NBTree [Kohavi (1996)] is an instance space decomposition method that induces a decision tree and Naïve Bayes hybrid classifier. Naïve Bayes, which is a classification algorithm based on Bayes' theorem and a Naïve independence assumption, is very efficient in terms of its processing time. To induce an NBTree, the instance space is recursively partitioned according to attributes values. The result of the recursive partitioning is a decision tree whose terminal nodes are Naïve Bayes classifiers. Since subjecting a terminal node to a Naïve Bayes classifier means that the hybrid classifier may classify two instances from a single hyperrectangle region into distinct classes, the NBTree is more flexible than a pure decision tree. In order to decide when to stop the growth of the tree, NBTree compares two alternatives in terms of error estimation — partitioning into a hyperrectangle regions and inducing a single Naïve Bayes classifier. The error estimation is calculated by cross—validation, which significantly increases the overall processing time. Although NBTree applies a Naïve Bayes classifier to decision tree terminal nodes, classification algorithms other than Naïve Bayes are also applicable. However, the cross—validation estimations make the NBTree hybrid computationally expensive for more time—consuming algorithms such as neural networks.

NBTree uses a simple stopping criterion according to which a split is not considered when the dataset consists of 30 instances or less. While splitting too few instances will not affect the final accuracy much, it will lead to a complex composite classifier. Moreover, since each subclassifier must generalize instances in its region, it must be trained on samples of sufficient size. [Kohavi (1996)] suggested a new splitting criterion: to select the attribute with the highest utility. Kohavi defined utility as the fivefold cross—validation accuracy estimate of using a Naïve Bayes algorithm for classifying regions generated by a split. The regions are partitions of the initial subspace according to particular attribute values.

Although different researchers have addressed the issue of instance space decomposition, there is no research that suggests an automatic procedure for mutually exclusive instance space decompositions, which can be employed for any given classification algorithm and implemented in a computationally efficient way. Next, we present an algorithm for space decomposition that exploits the k-means clustering algorithm.

4.2.1 *Partitioning the Instance Space*

This section presents a decomposition method that partitions the instance space using the k-means algorithm and subsequently employs an induction algorithm on each cluster. Because space decomposition is not necessarily suitable for any given dataset, and in some cases, it might reduce the classification accuracy, we suggest a homogeneity index that measures the initial reduction in the sum of square errors resulting from the clustering procedure. Consequently, the decomposition method is executed only if the homogeneity index obtained a certain threshold value. Additionally, the proposed procedure ensures that there is a sufficient number of instances in each cluster to induce a classifier. An empirical study conducted shows that the proposed method can lead to a significant increase in classification accuracy, particularly in numeric datasets.

One of the main issues arising when trying to address the problem formulated in the last section concerns the question of what sort of instance space division should be made in order to achieve the highest accuracy possible. There are a number of ways to divide the instance space, ranging from using one attribute at a time (similar to decision tree construction) to the use of different combinations of attribute values.

Inspired by the idea that similar instances should be assigned to the same subspace, we considered the use of a clustering method as a possible tool for detecting populations. Clustering is the grouping of similar objects or instances [Hartigan (1975)].

We choose to define the similarity of unlabeled data via the distance metric. More specifically, the metric used will be the Euclidean metric for continuous attributes, which involves simple matching for nominal attributes (very similar to the similarity measure used by [Haung (1998)] in the k-prototypes algorithm, except for the fact that there is no special cluster—dependent weight for the categorical attributes). The reason for the particular metric chosen lies in the clustering method we prefer for this work, namely the k-means algorithm.

4.2.1.1 *The k-Means Algorithm as a Decomposition Tool*

The k-means algorithm is one of the simplest and most commonly used clustering algorithms. It is a partitional algorithm, which heuristically attempts to minimize the sum of squared errors:

$$SSE = \sum_{k=1}^{K} \sum_{i=1}^{N_k} \|x_i - \mu_k\|^2 \qquad (4.17)$$

where N_k is the number of instances belonging to cluster k, and μ_k is the mean of k'th cluster calculated as the mean of all the instances belonging to that cluster:

$$\mu_{k,i} = \frac{1}{N_k} \sum_{q=1}^{N_k} x_{q,i} \forall i \qquad (4.18)$$

Figure 4.1 presents the pseudocode of the k-means algorithm. The algorithm starts with an initial set of cluster centers (Centroids) chosen at random or according to some heuristic procedure. In each iteration, each instance is assigned to its nearest cluster center according to the Euclidean distance between the two. Then, the cluster centers are re—calculated.

A number of convergence conditions are possible. For example, the search may stop when the partitioning error is not reduced by the relocation of the centers. This indicates that the present partition is locally optimal. Other stopping criteria, such as exceeding a predefined number of iterations, can also be used.

k-Mean Clustering

Input: S - Instances Set, k - Number of Clusters

1: Randomly initialize k cluster centers.
2: **while** termination condition is not satisfied **do**
3:   Assign instances to the closest cluster center.
4:   Update cluster centers using the instances assignment
5: **end while**

Fig. 4.1: The k-means algorithm.

The k-means algorithm may be viewed as a gradient—decent procedure, which begins with an initial set of k cluster—centers which is iteratively updated so as to decrease the error function. The algorithm starts with an initial set of cluster centers chosen at random or according to some heuristic. In each iteration, each instance is assigned to its nearest cluster center according to the Euclidean distance between the two. The cluster centers are then recalculated.

A number of convergence conditions are possible, including no reduction in error as a result of the relocation of centers, no (or minimal) reassignment of instances to new cluster centers, or exceeding a predefined number of iterations. A rigorous proof of the finite convergence of the k-means type algorithm is given in [Selim and Ismail (1984)]. The complexity of T iterations of the k-means algorithm performed on a sample size of m instances, each characterized by N attributes, is: $O(T * K * m * N)$.

For T iterations of the k-means algorithm performed on a dataset containing m instances each of which has n attributes, its complexity may be calculated as: $O(T * K * m * n)$. This linear complexity with respect to m is one of the reasons for the popularity of k-means: Even if the number of instances is quite large (which is currently often the case) this algorithm is computationally attractive. Thus, k-means has an advantage compared to other clustering methods (e.g., hierarchical clustering methods) which have nonlinear complexity with respect to the number of instances.

Other reasons for the algorithm's popularity are its ease of interpretation, simplicity of implementation, speed of convergence, and adaptability to sparse data [Dhillon and Modha (2001)].

Taking into account the availability, linear complexity, and high understandability of the k-means algorithm, we choose to use k-means for partitioning the space into subspaces.

The k-means algorithm may be considered a simplification of the expectation maximization algorithm [Dempster *et al.* (1977)], which a density-based clustering algorithm used for identifying the parameters of different distributions from which the data objects are assumed to be drawn. In the case of k-means, the objects are assumed to be drawn from a mixture of k multivariate normal distributions, sharing the same known variance, whereas the mean vectors of the k distributions are unknown [Estivill-Castro (2000)]. When employing the k-means on unlabeled data, this underlying assumption of the algorithm may be written as:

$$x \sim N(\mu_k, \sigma^2) \forall k = 1, 2, \ldots, K, x \in C_k \qquad (4.19)$$

According to Bayes' theorem:

$$p(y = c_j^* \,|x\,) = \frac{p(y = c_j^*, x)}{p(x)} \qquad (4.20)$$

Since $p(x)$ depends on the distribution from which the unlabeled instances are drawn, and it is plausible to assume that different clusters have different distributions. This means that $p(y = c_j^* \,|x\,)$ is distributed differently on different clusters. The latter distribution has a direct influence on the predicted value of the target attribute, since:

$$\hat{y}\,(x) = \underset{c_j^* \in dom(y)}{\arg\max} \; p\left(y = c_j^* \,|x\,\right) \qquad (4.21)$$

This supports the idea of using a clustering algorithm.

4.2.1.2 *Determining the Number of Subsets*

Recall that the k-means algorithm requires the value of the k parameter as input and is affected by its value. Various heuristics attempt to find an optimal number of clusters, and most of them refer to inter—cluster distance or intra—cluster similarity. Nevertheless, because in this case as we know the actual class of each instance, we suggest using the mutual information criterion for clustering [Strehl *et al.* (2000)]). The criterion value for m instances clustered using $C = \{C_1, \ldots, C_g\}$ and referring to the target attribute y whose domain is $dom(y) = \{c_1, \ldots, c_k\}$ is defined as follows:

$$C = \frac{2}{m} \sum_{l=1}^{g} \sum_{h=1}^{k} m_{l,h} \log_{g \cdot k}\left(\frac{m_{l,h} \cdot m}{m_{.,l} \cdot m_{l,.}}\right) \qquad (4.22)$$

where $m_{l,h}$ indicate the number of instances that are in cluster C_l and in class c_h. $m_{.,h}$ denotes the total number of instances in the class c_h. Similarly, $m_{l,.}$ indicates the number of instances in cluster C_l.

4.2.1.3 *The Basic k-Classifier Algorithm*

The basic k-classifier algorithm employs the k-means algorithm for the purpose of space decomposition and uses the mutual information criterion for clustering to determine the number of clusters. The algorithm follows the following steps:

Step 1 Apply the k-means algorithm to the training set S using $K = 2, 3, \ldots K_{max}$

Step 2 Compute the mutual information criterion for clustering for $K = 2, 3, \ldots, K_{max}$, and choose the optimal number of clusters K^*.

Step 3 Produce k classifiers of the induction algorithm I, each produced on the training data belonging to a subset k of the instance space. A decomposition of the space is defined as follows: $B_k = \{x \in X : k = \arg\min \|x - \mu_k\|\}$ $k = 1, 2, \ldots, K^*$, and therefore, the classifier constructed will be: $I(x \in S \cap B_k)$ $k = 1, 2, \ldots, K^*$

New instances are classified by the k-classifier as follows:

- The instance is assigned to the cluster closest to it: B_k : $k = \arg\min \|x - \mu_k\|$.
- . The classifier induced using B_k is employed for assigning a class to the instance.

We analyze the extent to which the conditions surrounding the basic k-classifier may lead to its success or failure. This is done using three representative classification algorithms: C4.5, neural network, and Naïve Bayes. These algorithms, denoted by "DT," "ANN," and "NB" respectively, are employed on eight databases from the UCI repository, once in their basic form and again when combined with the k-classifier. The classification error rate resulting from the decomposition is measured and compared to that achieved by the basic algorithm using the McNemar's test [Dietterich (1998)]. The maximum number of clusters is set to a sufficiently large number (25).

These experiments are executed five times for each database and classifying algorithm, in order to reduce the variability resulting from the random choice of the training set in the McNemar's test.

In order to analyze the causes for the k-classifier's success/failure, a metadataset, which contains a tuple for each experiment on each database with each classifying algorithm, was constructed. Its attributes correspond to the characteristics of the experiment:

Record—attribute ratio Calculated as a training set size divided by the attribute set size.

Initial PRE the reduction in the SSE resulting from partitioning the dataset from one cluster (the nonpartitioned form) to two. This characteristic was chosen, since we suspect it indicates whether the dataset should be partitioned at all.

Induction method the induction algorithm employed on the database.

In order to analyze the reduction in error rate as a function of the method and dataset characteristics, a metaclassifier is constructed. The inducer employed for this purpose is the C4.5 algorithm.

The target attribute in the metadataset represents the accuracy performance of the k-classifier algorithm relative to the appropriate accuracy performance of the inducer employed in the base form. The target attribute can have one of the following values: non—significant decrease/increase of up to ten percent ("small ns dec/inc"), non—significant decrease/increase of ten percent or more ("large ns dec/inc"), significant decrease/increase of up to ten percent ("small s dec/inc"), significant decrease/increase of ten percent or more ("large s dec/inc"), and a decrease rate of zero percent ("no change"). The resulting decision tree is presented in Figure 4.2.

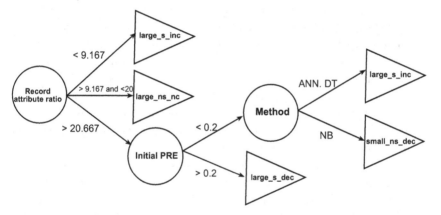

Fig. 4.2: A decision tree describing the change in error achieved by the k-classifier.

As may be learned from the tree, the two attributes that determine whether or not the k-classifier achieves a significant decrease in error rate are the record—attribute ratio and the initial PRE. A significant decrease in error rate may occur when the former characteristic exceeds 20.67 and the latter exceeds 0.2.

This result also answers the question: should there always be a recommended partition? This question may be viewed as a preliminary check of the dataset, aimed at discovering whether or not the dataset requires space decomposition.

When the record—attribute ratio is smaller than or equal to 20.67, the result will be a significant increase in the error rate or, at the very least, a non—significant increase. Therefore, it may be concluded that datasets containing a small number of records compared to their number of attributes should not be partitioned using the k-classifier algorithm.

Another conclusion that may be drawn from this stage is that the k-classifier algorithm works better on integer or continuous valued attributes. Although the algorithm did not significantly decrease the error for all numerical databases, the datasets for which the error decreased significantly all contained integer attributes, continuous valued attributes, or some combination of the two.

4.2.1.4   *The Heterogeneity Detecting k-Classifier (HDk-Classifier)*

An analysis of the error reduction rate provides the missing link regarding when clustering should be used. As we suspected, decomposition does not always yield an accuracy gain and may cause accuracy to deteriorate on many occasions. Such results may derive from the homogeneity, or lack of heterogeneity, of the dataset, i.e. there are no distinct clusters or populations in the dataset, and therefore it should not be partitioned.

The mutual information criterion used in the basic k-classifier does not examine whether heterogeneity exists. It simply assumes it exists and aims at finding the number of populations in the data, given that the dataset is indeed composed of different populations.

Should we detect nonheterogeneous datasets, there is no need for decomposing them, since their error will not decrease. The current k-classifier, which increases the running time complexity compared to the basic learning algorithm, only yields worse results on such datasets. In light of this, we refine the basic k-classifier and add another step. In this step, the k-means is employed for $k = 1$ and $k = 2$. If the resulting PRE is larger than 0.2, the rest of the k-classifier stages follow. If not, it is assumed that there is no use in decomposing, so the base form of the inducer is employed for the entire dataset. Thus, the algorithm maintains the accuracy of nonheterogeneous datasets at the cost of additional complexity which is, however, much less than the complexity of the basic k-classifier.

4.2.1.5   *Running–Time Complexity*

The proposed training algorithm requires the following computations:

- During the stages of determining the optimal number of clusters, the k-means algorithm is run $K_{max} - 1$ times. This leads to a complexity of $O(T * K_{max}^2 * n * m)$.
- Computation of the PRE's value for $K = 1$ and $K = 2$ is of $O(n * m)$ complexity and is therefore negligible.
- Constructing a classifier on each of the K^* partitions requires at most $O(K_{max} * G_I(m, n))$, where G_I is the classifier's training complexity time. For instance, when employing the decision tree algorithm, the time complexity of this stage will be at most $O(K_{max} * m\sqrt{l})$, where the number of leaves of the decision tree is l.

In light of the analysis above, the total running—time complexity of the training algorithm is $O(T * K_{max}^2 * n * m + K_{max} * G_I(m, n))$. In the case of decision trees classifiers, for instance, the time-complexity would be: $O(T * K_{max}^2 * n * m + K_{max} * m\sqrt{l})$.

4.3 Mixture of Experts and Metalearning

Metalearning is a process of learning from learners (classifiers). The training of a meta-classifier is composed of two or more stages, rather than one stage, as with standard learners. In order to induce a metaclassifier, first, the base classifiers are trained (stage one), and then, the meta classifier is trained (second stage). In the prediction phase, the base classifiers output their classifications, and then, the metaclassifier(s) make the final classification (as a function of the base classifiers). Metalearning methods are best suited for cases in which certain classifiers consistently correctly classify, or consistently misclassify, certain instances.

The following sections describe the most well-known metacombination methods.

4.3.1 *Stacking*

Stacking is probably the most-popular metalearning technique [Wolpert (1992)]. By using a metalearner, this method tries to induce which classifiers are reliable and which are not. Stacking is usually employed to combine models built by different inducers. The idea is to create a metadataset containing a tuple for each tuple in the original dataset. However, instead of using the original input attributes, it uses the predicted classifications by the classifiers as the input attributes. The target attribute remains as in the original training set. A test instance is first classified by each of the base classifiers. These classifications are fed into a metalevel training set from which a metaclassifier is produced. This classifier combines the different predictions into a final one. It is recommended that the original dataset be partitioned into two subsets. The first subset is reserved to form the meta-dataset, and the second subset is used to build the base level classifiers. Consequently, the metaclassifier predications reflect the true performance of base level learning algorithms. Stacking performance can be improved by using output probabilities for each class label from the base level classifiers. In such cases, the number of input attributes in the metadataset is multiplied by the number of classes. It has been shown that with stacking, the ensemble performs (at best) comparably to selecting the best classifier from the ensemble by cross-validation (Dzeroski and Zenko, 2004). In order to improve the existing stacking approach, they employed a new multiresponse model tree to learn at the metalevel and empirically showed that it performs better than existing stacking approaches and better than selecting the best classifier by cross-validation.

There are many variants of the basic stacking algorithm [Wolpert and Macready (1996)]. The most useful stacking scheme is specified in [Ting and Witten (1999)]. The metadatabase is composed of the posteriori class probabilities of each classifier. It has been shown that this schema, in combination with multiresponse linear regression as a metalearner, gives the best results.

Džeroski and Ženko (2004) demonstrated that the use of a metaclassifier based on multiresponse trees is required in order for this schema to work better than simply selecting the best classifier. Seewald (2002) showed that from a choice of seven classifiers it was possible for a stacking scheme using four of the classifiers that were considered as belonging to different classifier types, to perform equally as well as all seven classifiers. There has been considerably less attention given to the area of heterogeneity and stacking in the area of regression problems.

StackingC is a variation of the simple stacking method. In empirical tests, stacking showed significant performance degradation for multiclass datasets. StackingC was designed to address this problem. In StackingC, each base classifier outputs only one class probability prediction (Seewald, 2003). Each base classifier is trained and tested upon one particular class, while stacking output probabilities for all classes and from all component classifiers.

Seewald (2003) has shown that all ensemble learning systems, including StackingC (Seewald, 2002), grading (Seewald and Fuernkranz, 2001) and even bagging (Breiman, 1996), can be simulated by stacking (Wolpert, 1992). To do this, Seward gives functionally equivalent definitions of most schemes as metaclassifiers for stacking. Džeroski and Ženko (2004) indicated that the combination of SCANN (Merz, 1999), which is a variant of stacking, and MDT (Ting and Witten, 1999), plus selecting the best base classifier using cross-validation, seems to perform at about the same level as stacking with multilinear response (MLR).

Seewald (2003) presented strong empirical evidence that in the extension proposed by Ting and Witten (1999) stacking performs worse on multiclass than on two-class datasets for all but one metalearner he investigated. The explanation given was that when the dataset has a higher number of classes, the dimensionality of the metalevel data is increased proportionally. This higher dimensionality makes it harder for metalearners to induce good models, since there are more features to consider. The increased dimensionality has two more drawbacks. First, it increases the training time of the meta classifier; this problem is acute in many inducers. Second, it also increases the amount of memory which is used in the training process. This may lead to insufficient resources and therefore may limit the number of training instances from which an inducer may learn, thus damaging the accuracy of the ensemble.

During the learning phase of StackingC it is essential to use one-against-all class binarization and regression learners for each class model. This class binarization is believed to be a problematic method, especially when class distribution is highly nonsymmetric. It has been illustrated (Frnkranz, 2002) that handling many classes is a major problem for the one-against-all binarization technique, possibly because the resulting binary learning problems have increasingly skewed class distributions. An alternative to one-against-all class binarization is one-against-one binarization, in which the basic idea is to convert a multiple class problem into a series of two-class problems by training one classifier for each pair of classes, using only training examples of these two classes and ignoring all others. A new instance is classified by submitting it to each of the $\frac{k(k-1)}{2}$ binary classifiers and combining their predictions. Experimental studies show that this binarization method yields noticeably poor accuracy results when the number of classes in the problem increases. An explanation might be that as the number of classes in a problem increases, the greater the chance that any of the $\frac{k(k-1)}{2}$ base classifiers will provide an incorrect prediction. There are two reasons for this. First, when predicting the class of an instance, only $k-1$ out of $\frac{k(k-1)}{2}$ classifiers may predict correctly. This is because only

$k-1$ classifiers were trained on any specific class. The second reason is that in one-against-one binarization we only use instances that belong to either examined classes and ignore all other instances; while in one-against-all we use all instances. Thus, the number of training instances for each base classifier in one-against-one binarization is much smaller than when using the one-against-all binarization method; given this, the one-against-one binarization method may yield inferior base classifier.

StackingC improves on stacking in terms of accuracy and runtime. These improvements are more evident for multiclass datasets and have a tendency to become more pronounced as the number of classes increases. StackingC also addresses the weakness of stacking in the extension proposed by Ting and Witten (1999) and offers balanced performance on two-class and multiclass datasets.

The SCANN (Stacking, Correspondence Analysis and Nearest Neighbor) combining method [Merz (1999)] uses the strategies of stacking and correspondence analysis. Correspondence analysis is a method for geometrically modeling the relationship between the rows and columns of a matrix whose entries are categorical. In this context, correspondence analysis is used to explore the relationship between the training examples and their classification by a collection of classifiers.

A nearest neighbor method is then applied to classify unseen examples. Here, each possible class is assigned coordinates in the space derived by correspondence analysis. Unclassified examples are mapped into the new space, and the class label corresponding to the closest class point is assigned to the example.

4.3.2   *Arbiter Trees*

According to Chan and Stolfo's approach [Chan and Stolfo (1993)], an arbiter tree is built in a bottom-up fashion. Initially, the training set is randomly partitioned into k disjoint subsets. The arbiter is induced from a pair of classifiers, and a new arbiter is recursively induced from the output of two arbiters. Consequently, for k classifiers, there are $\log_2(k)$ levels in the generated arbiter tree.

The creation of the arbiter is performed as follows. For each pair of classifiers, the instances that belong to the union of their training sets are tested by the two classifiers. A selection rule compares the classifications of the two classifiers and selects instances from the comined set to form the training set for the arbiter. The arbiter is induced from this set with the same learning algorithm used in the base level. The purpose of the arbiter is to provide an alternate classification when the base classifiers present divergent classifications. This arbiter, together with an arbitration rule, decides on a final classification outcome based upon the base predictions. Figure 4.3 shows how the final classification is selected based on the classification of two base classifiers and a single arbiter.

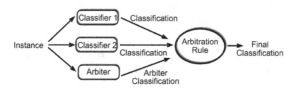

Fig. 4.3: A prediction from two base classifiers and a single arbiter.

The process of combining the data subsets, classifying it using a pair of arbiter trees, comparing the classifications, forming a training set, training the arbiter, and picking one of the predictions, is recursively performed until the root arbiter is formed. Figure 4.4 illustrates an arbiter tree created for $k = 4$. $T_1 - T_4$ are the four initial training datasets from which four classifiers $M_1 - M_4$ are generated concurrently. T_{12} and T_{34} are the training sets generated by the rule selection from which arbiters are produced, and A_{12} and A_{34} are the two arbiters. Similarly, T_{14} and A_{14} (root arbiter) are generated, and the arbiter tree is completed.

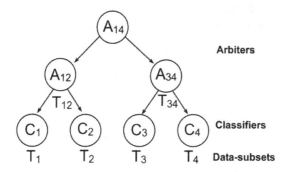

Fig. 4.4: Sample arbiter tree.

There are several schemes for arbiter trees, each of which is characterized by a different selection rule. Three versions of selection rules are presented below:

- Only instances with classifications that disagree are chosen (group 1).
- Group 1, as defined above, plus instances in which the classifications agree but are incorrect (group 2).
- Groups 1 and 2, as defined above, plus instances that have the same correct classifications (group 3).

Depending on the selection rule used for generating the training data, we can select the corresponding arbitration rules:

- For selection rules 1 and 2, a final classification is made by a majority vote of the classifications of the two lower levels and the arbiter's own classification, with preference given to the latter.
- For selection rule 3, if the classifications of the two lower levels are not equal, the classification made by the subarbiter based on the first group is chosen. In cases in which this is not true, and the classification of the subarbiter constructed on the third group equals the classification of the lower levels, this is the chosen classification. In any other case, the classification of the subarbiter constructed on the second group is chosen. In fact, it is possible to achieve the same accuracy level as that achieved when the same base learning algorithm is applied to the entire dataset but with less time and memory requirements [Chan and Stolfo (1993)]. More specifically, it has been shown that this metalearning strategy required only around 30% of the memory used by the single model case. This last fact, combined with the independent nature of the various learning processes, makes this method robust and effective for massive amounts of data. Nevertheless, the accuracy level depends on several factors, such as the distribution of the data among the subsets and the pairing scheme of learned classifiers and arbiters at each level. The decision regarding any of these issues may influence performance, but the optimal decisions are not necessarily known in advance, or set initially by the algorithm.

4.3.3   Combiner Trees

The way combiner trees are generated is very similar to arbiter trees. Both are trained bottom-up. However, a combiner, instead of an arbiter, is placed in each non-leaf node of a combiner tree [Chan and Stolfo (1997)]. In the combiner strategy, the classifications of the learned base classifiers form the basis of the metalearner's training set. A composition rule determines the content of training examples from which a combiner (metaclassifier) is be generated. In classifying an instance, the base classifiers first generate their classifications, and based on the composition rule, a new instance is generated. The aim of this strategy is to combine the classifications from the base classifiers by learning the relationship between these classifications and the correct classification. Figure 4.5 illustrates the result obtained from two base classifiers and a single combiner.

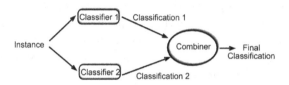

Fig. 4.5: A prediction from two base classifiers and a single combiner.

Two schemes for composition rules were proposed. The first one is the stacking scheme. The second is like stacking, with the addition of the instance input attributes. It has been shown that the stacking scheme per se does not perform as well as the second scheme [Chan and Stolfo (1995)]. Although there is information loss due to data partitioning, combiner trees can sustain the accuracy level achieved by a single classifier.

4.3.4 *Grading*

This technique uses "graded" classifications as metalevel classes [Seewald and Furnkranz (2001)]. The term "graded" is used in the sense of classifications that have been marked as correct or incorrect. The method transforms the classification made by the k different classifiers into k training sets by using the instances k times and attaching them to a new binary class in each occurrence. This class indicates whether the k-th classifier yielded a correct or incorrect classification compared to the instances actual class.

For each base classifier, one metaclassifier is learned whose task it is to classify when the base classifier misclassifies. At classification time, each base classifier classifies the unlabeled instance. The final classification is derived from the classifications of those base classifiers that are classified to be correct by the metaclassification schemes. In cases in which several base classifiers with different classification results are classified as correct, voting, or a combination considering the confidence estimates of the base classifiers, is performed. Grading may be considered a generalization of cross-validation selection [Schaffer (1993)], which divides the training data into k subsets, builds $k - 1$ classifiers by dropping one subset at a time, and then uses it to find a misclassification rate. Finally, the procedure simply chooses the classifier corresponding to the subset with the smallest misclassification. Grading tries to make this decision separately for each and every instance by using only those classifiers that are predicted to classify that instance correctly. The main difference between grading and combiners (or stacking) is that the former does not change the instance attributes by replacing them with class predictions or class probabilities. Instead, it modifies the class values. Furthermore, in grading several sets of metadata are created, one for each base classifier. Several metalevel classifiers are learned from those sets.

The main difference between grading and arbiters is that arbiters use information about the disagreements of classifiers for selecting a training set; in contrast, grading uses disagreement with the target function to produce a new training set.

4.3.5   *Gating Network*

Figure 4.6 illustrates an n-expert structure. Each expert outputs the conditional probability of the target attribute given the input instance. A gating network is responsible for combining the various experts by assigning a weight to each network. These weights are not constant but are functions of the input instance x. The gating network selects one or a few experts (classifiers) which appear to have the most appropriate class distribution for the example. In fact, each expert specializes on a small portion of the input space.

An extension to the basic mixture-of-experts, known as hierarchical mixtures-of-experts (HME), was proposed in [Jordan and Jacobs (1994)]. This extension decomposes the space into subspaces, and then recursively decomposes each subspace into subspaces.

Variations of the basic mixture of experts methods have been developed to accommodate specific domain problems. A specialized modular network called the Meta-p_i network has been used to solve the vowel-speaker problem [Hampshire and Waibel (1992); Peng *et al.* (1996)]. There have

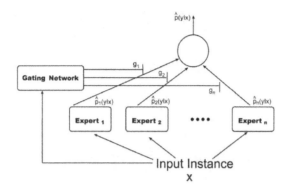

Fig. 4.6: Illustration of n-expert structure.

been other extensions to the mixture-of-experts, such as nonlinear gated experts for time-series [Weigend *et al.* (1995)], qrevised modular network for predicting the survival of AIDS patients [Ohno-Machado and Musen (1997)], and a new approach for combining multiple experts for improving handwritten numeral recognition [Rahman and Fairhurst (1997)].

Some of the weighting methods are trainable. Lin *et al.* (2005) propose using genetic algorithms in an attempt to find the optimal weights. They describe two different combinatorial schemes to improve the performance of handwritten Chinese character recognition: the accuracy rate of the first candidate class and the accuracy rate of top ten candidate classes. Their extensive study shows that this new approach can significantly improve the accuracy performance.

Reinforcement learning (RL) has been used to adaptively combine the base classifiers [Dimitrakakis (2005)]. The ensemble consists of a controlling agent that selects which base classifiers are used to classify a particular instance. The controlling agent learns to make decisions so that classification error is minimized. The agent is trained through a Q-learning inspired technique. The usage of reinforcement learning improves results when there are many base classifiers.

Chapter 5

Gradient Boosting Machines

5.1 Introduction

Among the ensemble methods used in practice, gradient boosting machine (GBM) is probably the most frequently used method in many real-world applications. GBM has been shown to achieve state of the art results on many supervised learning benchmarks.

Like other boosting methods, in gradient boosting machine, the training of each model is dependent on models that have already been trained. It includes a learning procedure in which the goal is to construct the base models so that they are maximally correlated with the negative gradient of the loss function associated with the whole ensemble. More specifically, a sequence of regression models is computed, where each successive model predicts the pseudo-residuals of the preceding models given an arbitrary differentiable loss function.

An arbitrary loss function requires the specification of the loss function by the user, as well as the function that calculates the corresponding negative gradient. Predictions are aggregated in an additive manner in which each added model is trained so it will minimize the loss function.

It is important to note that a GBM model usually has many simple models, as opposed to other ensemble approaches which have fewer but more complex models. Choosing the right number of models (i.e., number of iterations) is very important when training a gradient boosting model. Setting it too high can lead to overfitting, while setting it too low may result in underfitting. The selection of the most suitable number of iterations is usually done by using a validation set to evaluate the overall predictive performance. Overfitting can be reduced by applying a stochastic gradient boosting method in which models are consecutively trained with small subsets sampled from the original dataset.

Gradient boosting is typically used with decision trees as base learners. For this purpose a modified version of the generic GBM was developed to utilize the specific characteristics of decision trees. In particular, gradient boosting trees is optimized separately for each of the tree's regions, instead of trying to optimize the whole tree.

Gradient boosting trees became the method of choice for tabular supervised learning tasks when the XGBoost algorithm was introduced [Chen and Guestrin (2016)]. This is reflected by the fact that in 2015, 17 of the 29 Kaggles winning solutions used XGBoost. In this chapter, we discuss gradient boosting trees and get acquainted with the most popular open-source gradient boosting tree libraries available.

5.2   Gradient Boosting for Regression Tasks

We begin by examining the simplest form of GBM in which GBM is used to address a regression task by optimizing the mean squared error (MSE).

GBM is an additive model in the sense That it adds up the outputs of several simple models to create a more complicated model. One way to understand the intuition behind GBM is to think about how the game of golf is played [Parr and Howard (2018)]. The main goal of golf is to get the ball into the hole in as few strokes as possible. For the first shot, the golfer usually tries to move the ball a long distance. The subsequent hits are usually much gentler and are intended to correct the balls position based on its location relative to the hole after previous strokes. After each stroke, the golfer evaluates the balls position and distance to the hole, and based on that determines the right nudge. In GBM terms, the direction and distance represent the residual vector to be approximated by the next model.

In the context of regression setting, our goal is to train a model F to predict values of the form $\hat{y} = F(x)$ by minimizing the L2-loss (squared error): $\sum_{i=1}^{m} (\hat{y}_i - y_i)^2$, which goes over the entire training set and compares the actual values of the output variable y with the predicted value $\hat{y}_i$.

We begin with a constant function model $F_0(x)$ defined as:

$$F_0(x) = \arg\min_{\gamma} \sum_{i=1}^{m} L(y_i, \gamma) \tag{5.1}$$

Because our loss function is L2, the optimal value of γ is simply the mean of the target variable y.

In the next model, the gradient boosting algorithm improves on F_0 by constructing a new model which adds an estimator h_1 that, together with F_0, provides more accurate predictions: $F_1(x) = F_0(x) + h_1(x)$. To find h_1, we should recall that an optimal h satisfies the condition:

$$F_1(x) = F_0(x) + h_1(x) = y \tag{5.2}$$

or:

$$h_1(x) = y - F_0(x) \tag{5.3}$$

Thus, for training the model h_1 we need to fit it to the residual values: $r = y - F_0(x)$. For this purpose, we can use any regression algorithm that takes x as input and r as the target output values.

In each of the following iterations of the gradient boosting algorithm: $2 \leq j \leq T$, we adds an estimator h_j to construct a better model: $F_j(x) = F_{j-1}(x) + h_j(x)$, where $h_j(x)$ is trained to fit to the residuals $r = y - F_{j-1}(x)$.

We can generalize the idea presented above to any specified loss function $L(y, F(x))$. Figure 5.1 presents the pseudocode for building an ensemble of regression models using the GBM algorithm. Determining the optimal function h in each iteration for an arbitrary loss function L might be infeasible. Thus, we apply a steepest descent step to solve this minimization problem. In particular, we calculate the pseudo-residuals with respect to the functions F_{j-1}. We then use a regression algorithm I to approximate the pseudo-residuals given x. Note that the auxiliary training set $\{(x_i, r_{ij})\}_{i=1}^m$ is similar to the original one, but the original labels y_i are replaced with the gradients r_{ij}. Finally, we use line search to find the coefficient γ that represents the optimal step size. Note that in the case of L2 loss, the pseudo-residual is simply the difference between the actual y value and the corresponding predicted value.

5.3 Adjusting Gradient Boosting for Classification Tasks

In this section, we present how gradient boosted machines can be used for solving classification tasks. This is less straightforward than using gradient boosted machines for regression tasks.

Recall that in classification tasks the output variable y_i does not result in real values but rather class labels (e.g., positive and negative in the binary classification tasks). Class values are not additive, so we cannot use

GBM Training

Input: A base regression algorithm - I, number of iterations T, the training
    set, $S = \{(x_i, y_i)\}_{i=1}^{m}$, and a differentiable loss function $L(y, F(x))$
1:   Initialize model with a constant value: $F_0(x) = \arg\min_{\gamma} \sum_{i=1}^{n} L(y_i, \gamma)$
2:   $j \leftarrow 1$
3:   **repeat**
4:      For $i = 1, \ldots, m$, compute pseudo-residuals:
      $r_{ij} = -\left[\dfrac{\partial L(y_i, F(x_i))}{\partial F(x_i)}\right]_{F(x)=F_{j-1}(x)}$
5:      Construct regression model h_j using I using the training set
      $\{(x_i, r_{ij})\}_{i=1}^{m}$.
6:      Find multiplier γ_j by performing line search on the following one-
      dimensional optimization problem:
      $\gamma_j = \arg\min_{\gamma} \sum_{i=1}^{m} L\left(y_i, F_{j-1}(x_i) + \gamma h_j(x_i)\right).$
7:      Update the model: $F_j(x) = F_{j-1}(x) + \gamma_j h_j(x)$.
8:      $j \leftarrow j + 1$
9:   **until** $j > T$
10: Output $F_M(x)$

Fig. 5.1: The simple GBM algorithm for regression task.

them directly in the gradient boosting algorithm. Instead, we can model
the problem as a probability estimation using the following expression:

$$P(Y_i = +1 \mid X) = \frac{1}{1 + e^{-\hat{F}(x)}} \tag{5.4}$$

where $\hat{F}(x)$ is an additive model obtained by running the gradient boosting
algorithm:

$$\hat{F}(x) = F_0 + \sum_{i=1}^{T} \gamma_i h_i(x) \tag{5.5}$$

This function is called the sigmoid function, which maps all of the real
values into the range of zero and one, as required by probability. One way
to find the optimal model is to use the idea of maximum likelihood. Simply
put, we search the model space and look for a solution that maximizes the
known likelihood function given the observations in the training set.

Assuming that the observations are independent, the likelihood is expressed by:

$$Likelihood = \prod_{i=1}^{m} P(Y_i \mid x) \tag{5.6}$$

Instead of using the likelihood as is, it is easier from the computational perspective to maximize the logarithm of the likelihood. This logarithm transformation can be applied, because a logarithm is a monotone function:

$$Q = \sum_{i=1}^{m} L(y_i, f(x_i)) \tag{5.7}$$

where:

$$L(y_i, f(x_i)) = \log P(Y_i \mid x) \tag{5.8}$$

Given the above definitions, we can plug the loss function into the algorithm presented in Figure 5.1, once we express the initial estimation $F_0(x)$ and the pseudo-residuals using the new loss function.

In this case, the initial estimation $F_0(x)$ is estimated as:

$$F_0(x) = \log \frac{p_1}{1 - p_1} \tag{5.9}$$

where p_1 is the portion of instances in the training set that belong to the positive class. One can show that the above estimated $F_0(x)$ is an optimal initial approximation for the abovementioned likelihood function. Regarding the pseudo-residuals, we need to find the gradient of the loss function with respect to the functions F_{j-1}. More specifically, for positive training examples we get a gradient of $1 - \frac{1}{1+e^{-F_{j-1}(x)}}$, while for negative examples, we simply get the opposite value.

5.4 Gradient Boosting Trees

As indicated above, the gradient boosting algorithm is frequently applied to decision trees, particularly regression trees. The gradient boosting method can be adjusted specifically to decision trees, and in so doing, we can improve the quality of fit for each tree [Friedman (2001)].

In gradient boosting trees, the trees leaves predict the average of the residual values for all observations in that leaf. Let T_j represent the number of leaves of the tree that we obtained in iteration j, and let $R_{1j}, \ldots, R_{T_j j}$ represent the leaves. Thus, the output of $h(x)$ can be written as:

$$h_m(x) = \sum_{k=1}^{T_j} b_{kj} \mathbf{1}_{R_{kj}}(x) \tag{5.10}$$

where b_{kj} is the constant value predicted by the leaf R_{kj}.

Generic gradient boosting at the m-th step would fit a decision tree $h_m(x)$ to pseudo-residuals. Let J_m be the number of its leaves. The tree partitions the input space into J_m disjoint regions $R_{1m}, \ldots, R_{J_m m}$ and predicts a constant value in each region. Using the indicator notation, the output of $h_m(x)$ for input x can be written as the sum:

$h_m(x) = \sum_{j=1}^{J_m} b_{jm} \mathbf{1}_{R_{jm}}(x)$, where b_{jm} is the value predicted in the region R_{jm}.

Then, the coefficients b_{jm} are multiplied by some value γ_m chosen using line search so as to minimize the loss function, and the model is updated as follows:

$$F_m(x) = F_{m-1}(x) + \gamma_m h_m(x), \tag{5.11}$$

$$\gamma_m = \arg\min_{\gamma} \sum_{i=1}^{n} L(y_i, F_{m-1}(x_i) + \gamma h_m(x_i)) \tag{5.12}$$

Friedman proposed modifying this algorithm so that it chooses a separate optimal value γ_{jm} for each of the tree's regions, instead of a single γ_m for the whole tree. He calls the modified algorithm "TreeBoost." The coefficients b_{jm} from the tree fitting procedure can then be discarded, and the model update rule becomes:

$$F_m(x) = F_{m-1}(x) + \sum_{j=1}^{J_m} \gamma_{jm} \mathbf{1}_{R_{jm}}(x) \tag{5.13}$$

$$\gamma_{jm} = \arg\min_{\gamma} \sum_{x_i \in R_{jm}} L(y_i, F_{m-1}(x_i) + \gamma) \tag{5.14}$$

5.5   Regularization Methods for Gradient Boosting Machines

Running gradient boosting as is with too many models can lead to overfitting. Regularization can help us to address this challenge and serves as a stabilizer of the learning algorithm. We say that an algorithm is stable if slightly changing the training set does not change its predictions much.

Several regularization methods have been suggested to mitigate this effect. In the following subsections, we present the most popular methods.

5.5.1 *Number of Models*

One natural regularization parameter is limiting the number of gradient boosting iterations T. Simply reducing T may lead to underfitting. Thus, the optimal value of T is often determined by monitoring accuracy using a separate validation dataset. We can decrease the value of T until it leads to degradation of the model's validation accuracy.

5.5.2 *Shrinkage*

As indicated above, GBM requires many models. Due to the greedy nature of the algorithm, models that were added in early iterations have more impact than the models that were added later in the process.

The idea of shrinkage is to modify the update rule such that each iteration will have less impact on the total model. The contribution of each model is scaled by a factor of ν to control the learning rate:

$$F_j(x) = F_{j-1}(x) + \nu \cdot \gamma_j h_j(x) \quad 0 < \nu \leq 1 \tag{5.15}$$

Using low learning rates (less than 0.1) is recommended, as it has been shown to yield significant improvement in a model's generalization ability comparing to gradient boosting without shrinking. However, by setting ν to lower values, we will also need to increase the number of iterations at the cost of increased computational time.

5.5.3 *Stochastic Gradient Boosting*

Another approach for reducing the effect of overfitting, it to use the same idea used in the bagging algorithm and random forest. Specifically, the base learner should be fit on a subsample of the training set, drawn at random without replacement.

When the subsample ratio is set to values lower than 1 (usually between 0.5 and 0.8), it injects randomness into the algorithm and helps prevent overfitting. For example, setting it to 0.5 means that GBM randomly selects half of the data instances to train the models.

In addition to sampling the instances, the base learning can be trained on a subset of the input features, drawn at random without replacement. This ensures diversity among models. Both subsample methods help to reduce the training time, because a smaller dataset is used to train the models.

5.5.4 *Decision Tree Regularization*

When gradient boosting trees are used, we can further limit the number of iterations and reduce the chances of overfitting. In particular, we can set the minimum number of instances in the leaves. Thus, the tree's growth is stopped if any split leads to nodes containing fewer than the specified minimum number of training instances.

We can also mitigate overfitting by setting the maximum depth of the tree. For example, by setting this parameter to six, no tree can exceed six levels. This parameter can be used to keep the tree complexity low.

Another useful regularization technique for gradient boosted trees is to penalize the model complexity of the learned model. The model complexity can be defined as a function of the number of leaves in the trained trees. Thus, instead of simply minimizing the loss function, we can minimize an objective function that consists of both the loss and the tree's complexity. For example, the XGBoost algorithm adds the square of the scores associated with the leaves to the complexity.

5.6 Gradient Boosting Trees vs. Random Forest

Both random forest and gradient boosting trees are considered to be excellent decision forest algorithms. Thus, many practitioners have difficulty deciding which one to use. The main points to consider are listed below.

- Algorithm tuning: Every algorithm has its own hyperparameters, however the random forest algorithm has only one really important hyperparameter: the number of features that are randomly selected in each node. In contrast, gradient boosted trees have several hyperparameters that need to be tuned, including: the number of trees, the tree's depth, and the shrinkage ratio.
- Overfitting: Random forest is harder to overfit than gradient boosting trees. This can be explained by the fact that the trees in random forest are trained independently, whereas in gradient boosting trees they are dependent and thus can overfit the data.

- Model Complexity: Random forest usually reaches its best performance when it trains a few deep trees. The relatively large depth (20 to 40 levels) is required in order to reduce the bias error, while a relatively small number of trees (usually in the order of tens) is needed to reduce variance error. On the other hand, the best performance of gradient boosting trees is usually achieved when it trains many shallow decision trees. The relatively shallow trees (up to 10 levels) in gradient boosting trees are used to ensure low variance error, while a large number of trees (hundreds or even thousands) are needed to reduce bias error.
- Predictive Performance: In many regression and classification tasks, well-tuned gradient boosting trees outperform random forest.

To conclude, if one is interested in the best predictive performance, gradient boosting trees are the method of choice. However, this performance comes with a cost: a long hyperparameter tuning process. On the other hand, when time is limited, random forest might be the method of choice as it is considered to be "plug'n'play", i.e. hyperparameter tuning process is not required.

5.7 XGBoost Algorithm

XGBoost (short for eXtreme Gradient Boosting) is a scalable machine learning system for tree boosting that gained popularity among the Kaggle community where it has been used in a large number of competitions [Chen and Guestrin (2016)]. XGBoost added several optimizations and refinements to GBM in order to increase scalability. First, it features split finding algorithms that (a) handle sparse data with nodes default directions, (b) address weighted data using merge and prune operations, and (c) enumerate efficiently over all possible splits so the splitting threshold is optimized. XGBoost can run faster than other models as it supports distributed platforms such as Apache Hadoop and can be distributed across multiple machines.

But the most important refinement in XGBoost is that it adds a regularization component to the loss function presented in GBM, aimed at creating ensembles that are simpler and more generative. In particular, the objective function is defined as:

$$\mathcal{L}(\phi) = \sum_i l(\hat{y}_i, \ y_i) + \sum_k \Omega(f_k) \tag{5.16}$$

where l is a convex and differentiable loss function that measures how close the prediction $\hat{y}_i$ is to the target y_i. In particular l can be a quadratic loss function such as least squares error, i.e.:

$$l(\hat{y}_i,\ y_i) = (\hat{y}_i - y_i)^2 \qquad (5.17)$$

The second term in Eq. 5.16 (i.e. Ω) penalizes the complexity of the model and helps to avoid over-fitting. It is defined as:

$$\Omega(f) = \gamma T + \frac{1}{2}\lambda\|w\|^2 \qquad (5.18)$$

where T is the number of leaves in the tree and w is the leaf weights.

Since XGBoost model is trained in an additive manner, the loss function to be minimized in the t-th iteration is defined as:

$$\mathcal{L}^{(t)} = \sum_{i=1}^{n} l(y_i, \hat{y}_i^{(t-1)} + f_t(\mathbf{x}_i)) + \Omega(f_t) \qquad (5.19)$$

where $\hat{y}_i^{(t-1)}$ is the prediction of the i-th instance at the (t-1)-th iteration. Our goal is to find f_t that minimizes Eq. 5.19.

Instead of directly calculating the current loss $\mathcal{L}^{(t)}$ we can approximate its value by using Taylor expansion:

$$\mathcal{L}^{(t)} \simeq \sum_{i=1}^{n}[l(y_i, \hat{y}_i^{(t-1)}) + g_i f_t(\mathbf{x}_i) + \frac{1}{2}h_i f_t^2(\mathbf{x}_i)] + \Omega(f_t) \qquad (5.20)$$

where $g_i = \partial_{\hat{y}^{(t-1)}} l(y_i, \hat{y}_i^{(t-1)})$ and $h_i = \partial_{\hat{y}^{(t-1)}}^2 l(y_i, \hat{y}_i^{(t-1)})$ are the first and second order derivatives of the loss function with respect to $\hat{y}^{(t-1)}$.

Note that the first term in Eq. 5.20 (i.e. $l(y_i, \hat{y}_i^{(t-1)})$) is constant because we are in the iteration t and the loss of the previous iteration $t-1$ is already known. Thus, for our needs we can use the following goal function:

$$\tilde{\mathcal{L}}^{(t)} = \sum_{i=1}^{n}[g_i f_t(\mathbf{x}_i) + \frac{1}{2}h_i f_t^2(\mathbf{x}_i)] + \Omega(f_t) \qquad (5.21)$$

Using Eq. 5.18, we can expand Ω and rewrite Eq. 5.21 as:

$$\tilde{\mathcal{L}}^{(t)} = \sum_{i=1}^{n}[g_i f_t(\mathbf{x}_i) + \frac{1}{2}h_i f_t^2(\mathbf{x}_i)] + \gamma T + \frac{1}{2}\lambda\sum_{j=1}^{T} w_j^2 \qquad (5.22)$$

or simply:

$$\tilde{\mathcal{L}}^{(t)} = \sum_{j=1}^{T}[(\sum_{i\in I_j} g_i)w_j + \frac{1}{2}(\sum_{i\in I_j} h_i + \lambda)w_j^2] + \gamma T \qquad (5.23)$$

where $I_j = \{i|q(\mathbf{x}_i) = j\}$ is the instance set of leaf j and $q(\mathbf{x}_i)$ is a mapping function that assign every data instance $\mathbf{x}_i$ to its corresponding leaf in the tree.

By analytically solving Eq. 5.23, we get the optimal weight w_j^* of leaf j:

$$w_j^* = -\frac{\sum_{i\in I_j} g_i}{\sum_{i\in I_j} h_i + \lambda} \qquad (5.24)$$

The corresponding minimal value of the loss function is given by:

$$\tilde{\mathcal{L}}^{(t)}(q) = -\frac{1}{2}\sum_{j=1}^{T}\frac{(\sum_{i\in I_j} g_i)^2}{\sum_{i\in I_j} h_i + \lambda} + \gamma T \qquad (5.25)$$

Eq. 5.25 can be used for selecting the best split during the top-down induction of the tree. In particular each splitting candidate is evaluated according to the improvement in the objective value. More specifically, the gain is estimated as:

$$gain = \frac{1}{2}[\frac{(\sum_{i\in I_R} g_i)^2}{\sum_{i\in I_R} h_i + \lambda} + \frac{(\sum_{i\in I_L} g_i)^2}{\sum_{i\in I_L} h_i + \lambda} - \frac{(\sum_{i\in I} g_i)^2}{\sum_{i\in I} h_i + \lambda}] - \gamma \qquad (5.26)$$

where I_R and I_L are the instance sets of the right and left nodes after the split and $I = I_R \cup I_L$ represents all instances before the split.

5.8 Other Popular Gradient Boosting Tree Packages: LightGBM and CatBoost

LightGBM is another gradient boosting method recently developed by Microsoft researchers and engineers. It uses histogram-based algorithms to reduce duration and memory consumption when training the model. It also leverages network communication algorithms to optimize parallel learning [Ke *et al.* (2017); Meng *et al.* (2016)]. In particular, LightGBM consists of two new techniques: 1) exclusive feature bundling which addresses a training set with a large number of features. The idea is to look for features that never take nonzero values simultaneously and combine them into a new single feature. 2) gradient-based one-side sampling (GOSS) which aims to address a training set with a large number of instances; inspired by the idea behind the AdaBoost algorithm, in each iteration the training process focuses particularly on instances that were misclassified by preceding models. Similarly, when moving from one tree to the next, instead of using all instances, GOSS keeps all of the instances with large gradients but only a random sample of instances with small gradients.

CatBoost is an open-source gradient boosting tree library that was developed by Yandex researchers and engineers. As the name implies, this package can effectively handle categorical features. The simplest way to address categorical features is to convert them into one-hot encoding, namely having a dedicated binary variable for each category value. However, when the cardinality of the categorical feature is high, this encoding might run into various difficulties, including: large memory requirements, extensive computational costs, and difficulties that arise due to high-dimensional training data. CatBoost converts each category value to a numerical value that approximates the expected value of the target variable. For example, lets assume that we want to predict the age that an individual will get married based on various characteristics. One of the characteristics is the country in which the individual lives. This input feature is a categorical variable. Thus, instead of converting this categorical variable into a hot-vector of size 193 (the number of countries that are members of the UN), CatBoost converts each country to the corresponding expected age to get married. The expected age for a certain country is calculated based on the marriage age of the individuals that live in that country. To avoid data leakage in the estimation of the expected age, CatBoost uses a random permutation of the training set. Then, given a certain instance, it calculates the corresponding value by averaging the target variable value of the preceding instances in the permutation that share the same category value (lives in the same country in our example).

Formally, given a training set of n instances $\{(\mathbf{X}_i, Y_i)\}_{i=1\dots n}$, where each instance is represented by m features: $\mathbf{X}_i = (x_{i,1}, \dots, x_{i,m})$ and a corresponding label y_i. Let's assume that feature k is a categorical variable. Thus, given a random permutation $\sigma = (\sigma_1, \dots, \sigma_n)$, we substitute the category value of instance x_{σ_p} with the average label value of the same category in instances $X_{\sigma_1}, \dots, X_{\sigma_{p-1}}$:

$$\frac{\sum_{j=1}^{p-1} \left[x_{\sigma_j,k} = x_{\sigma_p,k} \right] y_{\sigma_j} + \alpha \cdot v}{\sum_{j=1}^{p-1} \left[x_{\sigma_j,k} = x_{\sigma_p,k} \right] + \alpha} \tag{5.27}$$

where v indicates a prior value, and $\alpha > 0$ is the weight of the prior. Adding a prior value aims to avoid overfitting in low frequency categories. In regression tasks where the output variable is numeric, the average y value in the entire dataset is used as the prior value. For binary classification tasks, the prior values represents the probability of encountering a positive class in the entire dataset.

In addition to addressing categorical variables, CatBoost also mitigates the bias problem that exists in the pointwise gradient estimates. In a regular gradient boosting tree algorithm, the gradients are estimated using the same data points that were used to train the tree. This means that the trees predictions and the gradient estimations are dependent. Moreover, the residuals estimated on the training set have absolute values that are less than those expected on unseen instances. Thus, the next tree that is trained to predict the gradient, will tend to underestimate the gradient.

Thus, CatBoost also uses the abovementioned idea of random permutation to address the bias issue. Specifically, the gradient estimate for a certain instance is based on the prediction learned using the preceding instances.

5.9 Training GBMs in R Using the XGBoost Package

In the previous section, we presented several popular and open-source implementations for gradient boosted trees. In this section, we illustrate how to use the XGBoost package in R. List 5.1 illustrates an R code for solving a regression task. The data used for this task is the U.S. Census Service data concerning housing in the area of Boston, Massachusetts. The data consists of 506 census tracts in Boston. Each tract is characterized by a set of features, such as: LSTAT: percentage values of lower status population, INDUS: the proportion of non-retail business acres per town, and CRIM: per capita crime. The goal is to predict the MEDV variable which represents the median price of a house.

In lines 9-10, we convert nominal variables to numeric variables, because XGboost works only with numeric variables. In lines 14-16, we split the data to training and test sets. In lines 19-20, we convert the data into XGBoost data objects. Instead of an R data frame, XGBoost uses its own structure called DMatrix. A DMatrix consists of both the input variables and the target variable.

In lines 23-24, we set the values of the XGBoost hyperparameters, particularly `max_depth` which limits the depth of the trees and `subsample` which defines the fraction of observations to be randomly sampled for each tree.

In line 27, we train 200 trees with early stopping of 10 trees. The idea of early stopping is to avoid overfitting by attempting to automatically select the optimal number of trees. The algorithm monitors the predictive performance after adding every new tree and stops the training once the performance on a separate test dataset has not improved in the last `early_stopping_rounds` trees.

In line 30, we use the trained model to predict the target value for the test dataset. In line 33, we calculate the importance of the variables. XGboost calculates the importance based on three metrics: 1) Gain - represents the relative contribution of each variable to the model based on the total gain of this variable's splits. 2) Cover - the number of observations in which the value of this variable was examined. 3) Frequency - the number of times a variable is used in all generated trees.

Finally, in line 36, we plot the first tree in the ensemble. Note that the `trees` parameter indicate which trees will be visualized. For example, `trees = 0:2` indicates that the first three trees in the forest will be presented.

Listing 5.1: Using XGBoost to solve a regression task

```
 1 library(xgboost)
 2 library(mlbench) # for getting the data
 3 library(DiagrammeR) # For plotting the tree
 4
 5 data(BostonHousing)
 6 df=BostonHousing
 7
 8 #convert all factors variables to numeric varaiables
 9 unfactorize<-names(df)
10 df[,unfactorize]<-lapply(unfactorize, function(x) as.numeric
      (as.character(df[,x])))
11
12
13 # split the data into to train and test
14 trainIndex<-sample(nrow(df), 2/3*nrow(df))
15 train <- df[trainIndex,]
16 test <- df[-trainIndex,]
17
18 # convert the data to the XGBoost object
19 dtrain <- xgb.DMatrix(as.matrix(train[,1:13]), label=train$
      medv)
20 dtest <- xgb.DMatrix(as.matrix(test[,1:13]), label=test$medv
      )
21
22 # setting the hyper-parameters and the list of datasets to
      use for evaluating model performance.
23 watchlist <- list(train = dtrain, eval = dtest)
24 param <- list(max_depth = 3, subsample=0.8, eta=0.3,
      objective="reg:linear")
25
26 #train the model
27 mdl <- xgb.train( param, dtrain, nrounds = 200, watchlist,
      early_stopping_rounds = 10 )
28
29 #use the model to get prediction
30 pred <- predict(mdl, dtest)
31
32 #presents the features importance
33 xgb.importance(model = mdl)
34
35 # plot only the first tree and display the node ID:
36 xgb.plot.tree(model = mdl, trees = 0, show_node_id = TRUE)
```

XGBoost has many hyperparameters which control the training process. We already used a few of them in the code above. We review the most important hyperparameters below.

- Tree Complexity Parameters: XGBoost has several hyperparameters that determine the complexity of the trees by adding constraints to the trees' structure. These parameters can help determine the right trade-off between a model's bias and variance. The parameter `max_depth` specifies the maximum number of levels in the tree. A large `max_depth` value lets us grow a complex tree which has low bias error at the cost of high variance error. The parameter `min_child_weight` specifies the minimum total weight threshold (or the number of training instances if the weights of all instances is 1) for growing a new node in the tree. A small `min_child_weight` value enables the algorithm to train a deep and complex tree which can potentially be overfitted. Another means of controlling the tree complexity is to tune the `gamma` parameter which specifies the minimum loss reduction required to make a further branching of a specific node in the tree. Setting `gamma` to a large value, will result in a small tree.

- Injecting Randomness: In an attempt to reduce the variance error and avoid overfitting, XGBoost has incorporated several components that inject randomness into the algorithm. In particular, instead of using the entire training set for growing the trees, in every iteration a subsample of training instances is randomly selected. The size of the subsample is controlled by the `subsample` which corresponds to the fraction of training instances that are used in each iteration. By default this is set to one, meaning that we use the whole training set. Another way to inject randomness is controlled by the `colsample_bytree` parameter which specifies the fraction of features that are randomly selected while training a tree. By default this is set to one, meaning that all features are being used. The `colsample_bylevel` also controls the fraction of columns used during the training, but in contrast to `colsample_bytree` which selects the features for each tree, `colsample_bylevel` selects the features for each split, at each level.

- Learning Rate: The `eta` parameter in XGBoost corresponds to the learning rate of the GBM algorithm. Recall that learning rate controls the step-size shrinkage of the feature weights and makes the learning process more conservative. Once we reduce the value of `eta`, the weight of every tree in the forest is decreased and their aggregation might be insufficient in size for correcting the initial target value. Thus, in this case, more training rounds are recommended; this can be accomplished by increasing the value of the `num_round` parameters at the cost of running time.

- Addressing Imbalance Classification Tasks: When our training dataset is extremely imbalanced (for example, when more than 95% of the training instances are labeled with the majority class) a regular decision forest may be overwhelmed by the majority class and disregard the minority class. XGBoost offers a simple mechanism to address this challenge. The idea is to increase the weights of the instances that belong to the minority class. This can be done by setting the parameter `scale_pos_weight` to the following ratio: number of negative samples divided by the number of positive samples. Note that this assumes that the positive class is the minority class. Another problem that can occur in imbalanced training sets is that the η-based learning rate update described above is not sufficient to correct extremely high weight values. Those high weight values tend to occur when the training set is imbalanced. For such cases, one can tune the `max_delta_steps` to a small positive number. This parameter introduces a regularization that caps the weight before applying the η correction.

Chapter 6

Ensemble Diversity

Ensemble methods are very effective, largely due to the fact that various types of classifiers have different "inductive biases" [Mitchell (1997)]. In order to make the ensemble more effective, there should be some sort of diversity between the classifiers [Kuncheva (2005b)]. Diversity may stem from different representations of the input data, as in bagging; variations in the learning algorithm (e.g. by using different hyperparameters settings); or by adding a penalty to the outputs to encourage diversity.

In fact, ensemble methods can make use of such diversity to reduce the variance-error [Tumer and Ghosh (1996); Ali and Pazzani (1996)] without increasing the bias-error. In certain situations, an ensemble can also reduce bias-error, as shown by the theory of large margin classifiers [Bartlett and Shawe-Taylor (1998)]. In this chapter we review the most common approaches for obtaining diversity and discuss advantages and disadvantages of each approach.

6.1 Overview

In an ensemble, the combination of the output of several classifiers is only useful if they disagree about some inputs [Tumer and Ghosh (1996)]. Creating an ensemble in which each classifier is as different as possible while still being consistent with the training set is known, theoretically, to be important for obtaining improved ensemble performance [Krogh and Vedelsby (1995)]. An ensemble of diverse classifiers lead to uncorrelated errors, which in turn improve classification accuracy [Hu (2001)].

Brown et al. [Brown et al. (2005)] indicate that for classification tasks, the concept of "diversity" remains an ill-defined concept. Nevertheless, it is believed to be closely related to the statistical concept of correlation.

Diversity is obtained when the misclassification events of the base classifiers are not correlated.

In the regression context, bias-variance-covariance decomposition has been suggested to explain why and how diversity between individual models contributes toward overall ensemble accuracy, however in the classification context, there is no complete and agreed upon theory [Brown *et al.* (2005)]. More specifically, there is no simple analogue of variance-covariance decomposition for the zero-one loss function. Instead, there are several ways to define such decomposition, each of which is based on its own assumptions.

Sharkey [Sharkey (1999)] suggests a taxonomy of methods for creating diversity in ensembles of neural networks. More specifically, Sharkey's taxonomy refers to four different aspects: the initial weights, training data used, architecture of the networks, and training algorithm used.

Brown *et al.* [Brown *et al.* (2005)] suggest a different taxonomy which consists of the following branches: varying the starting points within the hypothesis space, varying the set of hypotheses that are accessible by the ensemble members (for instance, by manipulating the training set), and varying the way each member traverses the space.

In this chapter, we extend the existing abovementioned taxonomies and suggest the following new taxonomy of methods for creating diversity in ensembles. Note, however, that the components of this taxonomy are not mutually exclusive; namely, there are a few algorithms which combine two components of the taxonomy.

(1) Manipulating the Inducer – We manipulate the way in which the base inducer is used. More specifically, each ensemble member is trained with an inducer that is manipulated differently.

(2) Manipulating the Training Sample – We vary the input that is used by the inducer for training. Each member is trained from a different training set.

(3) Changing the Target Attribute Representation – Each classifier in the ensemble solves a different target concept.

(4) Partitioning the Search Space – Each member is trained on a different search subspace.

(5) Hybridization – Diversity is obtained by using various base inducers or ensemble strategies.

6.2 Manipulating the Inducer

A simple method for increasing diversity is to manipulate the inducer used for creating the classifiers. Several strategies for obtaining such diversity are introduced in the following subsections.

6.2.1 *Manipulation of the Algorithm's Hyperparameters*

Usually, the base learning algorithm can be controlled by tuning a set of hyperparameters. For example, the well-known decision tree inducer C4.5 includes the confidence level hyperparameter which greatly affects learning and in particular this hyperparameter can be used for controlling the depth of the tree. Drucker [Drucker (2002)] examine the effect of depth of decision trees on the performance of the entire ensemble. When an algorithm (such as a decision tree algorithm) is used as a single strong learner, certain aspects (e.g. the predictive performance or model's comprehensibility) should be taken into consideration, but when the same algorithm is used as a weak learner for building and ensemble, other aspects should be taken into consideration (e.g. the level of diversity among the members).

In the neural network community, several attempts have been made to acquire diversity by using different numbers of nodes [Partridge and Yates (1996); Yates and Partridge (1996)], however this research concluded that varying the number of hidden nodes is not an effective method of creating diversity in neural network ensembles. In contrast, the CNNE algorithm [Islam *et al.* (2003)] which simultaneously determines the ensemble size, along with the number of hidden nodes in individual artificial neural networks (ANNs), has shown encouraging results.

Another effective approach for increasing diversity in ANNs involves the use of several network topologies. For instance, the Addemup algorithm [Opitz and Shavlik (1996)] uses a genetic algorithm to select the network topologies composing the ensemble. Addemup trains with standard backpropagation and then selects groups of networks based on the diversity measurement.

6.2.2 *Starting Point in Hypothesis Space*

Some inducers can gain diversity by starting the search in the hypothesis space from different points. For example, the simplest way to manipulate the backpropagation inducer is to assign different initial weights to the network [Kolen and Pollack (1991)]. Experimental studies indicate that the resulting networks differed in terms of the number of cycles it took to converge upon a solution, and whether they converged at all. While this is a very simple way to obtain diversity, it is now generally accepted that this method is insufficient for achieving good diversity [Brown *et al.* (2005)].

6.2.3   *Hypothesis Space Traversal*

Hypothesis space traversal techniques alter the way the learning algorithm traverses the space, thereby leading different classifiers to converge to different hypotheses [Brown *et al.* (2005)]. We differentiate between two types of strategies for manipulating space traversal in order to acquire diversity: random and collective performance-based strategies.

Random-based strategy

In this case, the idea is to "inject randomness" into the inducers in order to increase the independence among the ensemble's members. Ali and Pazzani [Ali and Pazzani (1996)] propose changing the rule learning HYDRA algorithm as follows. Instead of selecting the best attribute at each stage (using, for instance, an information gain measure), the attribute is selected randomly, such that its probability of being selected is proportional to its measured value. A similar idea has been implemented for C4.5 decision trees [Dietterich (2000a)]. Instead of selecting the best attribute in each stage, the algorithm randomly (with equal probability) selects an attribute from the set of the 20 best attributes.

Collective performance-based strategy

In this case, the evaluation function used in the induction of each member is extended to include a penalty term that encourages diversity. Negative correlation learning [Brown and Wyatt (2003); Rosen (1996)] is the most studied penalty method. The idea of negative correlation learning is to encourage different individual classifiers in the ensemble to represent different subspaces of the problem. While simultaneously creating the classifiers, the classifiers may interact with each other in order to specialize (for example, by using a correlation penalty term in the error function to encourage such specialization).

6.3   Manipulating the Training Samples

In this method, each classifier is trained on a different variation or subset of the original dataset. This method is useful for inducers whose variance-error factor is relatively large (such as decision trees and neural networks). That is to say, small changes in the training set may cause a major change in the classifier obtained. This category contains procedures such as bagging, boosting, and cross-validated committees.

6.3.1 *Resampling*

The distribution of tuples among the different classifiers could be random, as in the bagging algorithm or arbiter trees. Other methods distribute the tuples based on the class distribution, such that the class distribution in each subset is approximately the same as that in the entire dataset. It has been shown that proportional distribution, as used in combiner trees, [Chan and Stolfo (1995)] can achieve higher accuracy than random distribution.

Instead of performing sampling with replacement, some methods (like AdaBoost and wagging) manipulate the weights that are attached to each instance in the training set. In this case, the base inducer should be capable of taking these weights into account. Recently, a novel framework was proposed in which each instance contributes to the committee formation with a fixed weight, while contributing with different individual weights to the derivation of the constituent classifiers [Christensen *et al.* (2004)]. This approach encourages model diversity without inadvertently biasing the ensemble towards any particular instance.

The bagging using diversity (BUD) algorithm [Tang *et al.* (2006)] expands upon the bagging algorithm by considering the diversity among the base classifiers in order to achieve better results. It operates based on the assumption that the more diverse the classifiers are, the better the results achieved when the classifiers are combined. The algorithm generates a set of base classifiers from the training instances and selects a subset of the generated base classifiers by iteratively applying different diversity measures on the current ensemble and the candidate classifier that is being added to the ensemble.

Figure 6.1 presents the pseudocode of the BUD algorithm. First, a simple bagging ensemble with T base classifiers is created. The classifier with the least training error constitutes the initial output ensemble M'. Using either "disagreement," the "Kohavi-Wolpert variance," or "generalized diversity," additional $T/2 - 1$ base classifiers are added to M'. Classification of new instances is performed using distribution summation by taking the output of the base classifiers included in M' into account. Figures 6.2, 6.3, 6.4, 6.5, 6.6 present the pseudocode for calculating the diversity measures.

Bagging Using Diversity

Input: I (a base inducer), T (number of iterations), S (the original training set), and D (diversity measure).

1: **for** $t = 1$ to T **do**
2:    Create a dataset S' of size of S, created using random sampling with replacement.
3:    $M_t = I(S')$
4: **end for**
5: $M' = \arg\min_{t\in[1,T]} \sum_{x:M_t(x)\neq y} 1$
6: **for** $i = 1$ to $(\frac{T}{2} - 1)$ **do**
7:    **if** D="disagreement" OR D="kohavi wolpert variance" OR D="generalized diversity" **then**
8:        $M' = M' \bigcup \arg\max_{M_t \notin M'} \left[div\left(S, D, M' \cup M_t\right)\right]$
9:    **else**
10:       $M' = M' \bigcup \arg\min_{M_t \notin M'} \left[div\left(S, D, M' \cup M_t\right)\right]$
11:   **end if**
12: **end for**

Fig. 6.1: Bagging using diversity.

Calculating the Disagreement Measure

Input: S (the original training set), M' (examined set of classifiers)

1: $sum=0$
2: **for** each unique pair of base classifiers $\{a,b\} \subseteq M'|a \neq b$ **do**
3:    $sum=sum +$ number of instances where classifiers a and b disagree
4: **end for**
5: return $\frac{2sum}{|S|\times|M'|\times(|M'|-1)}$

Fig. 6.2: Calculating the disagreement measure.

6.3.2   *Creation*

The DECORATE algorithm [Melville and Mooney (2003)] is a dependent approach in which the ensemble is generated iteratively, learning a   clas-

Calculating the Double Fault Measure

Input: S (the original training set), M' (examined set of classifiers)

1: $sum=0$

2: **for** each unique pair of base classifiers $\{a,b\} \subseteq M'|a \neq b$ **do**

3:    $sum=sum$ + number of instances that were misclassified by both a and b.

4: **end for**

5: return $\frac{2sum}{|S|\times|M'|\times(|M'|-1)}$

Fig. 6.3: Calculating the double fault measure.

Calculating the Kohavi-Wolpert Variance

Input: S (the original training set), M' (set of classifiers examined)

1: $sum=0$

2: **for** each $\langle x_i, y_i \rangle \in S$ **do**

3:    l_i = number of classifiers misclassified x_i

4:    $sum = sum + l_i \times (|M'| - l_i)$

5: **end for**

6: return $\frac{sum}{|S|\times|M'|^2}$

Fig. 6.4: Calculating the Kohavi-Wolpert variance.

Calculating the Inter-Rater Measure

Input: S (the original training set), M' (examined set of classifiers)

1: $sum=0$

2: **for** each $\langle x_i, y_i \rangle \in S$ **do**

3:    l_i = number of misclassified classifiers x_i

4:    $sum = sum + l_i \times (|M'| - l_i)$

5: **end for**

6: $P = 1 - \frac{\sum l_i}{|S|\times|M'|}$

7: return $1 - \frac{sum}{|S|\times|M'|\times(|M'|-1)\times P\times(1-P)}$

Fig. 6.5: Calculating the inter-rater measure.

sifier in each iteration and adding it to the current ensemble. The first member is created by using the base induction algorithm on the original training set. The successive classifiers are trained on a dataset that consists of tuples from the original training set and artificial tuples that were

Calculating Generalized Diversity

Input: S (the original training set), M' (examined set of classifiers)
1: **for** each $\langle x_i, y_i \rangle \in S$ **do**
2:    l_i = number of misclassified classifiers x_i
3:    $V_i = \frac{|M'| - l_i}{|M'|}$
4: **end for**
5: return variance of V_i

Fig. 6.6: Calculating generalized diversity

synthesized by the algorithm. In each iteration, the input attribute values of the fabricated tuples are generated according to the original data distribution. On the other hand, the target values of these tuples are selected so as to differ maximally from the current ensemble predictions. Comprehensive experiments have demonstrated that this technique is consistently more accurate than the base classifier, bagging, and random forest. DEC-ORATE also achieves higher accuracy than boosting on small training sets and performs comparably on larger training sets.

6.3.3   *Partitioning*

Some argue that classic ensemble techniques (such as boosting and bagging) have limitations on massive datasets, because the size of the dataset become a bottleneck [Chawla *et al.* (2004)]. However, it has been suggested that partitioning the datasets into random, disjoint partitions will not only overcome the issue of exceeding the memory size but will also lead to the creation of an ensemble of diverse and accurate classifiers, each built from a disjoint partition. This can improve performance in a way that might not be possible by subsampling. More recently a framework for building thousands of classifiers that are trained on small subsets of data in a distributed environment was proposed in order to handle vast amounts of data [Chawla *et al.* (2004)]. The robust learning from bites (RLB) algorithm that was proposed by Christmann *et al.* [Christmann *et al.* (2007)] is also designed to work with large datasets.

Clustering techniques can be used to partition the original training set in order to make vast amounts of data more manageable. Recall that the goal of clustering is to group the data instances into subsets in such a way that similar instances are grouped together, while different instances belong to different groups. The instances are thereby organized into an efficient representation that characterizes the population being sampled. Formally, the clustering structure is represented as a set of subsets $C = C_1, \ldots, C_k$ of S, such that: $S = \bigcup_{i=1}^{k} C_i$ and $C_i \cap C_j = \emptyset$ for $i \neq j$. Consequently, any instance in S belongs to exactly one and only one subset.

Recall that the simplest and most commonly used algorithm employing a squared error criterion is the k-means algorithm. This algorithm partitions the data into k clusters $(C_1, C_2, \ldots, C_k)$ represented by their centers or means. The center of each cluster is calculated as the mean of all of the instances belonging to that cluster. The CBCD (cluster-based concurrent decomposition) algorithm [Rokach *et al.* (2005)] clusters the instance space by using the k-means clustering algorithm. Then, it creates disjoint sub-samples using the clusters in such a way that each subsample is comprised of tuples from all clusters and hence represents the entire dataset. An inducer is applied, in turn, to each subsample, and a voting mechanism is used to combine the classifiers' classifications. An experimental study performed shows that the CBCD algorithm outperforms the bagging algorithm.

Ahn *et al.* [Ahn *et al.* (2007)] indicate that randomly partitioning the input attribute set into several subsets, such that each classifier is induced from a different subset, is particularly useful for training an ensemble for high-dimensional datasets. Their experiments indicate that for unbalanced data, this partition approach maintains the balance between sensitivity and specificity better than many other classification methods.

Denison *et al.* [Denison *et al.* (2002)] examine two schemas for partitioning the instance space into disjoint subspaces: the Bayesian partition model (BPM) schema and the product partition model (PPM) schema. The BPM schema has been shown to be unsuitable when the training set is large or there are many input attributes. The PPM schema provides good results in several cases, especially in datasets where there are many irrelevant input attributes, however it is less suitable for situations in which there are strong interactions among input attributes.

6.4 Manipulating the Target Attribute Representation

In methods that manipulate the target attribute, instead of inducing a single complicated classifier, an ensemble of several classifiers with different, and usually simpler, representations of the target attribute are induced. This manipulation can be based on an aggregation of the original target's values (known as *concept aggregation*) or more complicated functions (known as *function decomposition*).

Basic concept aggregation replaces the original target attribute with a function, such that the domain of the new target attribute is smaller than the original one [Buntine (1996)].

The idea of converting k class classification problems into k two class classification problems was proposed by [Anand *et al.* (1995)]. Each problem considers the differentiation of one class to the other classes. Lu and Ito [Lu and Ito (1999)] extend Anand's method and propose a new method for manipulating the data based on the relations among the classes. By using this method, they divide a k class classification problem into a series of $k(k-1)/2$ two-class problems where each problem considers the differentiation of one class to each of the other classes. The researchers used neural networks to examine this idea.

A general concept aggregation algorithm called *Error-Correcting Output Coding* (ECOC) uses a code matrix to decompose a multiclass problem into multiple binary problems [Dietterich and Bakiri (1995)]. ECOC for multiclass classification hinges on the design of the code matrix. Please refer to Section 8.2 for additional details.

A general-purpose function decomposition approach for machine learning was proposed in [Zupan *et al.* (1998)]. According to this approach, attributes are transformed into new concepts in an iterative manner in order to create a hierarchy of concepts.

6.4.1   *Label Switching*

Breiman (2000) suggests generating an ensemble by using perturbed versions of the training set where the classes of the training examples are randomly changed to a different class label.

The classifiers generated by this procedure have statistically uncorrelated errors in the training set. The basic idea of this method is to choose a different set of examples for each run so that their class labels will be randomly changed to a different class label.

In contrast to Breiman (2000), Martinez-Munoz and Suarez (2005) suggest that the probability of switching class labels is kept constant (i.e., independent of the original label and class distribution) for every training instance. This idea makes it possible to use larger switching rate values in unbalanced datasets. Martinez-Munoz and Suarez (2005) also show that high accuracy can be achieved with ensembles generated by class switching, provided that fairly large ensembles are generated (around 1000 classifiers).

However, such large ensembles may slow down the entire learning process.

Figure 6.7 presents the pseudocode of label switching. In each iteration, the class value of some instances are randomly switched; in this case, an instance is chosen with a probability of p, where p is an input parameter. If an instance has been chosen to have its class changed, the new class is selected randomly from all of the other classes with equal probability.

Label Switching

Input: I (a base inducer), T (number of iterations), S (the original training set), and p (the rate of label switching).

1: **for** $t = 1$ to T **do**
2:   $S' =$ a copy of S
3:   **for** each $< x_i, y_i >$ in S' **do**
4:     $R = $ A new random number
5:     **if** $R < P$ **then**
6:       Randomly pick a new class label y' form $dom(y)$ that is different from the original class of x_i, i.e. $y' \neq y_i$
7:       Change the class label of x to be y'
8:     **end if**
9:   **end for**
10:   $M_t = I(S')$
11: **end for**

Fig. 6.7: Label switching algorithm.

6.5 Partitioning the Search Space

In this case, the idea is that each member in the ensemble explores a different part of the search space. Thus, the original instance space is divided into several subspaces. Each subspace is considered independently, and the total model is a (possibly soft) combination of such simpler models.

When using this approach, one should decide at what level the input subspaces will overlap. At one extreme, the original space is decomposed into several *mutually exclusive* subspaces, and each subspace is solved using a dedicated classifier; in such cases, the classifiers may have significant variations in their overall performance in different parts of the input space [Tumer and Ghosh (2000)]. At the other extreme, each classifier solves the same original task. In such cases, "If the individual classifiers are then appropriately chosen and trained properly, their performance will be (relatively) comparable in any region of the problem space. [Tumer and Ghosh (2000)]". Between these two extremes, one can decide that subspaces may have soft boundaries (i.e., subspaces are allowed to overlap).

There are two popular approaches for search space manipulation: divide and conquer approaches and feature subset-based ensemble methods.

6.5.1   *Divide and Conquer*

In the neural network community, Nowlan and Hinton [Nowlan and Hinton (1991)] examined the mixture of experts (ME) approach, which partitions the instance space into several subspaces and assigns different experts (classifiers) to the different subspaces. In ME, the subspaces have soft boundaries. A gating network then combines the experts' outputs and produces a composite decision. An extension of the basic mixture of experts approach, known as hierarchical mixtures of experts (HME),was proposed in [Jordan and Jacobs (1994)]. This extension decomposes the space into subspaces, and then recursively decomposes each subspace into additional subspaces.

Some researchers have used clustering techniques with the aim of partitioning the space [Rokach *et al.* (2003)]. The basic idea is to partition the instance space into mutually exclusive subsets using the k-means clustering algorithm. An analysis of the results shows that the proposed method is well-suited for datasets of numeric input attributes and that its performance is influenced by the dataset size and homogeneity.

NBTree [Kohavi (1996)] is an instance space decomposition method that induces a decision tree and a naïve Bayes hybrid classifier. To induce an NBTree, the instance space is recursively partitioned according to attributes values, resulting in a decision tree whose terminal nodes are naïve Bayes classifiers. Since subjecting a terminal node to a naïve Bayes classifier means that the hybrid classifier may classify two instances from a single hyperrectangle region into distinct classes, the NBTree is more flexible than a pure decision tree. More recently Cohen *et al.* (2007) generalized the NBTree approach and examined a decision -tree framework for space decomposition. According to this framework, the original instance space is hierarchically partitioned into multiple subspaces, and a distinct classifier (such as a neural network) is assigned to each subspace. Subsequently, an unlabeled, previously unseen instance is classified by employing the classifier that was assigned to the subspace to which the instance belongs.

The divide and conquer approach also includes many other methods such as local linear regression, CART/MARS, adaptive subspace models, etc. [Johansen and Foss (1992); Ramamurti and Ghosh (1999)].

6.5.2   *Feature Subset-based Ensemble Methods*

A less common strategy for manipulating the search space is to manipulate the input attribute set. Feature subset-based ensemble methods are those that manipulate the input feature set in order to create the ensemble members. The idea is simply to give each classifier a different projection of the training set. Tumer and Oza. [Tumer and Oza (2003)] claim that feature subset-based ensembles potentially facilitate the creation of a classifier for high-dimensional datasets without the feature selection drawbacks mentioned above. Moreover, these methods can be used to improve the classification performance due to the reduced correlation among the classifiers. Bryll *et al.* [Bryll *et al.* (2003)] also indicate that the reduced size of the dataset implies faster classifier induction. Feature subset-based ensemble methods avoid class underrepresentation which may occur in instance subset methods such as bagging. There are three popular strategies for creating feature subset-based ensembles: random-based, reduct-based and collective performance-based strategy.

6.5.2.1   *Random-based Strategy*

The most straightforward techniques for creating feature subset-based ensembles are based on random selection. Ho [Ho (1998)] used random subspaces to create a forest of decision trees. The ensemble is constructed systematically by pseudorandomly selecting subsets of features. The training instances are projected to each subset, and a decision tree is constructed using the projected training samples. This process is repeated several times to create the forest. The classifications of the individual trees are combined by averaging the conditional probability of each class at the leaves (distribution summation). Ho showed that simple random selection of feature subsets may be an effective technique, because the diversity of the ensemble members compensates for their lack of accuracy. Furthermore, random subspace methods are effective when the number of training instances is comparable to the number of features.

Bay [Bay (1999)] proposed Multiple Features Subsets (MFS) which uses simple voting in order to combine outputs from multiple kNN (k-nearest neighbors) classifiers, each having access to only a random subset of the original features. Each classifier employs the same number of features. This process is similar to that of random subspaces methods.

Bryll *et al.* [Bryll *et al.* (2003)] introduced attribute bagging (AB) which combines random subsets of features. AB first finds an appropriate subset size by randomly searching the feature subset space. It then randomly selects subsets of features, creating projections of the training set on which the classifiers are trained. A technique for building ensembles of simple Bayesian classifiers in random feature subsets was also examined [Tsymbal and Puuronen (2002)] for improving medical applications.

6.5.2.2 *Reduct-based Strategy*

A reduct is defined as the smallest feature subset that has the same predictive power as the entire feature set. By definition, the size of the ensembles created using reducts are limited to the number of features. There have been several attempts to create classifier ensembles by combining several reducts. Wu *et al.* [Wu *et al.* (2005)] introduced the worst-attribute-drop-first algorithm to find a set of significant reducts and combine them using naïve Bayes. Bao and Ishii [Bao and Ishii (2002)] examined the idea of combining multiple K-nearest neighbors classifiers for text classification by reducts. Hu *et al.* [Hu *et al.* (2005)] proposed several techniques to construct decision forests, in which every tree is built on a different reduct. The classifications of the various trees are combined using a voting mechanism.

6.5.2.3 *Collective Performance-based Strategy*

Cunningham and Carney [Cunningham and Carney (2000)] introduced an ensemble feature selection strategy that randomly constructs the initial ensemble. Then, an iterative refinement is performed based on a hill climbing search in order to improve the accuracy and diversity of the base classifiers. For all of the feature subsets, an attempt is made to switch (include or delete) each feature. If the resulting feature subset results in better performance on the validation set, the change is kept. This process is continued until there is no further improvement. Similarly, Zenobi and Cunningham [Zenobi and Cunningham (2001)] suggested that the search for various feature subsets should be guided by the disagreement among the ensemble members as well as the their predictive performance.

Tumer and Oza [Tumer and Oza (2003)] presented a new method called input decimation (ID), which selects feature subsets based on the correlations between individual features and class labels. This experimental study showed that ID can outperform simple random selection of feature subsets.

Tsymbal *et al.* [Tsymbal *et al.* (2004)] compared several feature selection methods that incorporate diversity as a component of the fitness function in the search for the best collection of feature subsets. This study shows that there are some datasets in which the ensemble feature selection method can be sensitive to the choice of the diversity measure. Moreover, their research showed that no particular measure is superior in all cases.

Gunter and Bunke [Gunter and Bunke (2004)] suggested employing a feature subset search algorithm in order to identify different subsets of the given features. The feature subset search algorithm not only takes the performance of the ensemble into account, but also directly supports diversity of subsets of features.

Combining genetic search with ensemble feature selection has also been examined in the literature. Opitz and Shavlik [Opitz and Shavlik (1996)] applied genetic algorithm (GA) to ensembles using genetic operators that were designed explicitly for hidden nodes in knowledge-based neural networks. In a later study, Opitz [Opitz (1999)] used genetic search for ensemble feature selection. Their genetic ensemble feature selection (GEFS) strategy begins by creating an initial population of classifiers where each classifier is generated by randomly selecting a different subset of features. Then, new candidate classifiers are continually produced by using the genetic operators of crossover and mutation on the feature subsets. The final ensemble is composed of the most accurate classifiers. Similarly, the genetic algorithm that Hu *et al.* [Hu *et al.* (2005)] used for selecting the reducts to be included in the final ensemble, creates N reducts and trains N decision trees using the reducts; a GA is then used for selecting which of the N decision trees are included in the final forest.

6.5.2.4 *Feature Set Partitioning*

Partitioning means dividing the original training set into smaller training sets. A different classifier is trained on each subsample. After all of the classifiers are constructed, the models are combined in some fashion [Maimon and Rokach (2005)]. There are two obvious ways to partition the original dataset: horizontal partitioning and vertical partitioning. In horizontal partitioning, the original dataset is partitioned into several datasets that have the same features as the original dataset, each containing a subset of the instances in the original. In vertical partitioning, the original dataset is partitioned into several datasets that have the same number of instances as the original dataset, each containing a subset of the original set of features.

In order to illustrate the idea of partitioning, recall the training set in Table 1.1 which contains a segment of the Iris dataset. This is one of the best known datasets in the pattern recognition literature. In this case, we are interested to classify flowers by Iris subgeni according to their characteristic features. The dataset contains three classes that correspond to three types of iris flowers: $dom\,(y) = \{IrisSetosa, IrisVersicolor, IrisVirginica\}$. Each pattern is characterized by four numeric features (measured in centimeters): $A = \{sepallength, sepalwidth, petallength, petalwidth\}$. Tables 6.1 and 6.2 respectively illustrate mutually exclusive horizontal and vertical partitions of the Iris dataset. Note that despite the mutual exclusivity, the class attribute must be included in each vertical partition.

Table 6.1: Horizontal partitioning of the Iris dataset.

Sepal Length	Sepal Width	Petal Length	Petal Width	Class (Iris Type)
5.1	3.5	1.4	0.2	Iris-setosa
4.9	3.0	1.4	0.2	Iris-setosa
6.0	2.7	5.1	1.6	Iris-versicolor

Sepal Length	Sepal Width	Petal Length	Petal Width	Class (Iris Type)
5.8	2.7	5.1	1.9	Iris-virginica
5.0	3.3	1.4	0.2	Iris-setosa
5.7	2.8	4.5	1.3	Iris-versicolor
5.1	3.8	1.6	0.2	Iris-setosa

Vertical partitioning (also known as feature set partitioning) is a particular case of feature subset-based ensembles in which the subsets are pairwise disjoint subsets. Feature set partitioning generalizes the task of feature selection which aims to provide a single representative set of features from which a classifier is constructed. Feature set partitioning, on the other hand, decomposes the original set of features into several subsets and builds a classifier for each subset. Thus, a set of classifiers is trained such that each classifier employs a different subset of the original feature set. An unlabeled instance is classified by combining the classifications of all classifiers.

Several researchers have shown that the partitioning methodology can be useful for classification tasks with a large number of features [Rokach (2006); Kusiak (2000)] due to the fact that the search space of feature set partitioning contains the search space of feature selection.

In the literature there are several works that deal with feature set par-

Table 6.2: Vertical partitioning of the Iris dataset.

Petal Length	Petal Width	Class (Iris Type)
1.4	0.2	Iris-setosa
1.4	0.2	Iris-setosa
5.1	1.6	Iris-versicolor
5.1	1.9	Iris-virginica
1.4	0.2	Iris-setosa
4.5	1.3	Iris-versicolor
1.6	0.2	Iris-setosa

Sepal Length	Sepal Width	Class (Iris Type)
5.1	3.5	Iris-setosa
4.9	3.0	Iris-setosa
6.0	2.7	Iris-versicolor
5.8	2.7	Iris-virginica
5.0	3.3	Iris-setosa
5.7	2.8	Iris-versicolor
5.1	3.8	Iris-setosa

titioning. In one study, the features are grouped according to the feature type: nominal value features, numeric value features, and text value features [Kusiak (2000)]. A similar approach was also used for developing the linear Bayes classifier [Gama (2000)]. The basic idea consists of aggregating the features into two subsets: the first subset contains only the nominal features and the second contains just the continuous features.

In another study, the feature set was decomposed according to the target class [Tumer and Ghosh (1996)]. For each class, the features with low correlation to that class were removed. This method was applied on a feature set of 25 sonar signals where the aim was to identify the meaning of the sound (whale, cracking ice, etc.).

The feature set decomposition can be obtained by grouping features based on pairwise mutual information, with statistically similar features assigned to the same group [Liao and Moody (2000)]. For this purpose one can use an existing hierarchical clustering algorithm to cluster the features into groups. Then a feature subset can be formed by selecting without replacement one representative feature from each group. This process can be repeated several times in order to obtain several features subsets. A neural network is then trained using the features of each subset, and all of the networks are combined.

In statistics literature, the most well-known feature oriented ensemble algorithm is the multivariate adaptive regression splines (MARS) algorithm [Friedman (1991)], in which a multiple regression function is approximated using linear splines and their tensor products. It has been shown that the algorithm performs an ANOVA decomposition, namely, the regression function is represented as a grand total of several sums. The first sum is the total value of all basic functions that involve only a single attribute. The second sum is the total value of all basic functions that involve exactly two attributes, representing (if present) two-variable interactions. Similarly, the third sum represents (if present) the contributions from three-variable interactions, and so on. In a recent study, several methods for combining different feature selection results have been proposed [Chizi *et al.* (2002)]. The experimental results of this study indicate that combining different feature selection methods can significantly improve the accuracy results.

The EROS (Ensemble Rough Subspaces) algorithm is a rough set-based attribute reduction algorithm [Hu *et al.* (2007)] which uses an accuracy-guided forward search strategy to sequentially induce base classifiers. Each base classifier is trained on a different reduct of the original dataset. Then a postpruning strategy is employed to filter out non-useful base classifiers. Experimental results show that EROS outperforms bagging and random subspace methods in terms of the accuracy and size of ensemble systems [Hu *et al.* (2007)].

A general framework that searches for helpful feature set partitioning structures has also been proposed [Rokach and Maimon (2005b)]. This framework nests many algorithms, two of which are tested empirically over a set of benchmark datasets. This work indicates that feature set decomposition can increase the accuracy of decision trees. More recently, a genetic algorithm was successfully applied for feature set partitioning [Rokach (2008a)]. This GA uses a new encoding schema and a Vapnik-Chervonenkis dimension bound to evaluate the fitness function. The algorithm also suggest a new caching mechanism to accelerate execution and avoid recreating the same classifiers.

6.5.2.5   *Rotation Forest*

Rotation forest is an ensemble generation method aimed at building accurate and diverse classifiers [Rodriguez (2006)] by applying feature extraction to subsets of features. Rotation forest ensembles tend to generate base classifiers which are more accurate than those created by AdaBoost and random forest, and more diverse than those created by bagging. Decision trees were chosen as the base classifiers for forming the rotation forest because of their ability to be sensitive to rotation of the feature axes while maintaining accuracy. The feature extraction in rotation forest is based on principal component analysis (PCA) which is a valuable diversifying heuristic.

Figure 6.8 presents the rotation forest pseudocode. For each of the T base classifiers to be built, we divide the feature set into K disjoint subsets $F_{i,j}$ of equal size M. For every subset, we randomly select a nonempty subset of classes and draw a bootstrap sample which includes three-quarters of the original sample. Then we apply PCA using only the features in $F_{i,j}$ and the selected subset of classes. The coefficients of the principal components, $a_{i,1}^1, a_{i,1}^2, \ldots$, are employed to create the sparse "rotation" matrix R_i. Finally, we use SR_i for training the base classifier M_i. In order to classify an instance, we calculate the average confidence for each class across all classifiers and assign the instance to the class with the largest confidence.

Zhang and Zhang (2008) present the RotBoost algorithm which blends the rotation forest and AdaBoost approaches. RotBoost achieves even lower prediction error than either of the two algorithms when implemented on their own. RotBoost is presented in Figure 6.9. In each iteration a new rotation matrix is generated and used to create a dataset. The AdaBoost ensemble is induced from this dataset.

6.6 Multiinducers

In the multiinducer strategy for building an ensemble, diversity is obtained by using different types of inducers [Michalski and Tecuci (1994)]. Each inducer contains an explicit or implicit bias that leads it to prefer certain generalizations over others. Ideally, this multiinducer ensemble would always perform as well as the best of its ingredients. Even more ambitiously, there is hope that this combination of paradigms might produce synergistic effects, leading to levels of accuracy that neither atomic approach would be able to achieve on its own.

Most research in this area has been concerned with combining empirical approaches with analytical methods (see, for instance, [Towell and Shavlik (1994)]. Woods *et al.* [Woods *et al.* (1997)] combined four types of base inducers (decision trees, neural networks, k-nearest neighbors, and quadratic Bayes) and estimated local accuracy in the feature space to choose the appropriate classifier for a given new unlabeled instance. Wang *et al.* [Wang *et al.* (2004)] examined the usefulness of adding decision trees to

Rotation Forest

Input: I (a base inducer), S (the original training set), T (number of iterations), and K (number of subsets),

1: **for** $i = 1$ to T **do**

2:   Split the feature set into K subsets: $F_{i,j}$ (for j=1..K)

3:   **for** $j = 1$ to K **do**

4:     Let $S_{i,j}$ be the data set S for the for the features in $F_{i,j}$

5:     Eliminate from $S_{i,j}$ a random subset of classes

6:     Select a bootstrap sample from $S_{i,j}$ of size 75% of the number of objects in $S_{i,j}$. Denote the new set by $S'_{i,j}$

7:     Apply PCA on $S'_{i,j}$ to obtain the coefficients in a matrix $C_{i,j}$

8:   **end for**

9:   Arrange the $C_{i,j}$, for j = 1 to K in a rotation matrix R_i as in the equation:

$$
R_i = \begin{bmatrix}
a_{i,1}^{(1)}, a_{i,1}^{(2)}, \ldots, a_{i,1}^{(M_1)} & [0] & \cdots & [0] \\
[0] & a_{i,2}^{(1)}, a_{i,2}^{(2)}, \ldots, a_{i,2}^{(M_2)} & \cdots & [0] \\
\cdots & \cdots & \cdots & \cdots \\
[0] & [0] & \cdots & a_{i,k}^{(1)}, a_{i,k}^{(2)}, \ldots, a_{i,k}^{(Mk)}
\end{bmatrix}
$$

10:   Construct R_i^a by rearranging the columns of R_i so as to match the order of features in F

11: **end for**

12: Build classifier M_i using (SR_i^a, X) as the training set

Fig. 6.8: The rotation forest.

an ensemble of neural networks. The researchers concluded that adding a few decision trees (but not too many) usually improved the performance. Langdon *et al.* [Langdon *et al.* (2002)] proposed using genetic programming to find an appropriate rule for combining decision trees with neural networks.

Another multiinducer approach was proposed by Brodley [Brodley (1995b)]. The model class selection (MCS) system fits different classifiers to different subspaces of the instance space by employing one of three classification methods (a decision tree, discriminant function, or instance-based method). In order to select the classification method, MCS uses the characteristics of the underlying training set, and a collection of expert rules. Brodley's expert rules are based on empirical comparisons of the methods'

RotBoost

Input: I (a base inducer), S (the original training set), K (number of attribute subsets), T_1 (number of iterations for rotation aorest), and T_2 (number of iterations for AdaBoost).

1: **for** $s = 1, \cdots T_2$ **do**

2:     Use the steps similar in rotation forest to compute the rotation matrix, R_s^a and let $S^a = [X R_s^a Y]$ be the training set for classifier C_s.

3:     Initialize the weight distribution over S^a as $D_1(i) = 1/N(i = 1, 2, \cdots N)$.

4:     **for** $t = 1, \cdots T_2$ **do**

5:         According to the distribution D_t, perform N extractions randomly f or S^a with replacement to compose a new set S_t^a.

6:         Apply I to S_t^a to train a classifier C_t^a and then compute the error of C_t^a as $\epsilon_t = \Pr_{i \sim D_t}(C_t^a(\mathbf{x}_i) \neq y_i) = \sum_{i=1}^N Ind(C_t^a(\mathbf{x}_i) \neq y_i)D_t(i)$.

7:         **if** $\xi i_t > 0.5$ **then**

8:             set $D_t(i) = 1/N(i = 1, 2, \cdots N)$ and continue with the next loop iteration

9:         **end if**

10:        **if** $\epsilon_t = 0\rangle$ **then**

11:           set $\epsilon_t = 10^{-10}$

12:        **end if**

13:        Choose $\alpha_t = \dfrac{1}{2} \ln(\dfrac{1 - \epsilon_t}{\epsilon_t})$

14:        Update the distribution D_t over S^a as $D_{t+1}(i) = \dfrac{D_t(i)}{Z_t} \times$ $\begin{cases} e^{-\alpha_t}, \text{if} C_t^a(\mathbf{x}_i) = y_i \\ e^{\alpha_t})\text{if} C_t^a(\mathbf{x}_i) \neq y_i \end{cases}$ where Z_t is a normalization factor such that D_{t+1} is a probability distribution over S^a.

15:     **end for**

16: **end for**

Fig. 6.9: The RotBoost algorithm.

performance (i.e., on prior knowledge).

    The NeC4.5 algorithm, which integrates decision trees with neural networks [Zhou and Jiang (2004)], trains a neural network ensemble. Then the trained ensemble is used to generate a new training set by replacing the desired class labels of the original training examples with the output from the trained ensemble. Some extra training examples are also generated from the trained ensemble and added to the new training set. Finally, a C4.5 decision tree is grown from the new training set. Since its learning results are decision trees, the comprehensibility of NeC4.5 is better than that of neural network ensembles.

Using several inducers can solve the dilemma that arises from the "no-free-lunch" theorem. This theorem implies that a certain inducer will be successful only insofar as its bias matches the characteristics of the application domain [Brazdil *et al.* (1994)]. Thus, given a certain application, the practitioner needs to decide which inducer should be used. Using the multiinducer eliminates the need to try each one and simplifies the entire process.

6.7   Measuring the Diversity

As stated earlier in the chapter, it is usually assumed that increasing diversity may decrease ensemble error [Zenobi and Cunningham (2001)]. For regression tasks, *variance* is usually used to measure diversity [Krogh and Vedelsby (1995)]. With regression tasks, it can easily be shown that the ensemble error can be reduced by increasing ensemble diversity while maintaining the average error of a single model.

In classification tasks, a more complicated measure is required to evaluate the diversity. There have been several attempts to define a diversity measure for classification tasks.

In the neural network literature two measures are presented for examining diversity:

- Classification coverage: An instance is covered by a classifier if the classifier yields a correct classification.
- Coincident errors: A coincident error among the classifiers occurs when more than one member misclassifies a given instance.

Based on these two measures, Sharkey [Sharkey and Sharkey (1997)] defined four diversity levels:

- Level 1 - There are no coincident errors, and the classification function is completely covered by a majority vote of the members.
- Level 2 - Coincident errors may occur, but the classification function is completely covered by a majority vote.
- Level 3 - A majority vote will not always correctly classify a given instance, but at least one ensemble member always classifies the instance correctly.

- Level 4 - The function is not always covered by the members of the ensemble.

Brown *et al.* [Brown *et al.* (2005)] claim that the above four-level scheme provides no indication of how typical the error behavior described by the assigned diversity level is. This claim holds particularly well when the ensemble exhibits different diversity levels on different subsets of instance space.

There are other more quantitative measures which categorize these measures into two types [Brown *et al.* (2005)]: pairwise and non-pairwise. Pairwise measures calculate the average of a particular distance metric, such as the Q-statistic [Brown *et al.* (2005)] or kappa statistic [Margineantu and Dietterich (1997)], between all possible pairings of members in the ensemble. The non-pairwise measures either use the idea of entropy (such as [Cunningham and Carney (2000)]) or calculate a correlation of each ensemble member with the averaged output. The comparison of several measures of diversity has resulted in the conclusion that most of the diversity measures are correlated [Kuncheva and Whitaker (2003)].

In this section, we mainly discuss pairwise diversity measures due to their popularity in practice. For an ensemble of n classifiers, the total pairwise diversity measure is calculated as the mean pairwise measure over all $n \cdot (n-1)/2$ pairs of classifiers: $F_{Total} = \frac{2}{n(n-1)} \sum_{\forall i \neq j} f_{i,j}$, where $f_{i,j}$ is a similarity or diversity measure of two classifiers' outputs i and j. Kuncheva and Whitaker (2003) find the following two diversity pairwise measures useful:

(1) The disagreement measure is defined as the ratio between the number of disagreements and the total number of instances: $Dis_{i,j} = \frac{m_{\bar{i}j} + m_{i\bar{j}}}{m_{ij} + m_{\bar{i}j} + m_{i\bar{j}} + m_{\bar{i}\bar{j}}}$ where m_{ij} specifies the number of instances in which both classifier i and classifier j are correct, while $m_{\bar{i}\bar{j}}$ indicates the number of instances that are misclassified by both classifiers. Similarly, $m_{i\bar{j}}$ and $m_{\bar{i}j}$ indicate the number of instances in which one classifier has correctly classified the instances but its counterpart has misclassified these instances.

(2) The double fault measure is defined as the proportion of cases that have been misclassified by both classifiers: $DF_{i,j} = \frac{m_{\bar{i}\bar{j}}}{m_{\bar{i}j} + m_{i\bar{j}} + m_{ij} + m_{\bar{i}\bar{j}}}$.

Instead of measuring the diversity, we can complementarily use the following pairwise similarity measures:

(1) The Q statistic varies between -1 and 1 and is defined as: $Q_{i,j} = \left(m_{ij} \cdot m_{\bar{i}\bar{j}} - m_{i\bar{j}} \cdot m_{\bar{i}j}\right) / \left(m_{ij} \cdot m_{\bar{i}\bar{j}} + m_{i\bar{j}} \cdot m_{\bar{i}j}\right)$. Positive values indicate that the two classifiers are correlated (namely, they tend to correctly classify the same instances). A value close to 0 indicates that the classifiers are independent.

(2) The correlation coefficient. The ρ measure is very similar to the Q measure. It has the same numerator as the Q measure. Moreover, it always has the same sign (both positive, or both negative), but the value magnitude is never greater than the corresponding Q value: $\rho_{i,j} = \dfrac{\left(m_{ij} \cdot m_{\bar{i}\bar{j}} - m_{i\bar{j}} \cdot m_{\bar{i}j}\right)}{\sqrt{\left(m_{ij} + m_{i\bar{j}}\right) \cdot \left(m_{ij} + m_{\bar{i}j}\right) \cdot \left(m_{\bar{i}\bar{j}} + m_{i\bar{j}}\right) \cdot \left(m_{\bar{i}\bar{j}} + m_{\bar{i}j}\right)}}$.

Kuncheva and Whitaker (2003) showed that these measures are strongly correlated. That said, on specific real classification tasks, the measures might behave differently, so they can be used as a complementary set. Nevertheless, Kuncheva and Whitaker (2003) were unable to identify a definitive connection between the measures and the improvement of the accuracy. Thus, they concluded that it is unclear whether diversity measures have any practical value in building classifier ensembles.

Tang *et al.* (2006) explained the relation between diversity measures and the concept of margin which is explicitly related to the success of ensemble learning algorithms. They presented the uniformity condition for maximizing both the diversity and the minimum margin of an ensemble and demonstrated theoretically and experimentally the ineffectiveness of the diversity measures for constructing ensembles with good generalization performance. Tang *et al.* (2006) mentioned three reasons for that:

(1) The change in the diversity measures does not afford consistent guidance on whether a set of base classifiers results in low generalization error.

(2) The existing diversity measures are correlated to the mean accuracy of the base classifiers. Thus, they do not provide any additional information for the accuracy measure.

(3) Most of the diversity measures have no regularization term. Thus, even if their values are maximized, the ensemble may be overfit.

Chapter 7

Ensemble Selection

7.1 Ensemble Selection

Determining the number of base classifiers to use is important when using ensemble methods.

Ensemble selection, also known as ensemble pruning or shrinkage, aims at reducing the size of the ensemble. There are three main reasons for thinning an ensemble: a) decreasing computational overhead (smaller ensembles require less computational overhead in terms of model's storage requirements and prolonged prediction time), b) reduced compressibility by the user, and c) improving accuracy (some members in the ensemble can reduce the predictive performance of the whole, and pruning these members can increase the accuracy). However, in some cases, shrinkage can actually cause the ensemble to overfit in a situation where the original ensemble would not have [Mease and Wyner (2008)].

There are several factors that may play a role in determining the size of the ensemble:

- Desired accuracy — In most cases, ensembles containing at least ten classifiers are capable of reducing the error rate. Nevertheless, there is empirical evidence indicating that when AdaBoost uses decision trees, error reduction can occur in relatively large ensembles containing 10s of classifiers [Opitz and Maclin (1999)]. Moreover, gradient boosting tree ensemble frequently consists of hundreds of classifiers. In disjoint partitioning approaches, there may be a tradeoff between the number of subsets and the final accuracy. However, the size of each subset cannot be too small, because sufficient data must be available in order for each learning process to produce an effective classifier.

- Computational cost — Increasing the number of classifiers usually increases their computational cost.

- Comprehensibility — large ensemble are considered to be less comprehensive compared to small ensembles.
- The nature of the classification sliding problem - In some ensemble methods, the nature of the classification problem to be solved determines the number of classifiers needed.
- Number of processors available — In independent methods, the number of processors available for parallel learning could be used as an upper bound on the number of classifiers.

The three approaches used to determine the ensemble size are described below. Each approach occurs at a different stage in the classification process.

7.2   Preselection of the Ensemble Size

This is the most common way to determine the ensemble size. Many ensemble algorithms, including bagging, have a controlling parameter such as "number of iterations," which can be set by the user. Since a new classifier is added in each iteration, this parameter actually determines the ensemble size.

7.3   Selection of the Ensemble Size During Training

There are ensemble algorithms that try to determine the best ensemble size during training. Usually, these algorithms determine whether the contribution of the last classifier added to the ensemble is significant (in terms of the ensemble's performance) as new classifiers are added to the ensemble. If the contribution of the classifier is not significant, the ensemble algorithm stops. In addition, these algorithms often have a controlling parameter that bounds the maximum size of the ensemble.

The random forest algorithm uses the out-of-bag (OOB) procedure to obtain an unbiased estimate of the test set error [Breiman (1999)]. The effectiveness of using the out-of-bag error estimate to decide when there are a sufficient number of classification trees was recently examined in [Banfield *et al.* (2007)]. The random forest algorithm works by smoothing the out-of-bag error graph with a sliding window in order to reduce the variance. After smoothing has been completed, the algorithm takes a larger window on the smoothed data points and determines the maximum accuracy within that window, continuing to process windows until the accuracy within a particular window no longer increases and the maximum accuracy has been reached. This serves as an indication that the stopping criterion has been met, and the algorithm returns the ensemble with the maximum raw accuracy from within that window. It has been shown that the out-of-bag procedure obtains an accurate ensemble for those methods that incorporate bagging in the construction of the ensemble.

Mease and Wyner (2008) found that using stopping rules may be harmful in certain cases; in their study, they stopped the algorithm after just a few iterations, when the overfitting initially occurs, despite the fact that the best performance is achieved after adding more base classifiers.

7.4 Pruning — Postselection of the Ensemble Size

As in decision tree induction, it is sometimes useful to let the ensemble grow freely and prune the ensemble later, in order to obtain more effective and compact ensembles. Postselection of the ensemble size allows ensemble optimization for performance metrics such as accuracy, cross entropy, mean precision, and the ROC area. Empirical examination indicates that pruned ensembles may achieve accuracy performance similar to that of the original ensemble [Margineantu and Dietterich (1997)]. An empirical study that was conducted in order to understand the effect of ensemble size on ensemble accuracy and diversity, showed that it is feasible to maintain a small ensemble with accuracy and diversity similar to that of a full ensemble [Liu et al. (2004)].

The challenge of ensemble pruning is to select the best subset of classifiers, such that when combined the ensemble will have the highest possible accuracy. Therefore, the problem can be formally phrased as follows:

Given an ensemble $\Omega = \{M_1, \ldots, M_n\}$, *a combination method* C, *and a training set* S *from a distribution* D *over the labeled instance space, the goal is to find an optimal subset* $Z_{opt} \subseteq \Omega$. *which minimizes the generalization error over the distribution* D *of the classification of classifiers in* Z_{opt} *combined using method* C.

Note that we assume that the ensemble is given, and we do not attempt to improve the way in which the ensemble is created.

In earlier research on ensemble pruning (Margineantu and Dietterich, 1997), the goal was to use a small ensemble size in order to achieve performance equivalent to that of a boosted ensemble. This has been shown to be NP-hard and difficult to approximate (Tamon and Xiang, 2000), and moreover, pruning may sacrifice the generalization capability of the final ensemble.

The "many-could-be-better-than-all" theorem proven by Zhou *et al* (2002) showed that it was possible to obtain a small yet strong ensemble. This led to the creation of many new ensemble pruning methods that will be described below. Tsoumakas *et al.* (2008) proposed organizing the various ensemble selection methods based on the following categories: a) ranking-based, b) search-based, c) clustering based, and d) other. In the following subsections, we will first discuss in detail the first two categories, which are the most popular in practice.

7.4.1 *Ranking-based Methods*

The idea of this approach is to rank the individual members of the ensemble according to a certain criterion and choose the top ranked classifiers according to a threshold. For example, Prodromidis *et al.* (1999) suggested ranking classifiers according to their classification performance on a separate validation set and their ability to correctly classify specific classes. Similarly, Caruana *et al.* (2004) presented a forward stepwise selection procedure in order to select the most relevant classifiers (those that maximize the ensemble's performance) among thousands of classifiers. The FS-PP-EROS (Forward Search and Postpruning Ensemble multiple ROugh Subspaces) algorithm generates a selective ensemble of rough subspaces (Hu *et al.*, 2007) and performs an accuracy-guided forward search to select the most relevant members. Their results show that the FS-PP-EROS algorithm outperforms bagging and random subspace methods in terms of the accuracy and size of ensemble systems. In attribute bagging (Bryll *et al.*, 2003), the classification accuracy of randomly selected m-attribute subsets is evaluated using the wrapper approach, and only the classifiers constructed from the highest ranking subsets participate in the ensemble voting. Margineantu and Dietterich (1997) present agreement-based ensemble pruning, which measures the kappa statistics between any pair of classifiers. Then, pairs of classifiers are selected in ascending order of their agreement level until the desired ensemble size is reached.

7.4.2 *Search-based Methods*

Instead of ranking the members separately, one can perform a heuristic search in the space of the possible different ensemble subsets while evaluating the collective merit of a candidate subset. The GASEN (Genetic

Algorithm based Selective ENsemble) algorithm was developed for select-ing the most appropriate classifiers in a given ensemble (Zhou *et al.*, 2002). In the initialization phase, GASEN assigns a random weight to each of the classifiers. Then, it uses genetic algorithms to update those weights, so that the weights can characterize, to some extent, the fitness of the classifiers in joining the ensemble. Finally, it removes those classifiers whose weight is less than a predefined threshold from the ensemble.

A revised version of the GASEN algorithm called GASEN-b was also suggested (Zhou and Tang, 2003). In this algorithm, instead of assigning a weight to each classifier, a bit is assigned to each of classifiers, indicating whether a given classifier will be used in the final ensemble. In an experi-mental study, the researchers showed that ensembles generated by a selec-tive ensemble algorithm that selects some of the trained C4.5 decision trees to form an ensemble may be smaller in size and stronger in terms of gener-alization than ensembles generated by non-selective algorithms. A similar approach can also be found in (Kim *et al.*, 2002). Rokach *et al.* (2006) suggested ranking the classifiers according to their ROC performance and evaluating the performance of the ensemble subset by using the top ranked members. The subset size is increased gradually until there are several sequential points with no improvement in performance. Prodromidis and Stolfo (2001) introduced backwards correlation-based pruning. The main idea is to remove the members that are least correlated to a metaclassifier which is trained based on the classifiers' outputs. In each iteration, they re-move one member and recompute the new reduced metaclassifier (with the remaining members). In this case, the metaclassifier is used to evaluate the collective merit of the ensemble. Zhang el al. (2006) formulated the ensem-ble pruning problem as a quadratic integer programming problem to look for a subset of classifiers that has the optimal accuracy-diversity tradeoff. Using a semidefinite programming (SDP) technique, they efficiently appro-ximate the optimal solution, despite the fact that the quadratic problem is NP-hard.

The ensemble pruning problem resembles the well-known feature se-lection problem. However, instead of selecting features, one selects the ensemble's members (Liu *et al.*, 2004). This led to the idea of adapting the correlation-based feature selection method (CFS) (Hall, 2000) that is known to be successful in feature selection tasks to the current problem of ensemble pruning. The CFS algorithm is suitable in this case, because there are many correlated base-classifiers in many ensembles. The next section describes this approach in more details.

Which approach to use? Search-based methods provide better classification performance than ranking-based methods (Prodromidis *et al.*, 1999). However, search-based methods are usually computationally expensive due to their need to search a large space. Thus, one should select a feasible search strategy depending on the resources available and problem to solve. Moreover, it is worth noting that independent from the search strategy chosen, the computational complexity for evaluating a single candidate subset is usually at least linear in the number of instances in the training set (see Tsoumakas *et al.*, 2008 for complexity analysis of existing evolution measures).

7.4.2.1   *Collective Agreement-based Ensemble Pruning Method*

In this section we would like to describe in more detail one of the simple yet effective method for ensemble selection. Collective agreement-based ensemble pruning (CAP) calculates the member-class and member-member agreements based on the training data. Member-class agreement indicates how much the members' classifications agree with the real label, while member-member agreement is the agreement between the classifications of two members. The merit of an ensemble subset Z with nz members can be estimated from:

$$Merit_z = \frac{n_z \bar{\kappa}_{cm}}{\sqrt{n_z + n_z(n_z - 1)\bar{\kappa}_{mm}}} \tag{7.1}$$

where $\bar{\kappa}_{cf}$ is the mean agreement between Z's members and the class, and $\bar{\kappa}_{mm}$ is the average of the member-member agreements in Z.

Adopted from test theory, Equation 2 is mathematically derived (Gulliksen, 1950, pages 74-89) from the Spearman formula (Spearman, 1913) in order to measure the augmented validity coefficient of a psychological test which consists of nz unit tests. Since its development, the Spearman formula was used in human relations studies to evaluate the validity of aggregating experts' opinions (Hogarth, 1977) which is similar to the ensemble selection problem addressed in this chapter. According to Equation 2, the following properties can be observed:

(1) The lower the intercorrelation among classifiers, the higher the merit value.
(2) The higher the correlation between the classifiers and the real class, the higher the merit value.

(3) As the number of classifiers in the ensemble increases (assuming the additional classifiers are the same as the original classifiers in terms of the average intercorrelation with the other classifiers and the real class), the higher the merit value. However, it is unlikely that a large ensemble of classifiers that are all highly correlated with the real class will, at the same time, yield low correlation with each other (Hogarth, 1977).

While the above properties indicate that removing a classifier from an ensemble might be beneficial, it might not necessarily pay to remove the classifier with the lowest individual agreement with the class.

Several measures can be incorporated in Equation 2 to measure the agreement among members and with the class. Specifically, the kappa statistics can be used to measure the agreement in Equation 2:

$$\kappa_{i,j} = \frac{\vartheta_{i,j} - \theta_{i,j}}{1 - \theta_{i,j}} \tag{7.2}$$

where $\vartheta_{i,j}$ is the proportion of instances on which the classifiers i and j agree with their classifications to the training set, and $\theta_{i,j}$ is the probability that the two classifiers agree by chance.

Alternatively, one can use the symmetrical uncertainty (a modified information gain measure) to measure the agreement between two members (Hall, 2000):

$$SU_{i,j} = \frac{H(\hat{y}_i) + H(\hat{y}_j) - H(\hat{y}_i, \hat{y}_j)}{H(\hat{y}_i) + H(\hat{y}_j)} \tag{7.3}$$

where $\hat{y}_i$ is the classification vector of classifier i, and H is the entropy function.

Although both kappa statistics and the entropy measure have been mentioned in the ensemble literature (Kuncheva, 2004), in the past they have merely been used to measure the diversity in classifier ensembles. Rokach (2009) suggested to incorporate them into the ensemble's merit estimation (Eq. 2). Instead of simply averaging the agreement measure across all pairs of classifiers ($\overline{\kappa}_{mm}$) to obtain a global pairwise agreement measure, we suggest taking the agreement between the classifier's outputs and the actual class ($\overline{\kappa}_{cm}$) into consideration. Thus, the CAP algorithm prefers subensembles whose members have greater agreement with the actual class (i.e., greater accuracy) and have less agreement among themselves.

In this sense, the merit measure presented in Equation 2 is reminiscent of Breiman's upper bound on the generalization error of random forest (Breiman, 2001) which is expressed *"in terms of two parameters that are measures of how accurate the individual classifiers are and the agreement between them."* While Brieman's bound is theoretically justified, it is not considered to be very tight (Kuncheva, 2004). Moreover, it is only designed for decision forests.

As the search space for ensemble selection is huge (2^n, where n is the number of members in the ensemble), the preferred strategy is the best-first search strategy which explores the search space by making local changes to the current ensemble subset. The best-first search strategy begins with an empty ensemble subset. If the path being explored does not improve the merit, the best-first strategy backtracks to a previous subset that is more promising and continues the search from there. The search stops if there is no improvement in the subsets of five consecutive iterations.

The pseudocode of the proposed algorithm is presented in Figure 7.1. As input, the algorithm receives the training set, ensemble of classifiers, method for calculating the agreement measure (for example, kappa statistics), and search strategy. First, the algorithm calculates the classifiers' output (prediction) for each instance in the training set. Then, it calculates the mutual agreement matrix among the classifiers' outputs and the agreement between each classifier's output and the actual class. Finally, the algorithm searches the space according to the given search strategy. The search procedure uses the merit calculation to evaluate a candidate solution (Figure 7.2).

The computational complexity of the agreement matrix calculation is $o(n^2 m)$, assuming that the complexity of the agreement measure is $o(m)$. This assumption is true for the two measures presented in equations 3 and 4. The computational complexity of the merit evaluation (Figure 7.2) is $o(n^2)$. If the search strategy imposes a partial ordering of the search space, the merit can be calculated incrementally. For example, if backward search is used, one addition to the numerator and up to n additions/subtractions to the denominator are required.

Note that the actual computational complexity of CAP algorithm depends on the computational complexity of the classifier making a classification and the computational complexity of the search strategy being used. Nevertheless, neither the computational complexity of evaluating a solution's merit nor the search space size depends on the training set size. Thus, the presented method makes it possible to thoroughly search the

CAP (S, Ω, Agr, Src)

Input: S – the training set, Ω – Ensemble of classifiers $\{M_1, \ldots, M_n\}$, Agr – A method for calculating the agreement measure, Src – A search strategy

Output: Z – Pruned ensemble set

1: **for all** $< x_q, y_q > \in S$ **do**
2:   **for all** $M_i \in \Omega$ **do**
3:     $\hat{y}_{i,q} \leftarrow M_i(x_q)$
4:   **end for**
5: **end for**
6: **for all** $M_i \in \Omega$ **do**
7:   $CM_i = Agr\,(y, \hat{y}_i)$
8:   **for all** $M_j \in \Omega \,;\, j > i$ **do**
9:     $MM_{i,j} = Agr\,(\hat{y}_i, \hat{y}_j)$
10:   **end for**
11: **end for**
12: $Z \leftarrow Src(\Omega, MM, CM)$
13: **return** Z

Fig. 7.1: Pseudocode of collective agreement-based pruning of ensembles.

space in problems with large training sets. For example, the complexity for a forward selection or backward elimination is $o(n^2)$. Best-first search is exhaustive, but the use of a stopping criterion makes the probability of exploring the entire search space low.

7.4.3 *Clustering-based Methods*

Clustering-based methods have two stages. In the first phase, a clustering algorithm is used in order to discover groups of classifiers that make similar classifications. Then in the second phase, each group of classifiers is pruned separately in order to ensure the overall diversity of the ensemble.

Lazarevic and Obradovic (2001) use the well-known k-means algorithm to cluster the classifiers. They increase k iteratively until the diversity among the classifiers starts to decrease. In the second phase, they prune the classifiers of each cluster by considering the classifiers in turn, from the least accurate to the most accurate. A classifier is kept in the ensemble if its disagreement with the most accurate classifier is more than a predefined threshold and it is sufficiently accurate.

EvaluateMerit (Z, CM, MM)

Input: Z – The Ensemble Subset, CM – Class-Member agreement vector, MM – Member-Member agreement matrix

Output: $Merit_z$ – The merit of Z.

1: $n_z \leftarrow |Z|$
2: $\overline{\kappa}_{cm} \leftarrow 0$
3: $\overline{\kappa}_{mm} \leftarrow 0$
4: **for all** $M_i \in Z$ **do**
5:      $\overline{\kappa}_{cm} \leftarrow \overline{\kappa}_{cm} + CM_i$
6:      **for all** $M_j \in Z; \ j > i$ **do**
7:          $\overline{\kappa}_{mm} \leftarrow \overline{\kappa}_{mm} + MM_{i,j}$
8:      **end for**
9: **end for**
10: $Merit_z \leftarrow \dfrac{n_z \overline{\kappa}_{cm}}{\sqrt{n_z + n_z(n_z - 1)\overline{\kappa}_{mm}}}$
11: **return** $Merit_z$

Fig. 7.2: Pseudocode for evaluating the merit of a candidate solution.

Giacinto *et al.* (2000) use hierarchical agglomerative clustering (HAC) to identify the groups of classifiers. HAC returns a hierarchy of different clustering results starting with as many clusters as there are classifiers and ending with a single cluster which is identical to the original ensemble. In order to create the hierarchy, they define a distance metric between two classifiers as the probability that the classifiers do not misclassify coincidentally and estimate this probability from a validation set. The distance between two groups is defined as the maximum distance between two classifiers belonging to these clusters. In the next phase, they prune each cluster by selecting the single best performing classifier. Similarly, Fu *et al.* (2005) use the k-means algorithm to cluster the classifiers into groups and select the best classifier from each cluster.

7.4.4   *Pruning Timing*

Pruning methods can be divided into two groups: precombining pruning methods and postcombining pruning methods.

7.4.4.1   *Precombining Pruning*

Precombining pruning is performed before combining the classifiers. Classifiers that seem to perform well are included in the ensemble. Prodromidis *et al.* [Prodromidis *et al.* (1999)] present three methods for precombining pruning: 1) methods based on an individual classification performance on a separate validation set, 2) methods based on diversity metrics among the classifiers, and 3) methods based on the ability of classifiers to classify correctly specific classes.

In attribute bagging [Bryll *et al.* (2003)], classification accuracy of randomly selected m-attribute subsets is evaluated by using the wrapper approach, and only the classifiers constructed on the highest ranking subsets participate in the ensemble voting.

7.4.4.2 *Postcombining Pruning*

In postcombining pruning methods, classifiers are removed based on their contribution to the collective.

Prodromidis [Prodromidis *et al.* (1999)] examines two methods for postcombining pruning, assuming that the classifiers are combined using a metacombination method which is based on decision tree pruning and the correlation of the base classifier to the unpruned metaclassifier.

A forward stepwise selection procedure can be used in order to select the most relevant classifiers (those that maximize the ensemble's performance) among thousands of classifiers [Caruana *et al.* (2004)]. Recall that for this purpose one can use feature selection algorithms, however instead of selecting features, one should select the ensemble's members [Liu *et al.* (2004)].

Rokach *et al.* [Rokach *et al.* (2006)] suggest a process that starts by ranking the classifiers according to their ROC performance. The results are then plotted in a graph in which the y-axis displays a performance measure for the integrated classification, and the x-axis presents the number of classifiers that participated in the ensemble, i.e., the first-best classifiers from the list are combined by voting (assuming equal weights) with the rest getting zero weights. The ensemble size is chosen when there are several sequential points with no improvement.

The abovementioned FS-PP-EROS algorithm is also considered to be a postcombining pruning. Recall that the FS-PP-EROS algorithm generates a selective ensemble of rough subspaces [Hu *et al.* (2007)]. The algorithm performs an accuracy-guided forward search and postpruning strategy to select some of the base classifiers to construct an efficient and effective ensemble system. The experimental results show that the FS-PP-EROS algorithm outperforms bagging and random subspace methods in terms of accuracy and the size of ensemble systems.

Recall the GASEN algorithm that was developed for selecting the most appropriate classifiers in a given ensemble [Zhou *et al.* (2002)]. In the initialization phase, GASEN assigns a random weight to each of the classifiers. Consequently, it uses genetic algorithms to update these weights and eventually removes those classifiers whose weight is less than a predefined threshold. In this sense, GASEN algorithm determines which classifier to remove after trying to combine it with the other classifiers. Thus, GASEN algorithm can also be considered as a postcombining pruning method.

The following postcombining pruning methods applied to boosting and bagging were compared in [Windeatt and Ardeshir (2001)]: minimum error pruning (MEP), error-based pruning (EBP), reduced-error pruning(REP), critical value pruning (CVP), and cost-complexity pruning (CCP). The results indicate that if a single pruning method needs to be selected then overall the popular EBP makes a good choice.

A comparative study of precombining and postcombining pruning methods when metacombining methods are used was performed in [Prodromidis *et al.* (1999)]. The results indicate that postcombining pruning methods tend to perform better in this case.

Zhang *et al.* [Zhang *et al.* (2009)] use boosting to determine the order in which the base classifiers are fused, and then they construct a pruned ensemble by stopping the fusion process early. Two heuristic rules are used to stop fusion: 1) select the upper twenty percent of the base classifiers from the ordered full double-bagging ensemble, and 2) stop the fusion when the weighted training error reaches 0.5. Recall that in each iteration of bagging, a bootstrap sample is drawn from the training set. Since sampling with replacement method is used in bootstrap sampling, a particular instance may appear multiple times in a certain sample, while other instances may not appear at all. Approximately a third of the instances in the original training set is not included in the sample. These instances form the out-of-bag sample. Double-bagging utilizes the out-of-bag sample to augment the input features. More specifically, it first trains a linear discriminant analysis (LDA) using the out-of-bag sample. Then it computes the discriminant variables for the instances in the bootstrap sample and adds them as additional variables for building the base classifier.

Croux *et al.* [Croux *et al.* (2007)] propose the idea of trimmed bagging which aims to prune classifiers that yield the highest error rates, as estimated by the out-of-bag error rate. It has been shown that trimmed bagging performs comparably to standard bagging when applied to unstable classifiers, such as decision trees, but yields improved accuracy when applied to more stable base classifiers, like support vector machines.

7.5 Back to a Single Model: Ensemble Derived Models

Ensemble pruning methods have been shown to significantly improve ensemble predictive performance and computational costs, however they do not solve the comprehensibility problem and fail to acquire knowledge from the pruned ensemble.

The subject of knowledge acquisition from an ensemble has been addressed by researchers. A simplified tree ensemble learner (STEL) provides the ability to extract rules from an ensemble of trees and search for frequent variable interactions [Deng (2014)]. STEL rules may subsequently be combined into a rule-based classifier that iteratively searches for the matching rule given a new observation.

The REEMTIC (Rule Extraction from Ensemble Methods via Tree Induction and Combination) method combines ensemble base classifiers into a comprehensible set of rules by applying pedagogical and decomposition methods. These rules are then combined and logically minimized [Iqbal (2012)].

The idea of building a single model that preserves the predictive performance of a given ensemble has also been presented in several studies. One approach for tackling this challenge is to use real or generated unlabeled data to train a simple model based on the ensemble predictions. An example is a method that uses an ensemble model to label a vast amount of unlabeled data and then uses the new labeled data to fit a neural network that is smaller and faster than the ensemble model while maintaining its accuracy [Bucilua *et al.* (2006)].

The same idea can be applied to decision trees. In their paper "born again trees", Breiman and Shang (1996) suggest to train a new decision tree from the ensemble. After training an ensemble with the available data, new unlabeled data is generated and then labeled by the ensemble. The final decision tree is trained using the synthesized data labels. In combined multiple models (CMM), a new model is trained by learning the data partitioning implicitly from the ensemble using the generated data.

Several methods can be used for generating synthetic unlabeled data that resembles the original dataset:

- Munging method: Each instance x in the original training set is visited once and its closest neighbor instance x' is selected. For each continuous variable a, with probability $1 - p$, x_a is left unchanged. However, with probability p, x_a is assigned a random value drawn from a normal distribution with mean x'_a and appropriate standard deviation. The values of each nominal or ordinal variables are swapped between x and x' with probability p and are left unchanged with probability $1 - p$.

- Smearing method is similar to the munging method as it also swaps the values of attributes with a given probability p. However, instead of swapping the values with the closest neighbor, the value is swapped with the corresponding value of randomly selected instance.

- Construct a kernel density estimate for each input variable separately, and sample from the product of the density estimates.

- GAN: Most recently, generative adversarial networks (GANs) are used to mimic the distribution of training set. GAN is a deep neural net consists of two neural networks, competing each other: The first generative neural network synthesizes candidate instances and the second discriminator neural network tries to determine if the generated instance is authentic or artificially synthesized. The aim of the generative network is to "fool" the discriminator network by generating instances that seem to have come from the original training set. Backpropagation is applied in both networks so that the generator produces better candidates, while the discriminator becomes more skilled at detecting synthetic instances.

There are also methods that do not require generating synthetic unlabeled data to train a simpler model. Instead, those approaches conduct a postprocessing procedure that uses the inner structure of the ensemble. One method that works in this manner is ISM [Van Assche and Blockeel (2007)], an algorithm that constructs a single decision tree that iteratively chooses the most informative node for splitting the new tree based on the ensemble structure. This results in a tree that achieves the same performance as the original ensemble for some datasets. GENESIM is another example of such an algorithm [Vandewiele *et al.* (2016)]. It applies genetic algorithms to transform ensemble inducers into a single decision tree. Experiments conducted show that GENESIM outperforms an optimized single decision tree in terms of generalized accuracy.

Chapter 8

Error Correcting Output Codes

Some machine learning algorithms are designed to solve binary classification tasks, i.e., to classify an instance into just two classes. For example, in the direct marketing scenario, a binary classifier can be used to classify potential customers as to whether they will positively or negatively respond to a particular marketing offer.

In many real problems, however, we are required to differentiate between more than two classes. Examples of such problems are the classification of handwritten letters [Knerr *et al.* (1992)], differentiating between multiple types of cancer [Statnikov *et al.* (2005)], and text categorization [Berger (1999); Ghani (2000)].

A multiclass classification task is more challenging than a binary classification task, since the induced classifier must classify the instances into a larger number of classes, which also increases the likelihood of misclassification. Let us consider, for example, a balanced classification problem with a similar amount of data per class, with equiprobable classes and a random classifier. If the problem is binary, the probability of obtaining a correct classification is 50%. For four classes, this probability drops to 25%.

Several machine learning algorithms, such as SVM [Cristianini and Shawe-Taylor (2000)], were originally designed to solve only binary classification tasks. There are two main approaches for applying such algorithms to multiclass tasks. The first approach, which involves extending the algorithm, has been applied to SVMs [Weston and Watkins (1999)] or boosting[Freund and Schapire (1997)]. However, extending these algorithms into a multiclass version may be impractical or, more frequently, be difficult to perform [Passerini *et al.* (2004)]. For SVMs, in particular, Hsu and Lin (2002) observed that the reformulation of this technique into multiclass versions leads to high costs in training algorithms.

The second approach is to convert the multiclass task into an ensemble of binary classification tasks whose results are then combined. There are several alternatives for decomposing the multiclass problem into binary subtasks [Allwein *et al.* (2000)]. The decomposition that has been performed can be generally represented by a code matrix $\vec{M}$ [Allwein *et al.* (2000)]. This matrix has k rows, representing codewords ascribed to each of the k classes in the multiclass task; the columns correspond to the desired outputs of the binary classifiers induced in the decomposition.

In order to illustrate the idea of multiclass decomposition, recall the training set in Table 1.1 which contains a segment of the Iris dataset. In this case, the goal is to classify flowers into Iris subspecies according to their characteristic features. The dataset contains three classes that correspond to three types of irises: $dom(y) = \{IrisSetosa, IrisVersicolor, IrisVirginica\}$. Table 8.1 illustrates a code matrix for the Iris dataset. It contains one row for each class and one column for each classifier to be built. The first classifier attempts to distinguish between $\{IrisSetosa, IrisVirginica\}$, which is represented by the binary value of 1 in column 1 and $\{IrisVersicolor\}$, which is represented by the value -1 in column 1. Similarly, the second classifier attempts to distinguish between $\{IrisVersicolor, IrisVirginica\}$, represented by the binary value of 1 in column 2 and $\{IrisSetosa\}$, represented by the value -1 in column 2. Finally, the third classifier attempts to distinguish between $\{IrisSetosa, IrisVersicolor\}$, represented by the binary value of 1 in column 3 and $\{IrisVirginica\}$, represented by the value -1 in column 3.

Table 8.1: Illustration of code matrix for the Iris dataset.

Class Label	First Classifier	Second Classifier	Third Classifier
Iris Setosa	1	-1	1
Iris Versicolor	-1	1	1
Iris Virginica	1	1	-1

In order to classify a new instance into one of the three classes, we first obtain the binary classification from each of the base classifiers. Based on these binary classifications, we search for the most probable class. We simply measure the Hamming distance from the obtained code to the codewords ascribed to each class. The class with the shortest distance is chosen to be the output class. In case of a tie, we arbitrarily select the class. This process is also known as decoding. Table 8.2 presents the Hamming distance for each possible output of an unseen instance. For example, if a certain instance is classified as $-1, 1, -1$ by classifiers 1 to 3 respectively, then its predicted class is either Versicolor or Virginica.

Table 8.2: Decoding process for the Iris dataset.

Output			Hamming Distance			
Classifier 1	Classifier 2	Classifier 3	Setosa	Versicolor	Virginica	Predicted Class
-1	-1	-1	4	4	4	Any Class
-1	-1	1	2	2	6	Setosa OR Versicolor
-1	1	-1	6	2	2	Versicolor OR Virginica
-1	1	1	4	0	4	Versicolor
1	-1	-1	2	6	2	Setosa OR Virginica
1	-1	1	0	4	4	Setosa
1	1	-1	4	4	0	Virginica
1	1	1	2	2	2	Any Class

8.1 Code Matrix Decomposition of Multiclass Problems

There are several reasons for using decomposition tactics in multiclass solutions. Mayoraz and Moreira (1996), Masulli and Valentini (2000) and Furnkranz (2002) state that implementing a decomposition approach may lessen the computational complexity required for inducing the classifier. Thus, even multiclass induction algorithms may benefit from converting the problem into a set of binary tasks. Knerr *et al.* (1992), claim that the classes in a digit recognition problem (such as the LED problem) can be linearly separated when the classes are analyzed in pairs. Consequently, they combine linear classifiers for all pairs of classes. This is simpler than using a single multiclass classifier that separates all classes simultaneously. Pimenta and Gama (2005) claim that the decomposition approach suggests new possibilities for parallel processing, since the binary subproblems are independent and can be solved in different processors.

Crammer and Singer (2002) differentiate between three subcategories:

(1) Type I - Given a code matrix, find a set of binary classifiers that result in low empirical loss;
(2) Type II - Find simultaneously both a set of binary classifiers and a code matrix that produces low empirical loss;
(3) Type III – Given a set of binary classifiers, find a code matrix that yields low empirical loss.

In this chapter we focus on type I and II tasks, as defined below.

8.2 Type I - Training an Ensemble Given a Code Matrix

The most simple decomposition tactic is one-against-one (1A1) decomposition, also known as the round robin classification. It consists of building $k(k-1)/2$ classifiers, each distinguishing a pair of classes i and j, where $i \neq j$ [Knerr *et al.* (2000); Hastie and Tibshirani (1998)]. To combine the outputs produced by these classifiers, a majority voting scheme can be applied [Kreβel (1999)]. Each 1A1 classifier provides one vote to its preferred class. The final classification result is the class with most of the votes. Table 8.3 illustrates the 1A1 matrix for a four-class classification problem.

In certain cases, only a subset of all possible pairwise classifiers should be used [Cutzu (2003)]. In such cases it is preferable to count the "against" votes, instead of counting the "for" votes, since there is a greater chance of making a mistake when counting the latter. If a certain classifier attempts to differentiate between two classes, neither of which is the true class, counting the "for" votes inevitably causes a misclassification. On the other hand, voting against one of the classes will not result in misclassification in such cases. Moreover, in the 1A1 approach, the classification of a classifier for a pair of classes (i, j) does not provide useful information when the instance does not belong to classes i or j [Alpaydin and Mayoraz (1999)].

1A1 decomposition is illustrated in Figure 8.1. For the four-class problem presented in Figure 8.1(a), the 1A1 procedure induces six classifiers, one for each pair of classes. Figure 8.1(b) shows the classifier of class 1 against 4.

Table 8.3: Illustration of one-against-one (1A1) decomposition for a four-class classification problem.

Class Label	Classifier 1	Classifier 2	Classifier 3	Classifier 4	Classifier 5	Classifier 6
Class 1	1	1	1	0	0	0
Class 2	-1	0	0	1	1	0
Class 3	0	-1	0	-1	0	1
Class 4	0	0	-1	0	-1	-1

Another common approach for converting a multiclass classification task into binary classification tasks is called one-against-all (1AA). In this case, given a problem with k classes, k binary classifiers are generated. Each binary classifier is responsible for differentiating a class i from the remaining classes. The classification is usually chosen according to the class with the highest probability. Table 8.4 illustrates the 1AA matrix for a four-class classification problem.

Table 8.4: Illustration of one-against-all code matrix for a four-class classification problem.

Class Label	Classifier 1	Classifier 2	Classifier 3	Classifier 4
Class 1	1	-1	-1	-1
Class 2	-1	1	-1	-1
Class 3	-1	-1	1	-1
Class 4	-1	-1	-1	1

Some difficulties arise in 1AA decomposition when the training set is unbalanced, and the number of instances that are associated with a certain class is much smaller than the number of instances in other classes. In such cases, it will be difficult to generate a classifier with good predictive performance in the considered class.

Figure 8.1(c) illustrates one of the classifiers that were obtained using the 1AA procedure, namely, the classifier that examine class 1 against all other classes. It is obvious that in the 1A1 procedure, each base classifier uses fewer instances and thus according to [Fürnkranz (2002)] "has more freedom for fitting a decision boundary between the two classes."

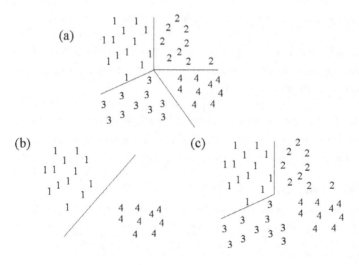

Fig. 8.1: Illustration of 1A1 and 1AA for a four-class problem.

8.2.1   *Error-Correcting Output Codes*

Error-correcting systems, which date back to the mid-20th century, have been used to increase the reliability of communication channels. Communication channels suffer from undesired noise that distorts the received message from the original. Due to noise, an arbitrary bit in a message will be changed from its original state. To reduce the possibility of this occurring, the submitted message should be encoded in such a way that simple errors can be detected, making it possible, in some cases, to correct the error on the receiver end.

Each submitted symbol is encoded as a different codeword that is known in advance to both ends. When a codeword is obtained, the receiver searches for the most similar codeword using the Hamming distance. The coding is designed in such a way that the probability that the receiver will misidentify the correct codeword is low. Peterson and Weldon (1972) noted that "much of binary coding theory has been based on the assumption that each symbol is affected independently by the noise, and therefore the probability of a given error pattern depends only on the number of errors."

Dietterich and Bariki (1995) employ communication techniques to transform multiclass problems into an ensemble of binary classification tasks. The idea is to transmit the correct class of a new instance via a channel composed of the instance attributes, the training data, and the learning algorithm. Due to errors that may be present in the attributes or training data and/or failures in the classifier learning process, the class information can be disrupted. To provide the system with the ability to recover from these transmission errors, the class is codified by an error- correcting code, and each of its bits is transmitted separately, that is, through separate executions of the learning algorithm.

Accordingly, a distributed output code is used to represent the k classes associated with the multiclass problem. A codeword of length l is ascribed to each class. Typically, the codeword has more bits than needed in order to uniquely represent each class. The additional bits can be used to correct eventual classification errors. For this reason, the method is called error-correcting output coding (ECOC).

The generated codes are stored in a matrix $\vec{M} \in \{-1, +1\}^{k \times l}$. The rows of this matrix represent the codewords of each class, and the columns correspond to the desired outputs of the l binary classifiers $(f_1(\vec{x}), \ldots, f_l(\vec{x}))$ induced.

A new pattern $\vec{x}$ can be classified by evaluating the classifications of the

l classifiers, which generate a vector $\vec{f}(\vec{x})$ of length l. This vector is then measured against the rows of $\vec{M}$. The instance is ascribed to the class with the lowest Hamming distance.

In order to assess the merit of a certain matrix of ECOC, Dietterich and Bariki (1995) propose two criteria for row separation and column diversity:

Row separation. Codewords should be well-separated in terms of Hamming distance.

Column diversity. Columns should be as uncorrelated as possible.

Dietterich and Bariki (1995) proposed that codewords should be designed in order to maximize their error-correcting capability and presented four techniques for constructing good error- correcting codes. The choice of technique is based upon the number of classes in the problem.

8.2.2 Code Matrix Framework

Allwein *et al* (2000) presented a framework that can generally be used to represent decomposition techniques. In this framework, the decomposition techniques are transformed into code matrix-based methods in which a value from the set $\{-1, 0, +1\}$ is ascribed to each entry of the matrix $\vec{M}$. An entry m_{ij} with +1 value indicates that the class corresponding to row i assumes a positive label in the classifier f_j induction. The -1 value designates a negative label, and the 0 value indicates that the data from class i does not participate in the classifier f_j induction. Binary classifiers are then trained to learn the labels represented in the columns of $\vec{M}$.

In 1AA decomposition, $\vec{M}$ has dimension $k\mathrm{x}k$, with diagonal entries equal to +1. All other entries receive the value -1. In the 1A1 case, $\vec{M}$ has dimension $k\mathrm{x}k(k-1g)/2$, and each column corresponds to a binary classifier for a pair of classes (i, j). In each column representing a pair (i, j), the value of the entries corresponding to lines i and j are defined as +1 and -1, respectively. The remaining entries are equal to 0, indicating that patterns from the other classes do not participate in the induction of this particular binary classifier.

The classification of a new pattern's class involves a decoding step, as with the ECOC technique. Several decoding methods have been proposed in the literature [Passerini *et al.* (2004); Allwein *et al.* (2000); Windeatt and Ghaderi (2003); Escalera *et al.* (2006); Klautau *et al.* (2003)].

No clear winner among the various coding strategies (e.g., 1AA, 1A1, dense random codes, and sparse random codes) has been found in previous studies [Allwein *et al.* (2000)]. Thus, finding an adequate combination of binary classifiers for a given multiclass task can still be considered a relevant and outstanding research issue.

The next section presents the code matrix design problem and discusses some of the main methods developed in this area. This problem can be defined as a search for codes to represent each class. Other issues to be addressed are the size of these codewords.

8.2.3   *Code Matrix Design Problem*

There are several methods that can be employed in order to decompose a multiclass problem into multiple binary subproblems. The most compact decomposition of a problem with k classes can be performed with the use of $l = \lceil \log_2(k) \rceil$ binary classifiers [Mayoraz and Moreira (1996)]. One instance of a compact matrix for a problem with four classes is presented in Table 8.5.

Table 8.5: Illustration of compact code matrix for a four-class classification problem.

Class Label	First Classifier	Second Classifier
Class 1	1	1
Class 2	1	-1
Class 3	-1	1
Class 4	-1	-1

The total number of different binary classifiers for a problem with k classes is $0.5\left(3^k + 1\right) - 2^k$, considering that $f = -f$. In other words, the inversion of the positive and negative labels produces the same classifier [Mayoraz and Moreira (1996)]. Among them, $2^{k-1} - 1$ include all classes simultaneously, i.e., these classifier have only the labels $+1$ and -1, without the 0 entry. An example of a code matrix constituted of such classifiers for a problem with four classes is illustrated in Table 8.6.

The next section reviews some strategies for obtaining ECOC matrices, i.e., code matrices with error-correcting capability and other strategies employed in obtaining code matrices. Section 8.3 describes techniques for adapting code matrices to each multiclass problem under consideration.

Unless it is explicitly stated, the described works use binary code matrices, that is, code matrices with only $+1$ and -1 entries.

Dietterich and Bariki (1995) recommend two characteristics necessary

Table 8.6: Illustration of compact code matrix for a four-class classification problem.

Class Label	Classifier 1	Classifier 2	Classifier 3	Classifier 4	Classifier 5	Classifier 6
Class 1	1	1	1	1	1	1
Class 2	1	1	-1	-1	-1	-1
Class 3	-1	-1	1	1	-1	-1
Class 4	1	-1	1	-1	1	-1

to ensure error-correcting capability when designing ECOC matrices:

- Row separation;
- Column separation.

where the separation is measured through the Hamming distance, which is equal to the differences between different bit strings.

Constant columns (with only positive or negative entries) should also be avoided, since they do not represent a binary decision problem.

Let d_m designate the minimum Hamming distance between any pair of rows of $\vec{M}$. The final ECOC multiclass classifier is able to correct at least $\lfloor \frac{d_m-1}{2} \rfloor$ errors of the binary classifier's outputs. Since, according to the Hamming distance, each incorrect classification implies a deviation of one unit from the correct class codeword, committing $\lfloor \frac{d_m-1}{2} \rfloor$ errors, the closest codeword will still be that of the correct class [Dietterich and Bakiri (1995)]. This is the reason why a high row separation is required. According to this principle, 1AA coding is unable to recover from any error, since its d_m is equal to 2. The row separation requirement is also needed in designing error-correcting code (ECC) in telecommunications [Alba and Chicano (2004)].

In addition to the requirement mentioned above, the errors of the binary classifiers that have been induced must be uncorrelated in order to obtain good error-correcting codes when solving the multiclass problem. In order to achieve this, column separation is also required, that is, the Hamming distance between each pair of columns of $\vec{M}$ must be high.

Based on these observations, Dietterich and Bariki (1995) propose four techniques for designing code matrices with good error-correcting capability. The choice of technique is determined by the number of classes in the multiclass problem. No justification is given as to how the number of classes was stipulated for each method.

- For $k \leqslant 7$, an exhaustive code is recommended. The first row (i.e., codeword of the first class) is composed of only $+1$ values. All other rows are composed of alternate runs of 2^{k-i} positive values and negative values when i is the row number. Table 8.5 illustrates the exhaustive code matrix for the four-class problem.
- If $8 \leqslant k \leqslant 11$, a method that selects columns from the exhaustive code is applied.
- For $k > 11$, there are two options: a method based on the *hill climbing* algorithm and the generation of BCH (Bose-Chaudhuri-Hocquenghem) codes [Boser and Ray-Chaudhuri (1960)]. The BCH algorithm employs polynomial functions to design nearly optimal error-correcting codes. One problem with BCH codes is that they do not ensure good column separation. Moreover, if the number of classes is not a power of two, the code must be shortened by removing rows (and possibly columns) while maintaining good row and column separations.

Pimenta and Gama (2005) present an algorithm for designing ECOCs that obtain competitive predictive performance in relation to traditional decomposition, using decision trees (DTs) [Quinlan (1986)] and SVMs as base classifiers. They used a function for evaluating the quality of ECOCs according to their error-correcting properties. An iterative persecution algorithm (PA) is used to construct the ECOCs by adding or removing columns from an initial ECOC, in order to maximize the quality function.

A good ECOC is an ECOC that maximizes the minimum Hamming distance among codewords. Thus, these ECOCs define a straight line $y = m.e + b$, where $n = \frac{2^{k-2}-1}{(2^{k-1}-1)-\lceil log_2(k) \rceil}$ and $b = 1 - m\lceil log_2(k) \rceil$. This line represents the best minimum Hamming distance for a certain k (number of classes) and e (the codeword size). Because the Hamming distance gets integer values, the support function $a(k, e)$ is defined as $y(k_1 e)$, rounded down. Based on this support function, a quality function $q(k, e)$ of an ECOC can be defined (assuming the values $W, B, B+$ comply with $W < B < B+$):

- $q(k, e) = W$ when the minimum Hamming distance of the ECOC is under the support function $a(k, e)$ at a distance greater than 1.
- $q(k, e) = B$ when the minimum Hamming distance of the ECOC is under the support function $a(k, e)$ at a distance less than 1.
- $q(k, e) = B+$ when the minimum Hamming distance of the ECOC is in or over the support function $a(k, e)$.

Pimenta and Gama (2005) compared the performance of the repulsion algorithm (RA) to the performance of the persecution algorithm (PA). The RA tries to maximize an evaluation function that gets higher as d_m increases. Since row separation is not required in the design of an ECC, the evaluation function is used to penalize matrices with identical or complementary columns. Moreover, genetic algorithms (GAs) are used to design the code matrices for maximizing the evaluation function. The RA is used in the mutation step of the GA. A comparative study indicated that the PA performed better in finding valid ECOCs, where the validity was measured by the criteria of avoiding equal, complementary, and constant columns; the RA was the worst performing method overall. Among the valid ECOCs generated, the PA still generally performed Better than RA, obtaining ECOCs with good quality according to the evaluation function proposed by Pimenta and Gama (2005). Nevertheless, GARA (GA with RA) method also designes ECOCs of good quality. Pimenta and Gama (2005) also suggested a method of determining the number of columns in the ECOC (i.e., the number of classifiers employed in the decomposition). This method involves examining an evaluation function based on the number of errors that can be corrected by ECOCs of different sizes.

There are some studies that claim that randomly designed ECOCs show good multiclass predictive performance [Berger (1999); Windeatt and Ghaderi (2003); Tapia *et al.* (2003)]. Allwein *et al* (2000) evaluated the performance of two randomly designed matrices: dense and sparse. In the dense matrix, 10,000 random matrices were generated, with $\lceil 10 * \log_2(k) \rceil$ columns and entries receiving the values -1 or $+1$ with the same probability. The matrix with the higher d_m and without identical or complementary columns is chosen, following the recommendations of Dietterich and Bariki (1995) . In the sparse matrix, which uses the ternary alphabet, the number of columns in the code matrix is $\lceil 15 \log_2 k \rceil$, and the entries are chosen as 0 with probability 0.5 and $+1$ or -1 with probability 0.25. Again, 10,000 random matrices are generated, and the one with higher d_m is chosen.

Berger (1999) gives statistical and combinatorial arguments for why random matrices can perform well. Among these arguments, are theorems that state that random matrices are likely to show good row and column separation, particularly as the number of columns increases. Nevertheless, it is assumed that the errors of the individual classifiers are uncorrelated, a state which does not hold for real applications.

Windeatt and Ghaderi (2002) also note the desirability of using equidistant codes in which the Hamming distance between rows is approximately constant. They showed that if $\vec{M}$ is an equidistant code matrix, the number of +1's in different rows is the same, and the number of common +1's between any pair of rows is equal. They used this heuristic to select a subset of rows from BCH codes, producing equidistant code matrices. Experimentally, they verified that equidistant codes were superior to 1AA and random codes for shorter codes (with fewer columns), using multilayer perceptron (MLP) neural networks (NNs) [Haykin (1999)] as base classifiers. As the length of the codes increases, the coding strategy seems to be less significant, favoring a random design.

8.2.4   *Orthogonal Arrays (OA)*

In designing experiments, the aim is to minimize the number of experiments required to collect useful information about an unknown process (Montgomery, 1997). The data collected is typically used to construct a model for the unknown process. The model may then be used to optimize the original process.

A *full factorial design* is an experiment design in which the experimenter chooses n attributes that are believed to affect the target attribute. Then, all possible combinations of the selected input attributes are acquired [Montgomery (1997)]. Applying a full factorial design is impractical when there are many input attributes.

A *fractional factorial design* is a design in which only a fraction of the combinations required for the complete factorial experiment is selected. One of the most practical forms of fractional factorial design is the orthogonal array. An orthogonal array OA(n,k,*d,t)* is a matrix of k rows and n columns, with every entry being one of the d values. The array has strength t if, in every t by n submatrix, the d^t possible distinct rows all appear the same number of times. An example of an OA of strength 2 is presented in Table 8.7. Any two classes in this array have all possible combinations ("1,1," "1,-1," "-1,1," "-1,-1"). Each of these combinations appears an equal number of times. In the orthogonal array of strength 3 presented in Table 8.8, we can find all combinations of any three classes.

The columns, called runs of the OA matrix, represent tests which require resources, such as time, money, and hardware. OA aims to create the minimum number of runs to ensure the required strength. The advantage of compact representation of the OA is that we can use it to create the minimal number of binary classifiers.

The number of rows k in the OA should be equal to the cardinality of the

Table 8.7: The OA(8,7,2,2) design.

+1	+1	+1	+1	-1	-1	-1	-1
+1	+1	-1	-1	+1	+1	-1	-1
+1	+1	-1	-1	-1	-1	+1	+1
+1	-1	+1	-1	+1	-1	+1	-1
+1	-1	+1	-1	-1	+1	-1	+1
+1	-1	-1	+1	+1	-1	-1	+1
+1	-1	-1	+1	-1	+1	+1	-1

Table 8.8: The OA(8,7,2,3) design.

-1	-1	-1	-1	-1	-1	-1	-1	+1	+1	+1	+1	+1	+1	+1	+1
-1	+1	-1	+1	-1	+1	-1	+1	+1	-1	+1	-1	+1	-1	+1	-1
-1	-1	+1	+1	-1	-1	+1	+1	+1	+1	-1	-1	+1	+1	-1	-1
-1	+1	+1	-1	-1	+1	+1	-1	+1	-1	-1	+1	+1	-1	-1	+1
-1	-1	-1	-1	+1	+1	+1	+1	+1	+1	+1	+1	-1	-1	-1	-1
-1	+1	-1	+1	+1	-1	+1	-1	+1	-1	+1	-1	-1	+1	-1	+1
-1	-1	+1	+1	+1	+1	-1	-1	+1	+1	-1	-1	-1	-1	+1	+1
-1	+1	+1	-1	+1	-1	-1	+1	+1	-1	-1	+1	-1	+1	+1	-1

class set. The number of columns is equal to the number of classifiers that will be trained. Constructing a new OA design for any number of classes is not an easy task. Usually, it is possible to use a ready-made design for a specific number of classes. The orthogonal designs can be taken from Sloane's library of OAs (Sloane 2007). If no OA with the required number of rows k can be found, then we can still use an OA with a larger number of rows and reduce it to the appropriate size. Note that any $N x k'$ subarray of an $OA(N, k, s, t)$ is an $OA(N, k', s, t')$, where $t' = min\{k', t\}$.

Before using the OA, we first need to remove columns that are the inverse of other columns, because the inversion of the positive and negative labels produces the same classifier [Mayoraz and Moreira (1996)]. For example, columns 9 to 16 in Table 8.8 should be removed as they are an inversion of columns 1 to 8 respectively. Moreover, columns that are labeled entirely with +1 or −1 also need to be removed, since there is no meaning to training a classifier with a single class. Accordingly, the first column in Table 8.7 should be removed.

8.2.5 *Hadamard Matrix*

Zhang *et al.* (2003) study the usefulness of Hadamard matrices for generating ECOCs in ensemble learning. Hadamard matrices may be regarded as special classes of two-level orthogonal arrays of strengths 2 and 3. These matrices are named after the French mathematician, Jacques Hadamard (1865–1963).

They point out that these matrices can be considered optimal ECOCs within the pool of k class codes that combine $k - 1$ base learners, where the optimality is measured according to the row and column separation criteria. Nevertheless, Hadamard matrix can be used as-is when the number of classes is exactly power two. For other numbers of classes, some rows have to be deleted. The Hadamard matrix provided a higher accuracy than random and 1AA matrices when the SVM algorithm is used as the binary learning algorithm.

A Hadamard matrix (HM) H_n consists of square matrices of $+1's$ and $-1's$ whose rows are orthogonal, which satisfies $H_n H_n^T = nI_n$, where $\mathbf{I}n$ is the nth order identity matrix. A Hadamard matrix $\mathbf{H}n$ is often written in the normalized form with both the first row and column consisting of all $+1$'s.

A Hadamard output code, obtained by removing the first column from any normalized Hadamard matrix, has two beneficial properties: a) every pair of codewords has the same Hamming distance; and b) every pair of columns is orthogonal.

8.2.6 *Probabilistic Error-Correcting Output Code*

Up until this point we assumed that the binary classifiers were crisp classifiers and provided only the class label 1 or -1. However, most binary classifiers are probabilistic and thus provide the class distribution in addition to the class label. This distribution can be used to better select the appropriate class in case of ambiguous output code. For example rows 1, 2, 3, 5 and 8 in Table 8.2 have more than one predicted class.

We assume that the output of each classifier i is a 2-long vector $p_{i,1}(x), p_{i,2}(x)$. The values $p_{i,1}(x)$ and $p_{i,2}(x)$ represent the support that instance x belongs to class -1 and $+1$ respectively according to the classifier i. For the sake of simplicity, we assume the provided vector is the correct distribution i.e., $p_{i,1}(x) + p_{i,2}(x) = 1$. Kong and Dieterich (1995) use the following revised Hamming distance between the classifier outputs and the codeword of class j:

$$HD\left(x,j\right) = \sum_{i=1}^{l} \begin{cases} p_{i,2}\left(x\right) & \text{If } \tilde{M}_{j,i} = -1 \\ p_{i,1}\left(x\right) & \text{If } \tilde{M}_{j,i} = +1 \end{cases} \tag{8.1}$$

where $\vec{M}$ represents the code matrix such as in Table 8.1. We now return to the decoding process presented in Table 8.2. However, we now assume that the classifier provides a classification distribution. Thus, instead of the classification outputs of $(-1, -1, -1)$ as in row 1 of Table 8.2 we obtain, for the sake of the example, the following distributions $0.8, 0.2, 0.6, 0.4$ and $0.7, 0.3$ from classifiers 1 to 3 respectively. Note that these distributions correspond to the classification outputs of row 1. Using equation 8.1, we conclude that the distance from class Setosa (with codeword of $1, -1, 1$) is $0.8 + 0.4 + 0.7 = 1.9$. The distance from class Versicolor (with codeword of $-1, 1, 1$) is $0.2 + 0.4 + 0.7 = 1.3$. The distance from class Virginica (with codeword of $1, 1, -1$) is $0.8 + 0.4 + 0.3 = 1.5$. Therefore the selected class is Versicolor. Recall from Table 8.2 that if we use only the corresponding classification outputs of $(-1, -1, -1)$, any class could have been chosen (ambiguous case).

8.2.7 *Other ECOC Strategies*

This section presents code matrix design works that could not be fully characterized into one of the classes described in the previous sections, either because they employ alternative criteria in the code matrix design or because a combination of the error-correcting and adaptiveness criteria is used.

Sivalingam *et al.* [Sivalingam *et al.* (2005)] propose transforming a multiclass recognition problem into a minimal binary classification problem using the minimal classification method (MCM) aided by error-correcting codes. Instead of separating only two classes at each classification, MCM requires only $log_2 K$ classifications since this method separates two groups of multiple classes. Thus the MCM requires a small number of classifiers but can still provide similar accuracy performance to binary ECOC.

Mayoraz and Moreira (1996) introduce an iterative algorithm for code matrix generation. The algorithm takes into account three criteria. The first two are the same criteria suggested by Dietterich and Bariki (1995). The third criterion is that each inserted column should be pertinent, according to the positions of the classes in the input space. A binary partition of classes is considered pertinent if it is easy to learn. The most important contribution of this algorithm is that the obtained classifiers are usually simpler than those induced by the original ECOC procedure.

Using concepts from telecommunications coding theory, Tapia *et al* (2001) present a particular class of ECOCs, recursive ECOCs (RECOC). The recursive codes are constructed from component subcodes of small lengths, which may be weak when working on their own, but strong when working together. This results in an ensemble of ECOCs, where each component subcode defines a local multiclass learner. Another interesting feature of RECOCs, noted by the authors, is that they allow a regulated degree of randomness in their design. Tapia *et al* (2003) indicate that a random code is the ideal way to protect information against noise.

As in channel coding theory, a puncturing mechanism can be used to prune the dependence among the binary classifiers in a code matrix [Pérez-Cruz and Artés-Rodríguez (2002)]. This algorithm eliminates classifiers that degrade the performance of a previously designed code matrix, deleting columns from it. As a result, less complex multiclass schemes can be obtained. In order to obtain these schemes, a ternary coding was employed, that is, the code matrices could have positive, negative and null entries. Experimentally, they achieved a good performance when puncturing 1A1 and BCH ECOC codes.

Several attempts have been made to design code matrices by maximizing certain diversity measures of classifier ensembles [Kuncheva (2005a)]. Specifically, the search for code combinations, in conjunction with the number of binary classifiers to compose the multiclass solution, constitute a combinatorial problem. In order to solve this combinatorial problem, we can employ genetic algorithms (GAs) [Mitchell (1999); Lorena and Carvalho (2008)]. The GAs are used to determine code matrices according to: their accuracy performance; diversity measures among columns defined by Kuncheva (2005); or the margins of separation among codes of different classes [Shen and Tan (2005)]. Since the implemented GA also aims to minimize the ensemble size, the code matrices are tailor-made for each multiclass problem.

8.3   Type II - Adapting Code Matrices to Multiclass Problems

A common criticism of the 1AA, 1A1 and other ECOC strategies is that all of them perform the multiclass problem decomposition a priori, without taking into account the properties and characteristics of each application

[Allwein *et al.* (2000); Mayoraz and Moreira (1996); Alpaydin and Mayoraz (1999); Mayoraz and Alpaydim (1998); Dekel and Singer (2003); Rätsch *et al.* (2003); Pujol *et al.* (2006)]. Furthermore, as Allwein *et al.* (2000) point out, although the ECOC codes have good error-correcting properties, several of the binary subproblems created may be difficult to learn.

Data-driven error-correcting output coding (DECOC) [Zhoua *et al.* (2008)]. explores the distribution of data classes and optimizes both the composition and number of base learners needed to design an effective and compact code matrix. Specifically, DECOC calculates the confidence score of each base classifier based on the structural information of the training data and use sorted confidence scores to assist in determining the code matrix of ECOC. The results show that the proposed DECOC is able to deliver competitive accuracy compared with other ECOC methods, using parsimonious base learners rather than the pairwise coupling (one-vs-one) decomposition scheme.

The key idea of DECOC is to reduce the number of learners by selectively including some of the binary learners into the code matrix. This optimizes both the composition and the number of base learners necessary to design an effective and compact code matrix. Classifier selection is done by calculating a quality measure for each classifier which predicts how well each base-learner separates the training-set into two relatively homogenous groups. The main strength of DECOC is its ability to provide a competitive accuracy compared with other ECOC methods, using parsimonious base-learners. But this does not come for free. In the process of building, the DECOC uses cross-validation procedures. This process takes a lot of time, because in every iteration it builds a classifier for every base learner. This latter step is done as a preprocess and doesn't affect the running time for testing samples. But if there are time and space limitations for our preprocess with the training-set, it might be a problem.

Some attempts have been made to simultaneously find a code matrix and the set of binary classifiers that produce the lowest empirical loss. Usually the columns of the code matrix and binary classifiers are created in a stage-wise manner.

Finding the optimal solution for this problem has been shown to be NP-hard [Crammer and Singer (2002)]. Nevertheless, several heuristics have been developed. The most popular heuristics attempt to combine the ECOC framework with the AdaBoost framework. More specifically, two algorithms are very widely used: output-code AdaBoost (AdaBoost.OC) [Schapire (1997)], and error-correcting code AdaBoost (AdaBoost.ECC)

[Guruswami and Sahai (1999)].

Figure 8.2 presents the AdaBoost.OC algorithm. In each iteration, a weak classifier is induced. The instances are reweighted by focusing on the misclassified instances. Then, as in ECOC, a new binary decomposition (coloring) is selected in each iteration . There are several ways to find the coloring function. The simplest option is to uniformly and independently choose each value at random from $\{-1, 1\}$. A better option is to choose at random but to ensure an even split of the labels, i.e. half should be labeled as -1 and half as 1. The third option is to maximize the value of U_t by using optimization algorithms.

Given: $(x_1, y_1), \ldots, (x_m, y_m) : x_i \in X, y_i \in Y, |Y| = k$
Initialize: $\tilde{D}_1(i, l) = 1/m(k-1)$ if $l \neq y_i$, $\tilde{D}_1(l, l) = 0 \; \forall l \in Y$.

For $t = 1, 2, \ldots, T$:
    Compute coloring $\mu_t : Y \longrightarrow \{-1, +1\}$.
    Let $U_t = \sum_{i=1}^{m} \sum_{l \in Y} \tilde{D}_t(i, l) [\![\mu_t(y_i) \neq \mu_t(l)]\!]$.
    Let $D_t(i) = \frac{1}{U_t} \cdot \sum_{l \in Y} \tilde{D}_t(i, l) [\![\mu_t(y_i) \neq \mu_t(l)]\!]$.
    Get hypothesis $h_t : X \longrightarrow \{-1, +1\}$ from the weak learner for distribution D_t.
    Let $\tilde{h}_t(x) = \{l \in Y : h_t(x) = \mu_t(l)\}$.
    Let $\tilde{\varepsilon}_t = \frac{1}{2} \sum_{i=1}^{m} \sum_{l \in Y} \tilde{D}_t(i, l) \cdot \left([\![y_i \notin \tilde{h}_t(x_i)]\!] + [\![l \in \tilde{h}_t(x_i)]\!] \right)$.
    Let $\alpha_t = \frac{1}{2} \ln \left(\frac{1 - \tilde{\varepsilon}_t}{\tilde{\varepsilon}_t} \right)$.
    Update:
$$\tilde{D}_{t+1}(i, l) = \frac{1}{\tilde{Z}_t} \cdot \tilde{D}_t(i, l) \exp \left\{ \alpha_t ([\![y_i \notin \tilde{h}_t(x_i)]\!] + [\![l \in \tilde{h}_t(x_i)]\!]) \right\}$$
    where $\tilde{Z}_t$ is a normalization factor.

Fig. 8.2: The algorithm AdaBoost.OC combining boosting and output coding.

Figure 8.3 presents the AdaBoost.ECC algorithm. The AdaBoost.ECC algorithm works similarly to AdaBoost.OC. However, instead of reweighting the instances based on the pseudo-loss, it uses the structure of the current classifier and its performance on the binary learning problem.

Sun *et al* (2005) prove that AdaBoost.ECC performs stage-wise functional gradient descent on a cost function, defined in the domain of margin values. Moreover Sun *et al.* (2005) prove that AdaBoost.OC is a shrinkage version of AdaBoost.ECC. Shrinkage can be considered as a method, for improving accuracy in the case of noisy data. Thus, Sun *et al.* (2005) conclude that in low noise datasets, AdaBoost.ECC may have some advantages over AdaBoost.OC. Yet, in noisy data sets, AdaBoost.OC should outperform AdaBoost.ECC.

Given: $(x_1, y_1), \ldots, (x_m, y_m) : x_i \in X, y_i \in Y, |Y| = k$
Initialize: $\tilde{D}_1(i, l) = 1/m(k-1)$ if $l \neq y_i$, $\tilde{D}_1(i, l) = 0$ if $l = y_i$.

For $t = 1, 2, \ldots, T$:
    Compute coloring $\mu_t : Y \longrightarrow \{-1, +1\}$.
    Let $U_t = \sum_{i=1}^{m} \sum_{l \in Y} \tilde{D}_t(i, l) [\![\mu_t(y_i) \neq \mu_t(l)]\!]$.
    Let $D_t(i) = \frac{1}{U_t} \cdot \sum_{l \in Y} \tilde{D}_t(i, l) [\![\mu_t(y_i) \neq \mu_t(l)]\!]$.
    Get hypothesis $h_t : X \longrightarrow \{-1, +1\}$ from the weak learner for distribution D_t.
    Compute the weight of positive and negative votes α_t and β_t respectively.
    Define:
        $g_t(x) = \alpha_t$ if $h_t(x) = +1$
                $= -\beta_t$ if $h_t(x) = -1$.
    Update:
        $\tilde{D}_{t+1}(i, l) = \frac{1}{\tilde{Z}_t} \cdot \tilde{D}_t(i, l) \exp\left\{ (g_t(x_i)\mu_t(l) - g_t(x_i)\mu_t(y_i))/2 \right\}$
    where $\tilde{Z}_t$ is a normalization factor.

Fig. 8.3: The algorithm AdaBoost.ECC combining boosting and output coding.

Crammer and Singer (2000) explain how to design code matrix by adapting it to each multiclass problem under consideration. Finding a discrete code matrix can be considered a NP-hard problem. Thus, they relaxed the problem, by allowing the matrix elements having continuous values. Thereupon, they obtained a variant of SVMs for the direct solution of multiclass problems. The predictive performance of this technique is comparable to those of the 1AA and 1A1 strategies [Hsu and Lin (2002)]. Nevertheless, the computational cost of this adaptive training algorithm is higher than the ready made matrices.

One can also combine linear binary classifiers in order to obtain a nonlinear multiclass classifier [Alpaydin and Mayoraz (1999)] . In this process, a MLP NN is obtained in which the first weight layer represents the parameters of the linear classifiers; the internal nodes correspond to the linear classifiers; and the final weight layer is equivalent to the code matrix. This NN has an architecture and second layer weights initialized according to a code matrix. As a result, the code matrix and classifiers parameters are optimized jointly in the NN training. The proposed method showed higher accuracy than those of 1AA, 1A1 and ECOC decompositions employing linear binary classifiers.

Dekel and Singer (2003) develop a bunching algorithm which adapts code matrices to the multiclass problem during the learning process. First, the training instances are mapped to a common space where it is possible to measure the divergence between input instances and their labels. Two matrices are used in the mapping process, one for the data and the other

for the labels, which is the code matrix. These two matrices are iteratively adapted by the algorithm in order to obtain a minimum error for
the training data. This error is measured by the divergence between the
training data and their labels in the common space. The code matrices are
probabilistic. Given an initial code matrix, the the algorithm modifies it
according to the previous procedure. Given a new instance, it is mapped
to the new space and the predicted class is the one closer to the instance
in this space. This algorithm was used for improving the performance of
logistic regression classifiers [Collins *et al.* (2002)].

Rätsch *et al.* (2003) define an optimization problem, in which the codes
and the embedding functions f are determined jointly by maximizing a
margin measure. The embedding functions ensure that instances from the
same class are close to their respective codeword vector. The margin is
defined as the difference between the distance of $\vec{f}(\vec{x})$ from the actual class
and the to closer incorrect class.

In [Pujol *et al.* (2006)] a heuristic method for designing ternary code
matrices is introduced. The design is based on a hierarchical partition of the
classes according to a discriminative criterion. The criterion used was the
mutual information between the feature data and its class label. Initiating
with all classes, they are recursively partitioned into two subsets in order
to maximize the mutual information measure until each subset contains
one class. These partitions define the binary classifiers to be employed in
the code matrix. For a problem with k classes, $k - 1$ binary classifiers are
generated in this process. Experimental results demonstrated the potential
of the approach using DTs and boosted decision stumps (BDS) [Freund
and Schapire (1997)] as base classifiers. The algorithm showed results that
were competitive to 1AA, 1A1 and random code matrices.

In [Lorena and Carvalho (2007)], GAs were used to determine ternary
code matrices according to their performance in multiclass problem solution. In such cases, the code matrices are adapted to each multiclass
problem. Another goal in implementing GAs is to minimize the number of
columns in the matrices in order to produce simpler decompositions.

Chapter 9

Evaluating Ensembles of Classifiers

In this chapter, we introduce the main concepts and quality criteria in ensemble classifier evaluation. Evaluating the performance of an ensemble is a fundamental aspect of pattern recognition. The evaluation is important for understanding the quality of a certain ensemble algorithm and tuning its parameters.

While there are several criteria for evaluating the predictive performance of ensemble classifiers, other criteria such as the computational complexity or the comprehensibility of the generated ensemble can be important as well.

9.1 Generalization Error

Historically, predictive performance measures have been the main criteria for selecting inducers. Moreover, predictive performance measures, such as accuracy, are considered to be objective and quantifiable, and thus are frequently used to benchmark algorithms.

In addition to the experimental studies performed to validate the contribution of a new ensemble method, several large comparative studies have been conducted, which aim to assist the practitioner in his/her decision-making.

Let $E(S)$ represent an ensemble trained on dataset S. The generalization error of $E(S)$ is its probability to misclassify an instance selected according to the distribution D of the labeled instance space. The *classification accuracy* of an ensemble is one minus the generalization error. The *training error* is defined as the percentage of examples in the training set correctly classified by the ensemble, formally:

$$\hat{\varepsilon}(E(S), S) = \sum_{\langle x,y \rangle \in S} L\left(y, E(S)(x)\right) \qquad (9.1)$$

where $L(y, E(S)(x))$ is the zero-one loss function defined in Chapter 1 (Equation 1.3).

In this book, classification accuracy and generalization error are the primary evaluation criteria. Although generalization error is a natural criterion, its actual value is only known in rare cases (mainly synthetic cases). The reason for that is that the distribution D of the labeled instance space is not known.

One can take the training error as an estimation of the generalization error. However, using the training error as is will typically provide an optimistically biased estimate, especially if the inducer *overfits* the training data. There are two main approaches for estimating the generalization error: theoretical and empirical. In this book we utilize both approaches.

9.1.1 *Theoretical Estimation of Generalization Error*

Low training error does not guarantee low generalization error. There is often a tradeoff between the training error and the confidence assigned to the training error as a predictor for the generalization error, measured by the difference between the generalization and training errors. The capacity of the inducer is a major factor in determining the degree of confidence in the training error. In general, the capacity of an inducer indicates the variety of classifiers it can induce. Breiman's upper bound on the generalization error of random forest (Breiman, 2001) which is expressed "in terms of two parameters that are measures of how accurate the individual classifiers are and of the agreement between them." While Breiman's bound is theoretically justified, it is not considered to be very tight (Kuncheva, 2004).

Bartlett and Traskin (2007) showed that AdaBoost is almost certainly consistent (i.e., the ensemble's risk usually converges to the Bayes risk), if stopped sufficiently early, after $m^{1-\alpha}$ iterations where m is the training set size. However, they could not determine whether this number can be increased.

Large ensembles with many members relative to the size of the training set are likely to obtain low training error. On the other hand, they might simply be memorizing or overfitting the patterns and hence exhibit poor generalization ability. In such cases, low error is likely to be a poor predictor of higher generalization error. When the opposite occurs, that is to say, when capacity is too small for the given number of examples, inducers may underfit the data and exhibit both poor training and generalization error.

In "Mathematics of Generalization," [Wolpert (1995)] discuss four theoretical frameworks for estimating the generalization error: probably approximately correct (PAC), VC , Bayesian, and statistical physics. All of these frameworks combine the training error (which can be easily calculated) with some penalty function expressing the capacity of the inducers.

9.1.2 *Empirical Estimation of Generalization Error*

Another approach for estimating the generalization error is the holdout method in which the given dataset is randomly partitioned into two sets: training and test sets. Usually, two-thirds of the data is considered for the training set and the remaining data is allocated to the test set. First, the training set is used by the inducer to construct a suitable classifier, and then the misclassification rate of this classifier on the test set is measured. This test set error usually provides a better estimation of the generalization error than the training error. The reason for this is the fact that the training error usually underestimates the generalization error (due to the overfitting phenomena). Nevertheless, since only a proportion of the data is used to derive the model, the test accuracy estimate tends to be pessimistic. It is important to remember that the test set cannot be used for tuning the learning algorithm nor for selecting the best performing approach. For this purpose we can define a third set known as validation set.

The validation set provides a predictive performance evaluation of the trained model while tuning its hyperparameters (e.g. selecting the loss function to be minimized). The validation set is frequently used for regularization to avoid overfitting. For example, it can be used to tune the number of iterations in gradient boosting trees that yields the best performance. For this purpose we can use an early stopping procedure, where after each learning iteration we test the model's predictive performance on the validation set. We stop the training when the error on the validation set cease to decrease and start to increase.

A variation of the holdout method can be used when data is limited. It is common practice to resample the data, that is, partition the data into training and test sets in different ways. An inducer is trained and tested for each partition, and the accuracies are averaged. By doing this, a more reliable estimate of the true generalization error of the inducer is provided.

Random subsampling and n-fold cross-validation are two common methods of resampling. In random subsampling, the data is randomly partitioned several times into disjoint training and test sets. Errors obtained from each partition are averaged. In n-fold cross-validation, the data is randomly split into n mutually exclusive subsets of approximately equal size. An inducer is trained and tested n times; each time it is tested on one of the k folds and trained using the remaining $n-1$ folds.

The cross-validation estimate of the generalization error is the overall number of misclassifications divided by the number of examples in the data. The random subsampling method has the advantage that it can be repeated an indefinite number of times. However, a disadvantage is that the test sets are not independently drawn with respect to the underlying distribution of examples. Because of this, using a t-test for paired differences with random subsampling can lead to an increased chance of type I error, i.e., identifying a significant difference when one does not actually exist. Using a t-test on the generalization error produced on each fold lowers the chances of type I error but may not give a stable estimate of the generalization error. It is common practice to repeat n-fold cross-validation n times in order to provide a stable estimate. However, this, of course, renders the test sets non-independent and increases the chance of type I error. Unfortunately, there is no satisfactory solution to this problem. Alternative tests suggested by [Dietterich (1998)] have a low probability of type I error but a higher chance of type II error, that is, failing to identify a significant difference when one does actually exist.

Stratification is a process often applied during random subsampling and n-fold cross-validation. Stratification ensures that the class distribution from the whole dataset is preserved in the training and test sets. Stratification has been shown to help reduce the variance of the estimated error especially for datasets with many classes.

Another well-known validation procedure is the bootstrapping. Given that n is the number of samples in the original set, bootstrapping method repeatedly samples with replacement n instances from the original training set . In each repetition, instances that were chosen by the sampling procedure are used to train the model. Testing is performed using the remaining instances that were not included in the training set.

Dietterich [Dietterich (2000a)] has compared three methods for constructing a forest of C4.5 classifiers: randomizing, bagging, and boosting. The experiments show that when there is little noise in the data, boosting gives the best results. Bagging and randomizing are usually equivalent.

Another study [Bauer and Kohavi (1999)], which compared bagging and boosting using decision trees and naive Bayes, determined that bagging reduced the variance of unstable methods, while boosting methods reduced both the bias and variance of unstable methods but increased the variance for stable methods.

Additional study [Opitz and Maclin (1999)] that compared bagging with boosting using neural networks and decision trees indicates that bagging is sometimes significantly less accurate than boosting. The study indicates that the performance of boosting methods is much more sensitive to the characteristics of the dataset, finding more specifically that boosting may overfit noisy data sets and reduce classification performance.

Villalba *et al.* (2003) compared seven different boosting methods. They conclude that for binary classification tasks the well-known AdaBoost is preferred. However, for multiclass tasks other boosting methods such as Gentle AdaBoost should be considered.

A recent study experimentally evaluated bagging and seven other randomization-based approaches for creating an ensemble of decision tree classifiers [Banfield *et al.* (2007)]. Statistical tests were performed on experimental results using 57 publicly available datasets. When cross-validation comparisons were tested for statistical significance, the best method was statistically more accurate than bagging on only eight of the 57 datasets. Alternatively, examining the average ranks of the algorithms across the group of datasets, Banfield *et al* found that boosting, random forest, and randomized trees are significantly better than bagging.

Sohna and Shinb [Sohna (2007)] compared the performance of several ensemble methods (bagging, modified random subspace method, classifier selection, and parametric fusion) to a single classifier, assuming that the base inducer is logistic regression. They argue that several factors should be taken into consideration when performing such comparison, including correlation between input variables, variance of observation, and training dataset size. They show that for large training sets, the performance of a single logistic regression and bagging are not significantly different. However, when the training set size is small, bagging is superior to a single logistic regression classifier. When the training dataset size is small and correlation is strong, both the modified random subspace method and bagging perform better than the other methods. When correlation is weak and variance is small, both parametric fusion and the classifier selection algorithm appear to perform the worst.

9.1.3   *Alternatives to the Accuracy Measure*

Accuracy is not a sufficient measure for evaluating a model with an imbalanced distribution of the class. There are cases where the estimation of the accuracy rate may be misleading in terms of the quality of a derived classifier. In circumstances where the dataset contains significantly more majority class than minority class instances, one can always select the majority class and obtain good accuracy performance. Therefore, in these cases, sensitivity and specificity measures can be used as an alternative to accuracy measures [Han and Kamber (2001)]. *Sensitivity*, (also known as recall), assesses how well the classifier can recognize positive samples and is defined as:

$$Sensitivity = \frac{true\_positive}{positive} \qquad (9.2)$$

where *true_positive* corresponds to the number of true positive samples, and positive is the number of positive samples.

Specificity measures how well the classifier can recognize negative samples. It is defined as

$$Specificity = \frac{true\_negative}{negative} \qquad (9.3)$$

where *true_negative* corresponds to the number of cases where the model predicts negative and the actual outcome was negative. The *negative* corresponds to the number of samples that are actually negative (regardless of the model's prediction).

Precision is another well-known performance measure. Precision measures how many examples classified as "positive" class are indeed "positive." This measure is useful for evaluating crisp classifiers that are used to classify an entire dataset. Formally:

$$Precision = \frac{true\_positive}{true\_positive + false\_positive} \qquad (9.4)$$

Based on the above definitions, the *accuracy* can be defined as a function of *sensitivity* and *specificity*:

$$Accuracy = Sensitivity \cdot \frac{positive}{positive+negative} + \\ Specificity \cdot \frac{negative}{positive+negative} \qquad (9.5)$$

9.1.4 *The F-Measure*

Usually there is a tradeoff between the precision and recall measures. Trying to improve one measure often results in the deterioration of the second measure. Figure 9.1 illustrates a typical precision-recall curve. This two-dimensional graph is closely related to the well-known receiver operating characteristics (ROC) graphs in which the true positive rate (recall) is plotted on the y-axis, and the false positive rate is plotted on the x-axis [Ferri *et al.* (2002)]. However, unlike the precision-recall graph, the ROC diagram is always convex.

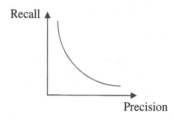

Fig. 9.1: A typical precision-recall diagram.

Given a probabilistic classifier, this tradeoff graph may be obtained by setting different threshold values. In a binary classification problem, the classifier prefers the "not pass" class over the "pass" class if the probability for "not pass" is at least 0.5. However, by setting a threshold value other than 0.5, the tradeoff graph can be obtained.

The problem here is described as multicriteria decision-making (MCDM). The simplest and most commonly used method to address MCDM is the weighted sum model. This technique combines the criteria into a single value by using appropriate weighting. The basic principle behind this technique is the additive utility assumption. The criteria measures must be numerical, comparable, and expressed in the same unit. Nevertheless, in the case discussed here, the arithmetic mean can be misleading. Instead, the harmonic mean provides a better notion of "average." More specifically, this measure is defined as [Van Rijsbergen (1979)]:

$$F = \frac{2 \cdot P \cdot R}{P + R} \tag{9.6}$$

The intuition behind the F-measure can be explained using Figure 9.2. Figure 9.2 presents a diagram of a common situation in which the right ellipsoid represents the set of all defective batches, and the left ellipsoid represents the set of all batches that were classified as defective by a certain classifier. The intersection of these sets represents the true positive (TP), while the remaining parts represent the false negative (FN) and false positive (FP). An intuitive way of measuring the adequacy of a certain classifier is to measure the extent to which the two sets match, namely to measure the size of the unshaded area. Since the absolute size is not meaningful, it should be normalized by calculating the proportional area. This value is the F-measure:

$$\text{Proportion of unshaded area} = \frac{2 \cdot (True\ Positive)}{False\ Positive + False\ Negative + 2 \cdot (True\ Positive)} = F \qquad (9.7)$$

The F-measure can have values ranging from zero to one. It obtains its highest value when the two sets presented in Figure 9.2 are identical, and it obtains its lowest value when the two sets are mutually exclusive. Note that each point on the precision-recall curve may have a different F-measure. Furthermore, different classifiers have different precision-recall graphs.

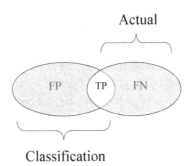

Fig. 9.2: A graphic explanation of the F-measure.

9.1.5 *Confusion Matrix*

The confusion matrix is used as an indication of the properties of a classification (discriminant) rule. It contains the number of elements that have been correctly or incorrectly classified for each class. On its main diagonal we can see the number of observations that have been correctly classified for each class; the off-diagonal elements indicate the number of observations that have been incorrectly classified. One benefit of a confusion matrix is that it makes it is easy to see if the system is confusing two classes (i.e., consistently mislabeling one as another).

For every instance in the test set, we compare the actual class to the class that was assigned by the trained classifier. A positive (negative) example that is correctly classified by the classifier is called a true positive (true negative); a positive (negative) example that is incorrectly classified is called a false negative (false positive). These numbers can be organized in a confusion matrix as shown in Table 9.1.

Table 9.1: A confusion matrix.

	Predicted negative	Predicted positive
Negative Examples	A	B
Positive Examples	C	D

Based on the values in Table 9.1, one can calculate all of the measures defined above:

- Accuracy is: $(a+d)/(a+b+c+d)$
- Misclassification rate is: $(b+c)/(a+b+c+d)$
- Precision is: $d/(b+d)$
- True positive rate (Recall) is: $d/(c+d)$
- False positive rate is: $b/(a+b)$
- True negative rate (Specificity) is: $a/(a+b)$
- False negative rate is: $c/(c+d)$

9.1.6 *Classifier Evaluation Under Limited Resources*

The abovementioned evaluation measures are insufficient when probabilistic classifiers are used to select the objects to be included in a limited quota. This is a common situation that arises in real-life applications due to resource limitations that require cost-benefit considerations. Resource limitations prevent the organization from choosing all of the instances. For example, in direct marketing applications, instead of mailing everybody on the list, marketing efforts must implement a limited quota, i.e., target the mailing audience with the highest probability of positively responding to the marketing offer without exceeding the marketing budget.

Another example deals with a security officer in an air terminal. Following September 11th, security officers need to search every passenger that might be carrying a dangerous instrument (such as scissors, penknives, and razor blades). For this purpose, security personnel use a classifier that is capable of classifying each passenger as class A, which means, "carries dangerous instruments" or class B, "safe."

Suppose that searching a passenger is a time-consuming task, and the security officer can only check 20 passengers prior to each flight. If the classifier has labeled exactly 20 passengers as class A, the officer can check all of these passengers. However, if the classifier has labeled more than 20 passengers as class A, the officer must decide which class A passengers should be ignored. On the other hand, if less than 20 passengers are classified as A, the officer, who must work constantly, has to determine which of the class B passengers to check after he/she has finished checking the class A passengers.

There also cases in which a quota limitation is known to exist but its size is not known in advance. Nevertheless, the decision maker would like to evaluate the expected performance of the classifier. Such situations may occur in some countries regarding the number of undergraduate students that can be accepted to specific departments at a state university. The actual quota for a given year is set according to different parameters, including the budget allocated by the government. In this case, the decision maker would like to evaluate several classifiers for selecting the applicants, while not knowing the actual quota size. Identifying the most appropriate classifier in advance is important, because the chosen classifier can dictate the important attributes, i.e., the information that the applicant should provide in the application process.

In probabilistic classifiers, the abovementioned definitions of precision and recall can be extended and defined as a function of a probability threshold τ. If we evaluate a classifier based on a given a test set which consists of n instances denoted as $(< x_1, y_1 >, \ldots, < x_n, y_n >)$, such that x_i represents the input feature vector of instance i, and y_i represents its true class ("positive" or "negative"), then:

$$\text{Precision } (\tau) = \frac{\left| \{ < x_i, y_i >: \hat{P}_E(pos \,|x_i) > \tau, y_i = pos \} \right|}{\left| \{ < x_i, y_i >: \hat{P}_E(pos \,|x_i) > \tau \right|} \tag{9.8}$$

$$\text{Recall }(\tau) = \frac{\left|\{< x_i, y_i >: \hat{P}_E(pos\,|x_i) > \tau, y_i = pos\}\right|}{\left|\{< x_i, y_i >: y_i = pos\}\right|} \qquad (9.9)$$

where E represents a probabilistic ensemble that is used to estimate the conditional likelihood of an observation x_i to be assigned to the "positive" class which is denoted as $\hat{P}_E(pos\,|x_i)$. The typical threshold value of 0.5 means that the predicted probability of "positive" must be higher than 0.5 for the instance to be predicted as "positive." By changing the value of τ, one can control the number of instances classified as "positive." Thus, the τ value can be tuned to the required quota size. Nevertheless, because there might be several instances with the same conditional probability, the quota size is not necessarily incremented by one.

The discussion above is based on the assumption that the classification problem is binary. In cases where there are more than two classes, adaptation could be easily made by comparing one class to all of the others.

9.1.6.1 *ROC Curves*

Another measure is the receiver operating characteristic (ROC) curve which illustrates the tradeoff between true positive to false positive rates [Provost and Fawcett (1998)]. Figure 9.3 illustrates a ROC curve in which the x-axis represents a false positive rate, and the y-axis represents a true positive rate. The ideal point on the ROC curve would be (0,100), that is, all positive examples are classified correctly, and no negative examples are misclassified as positive.

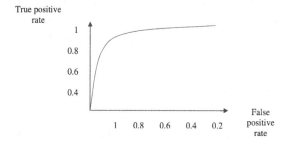

Fig. 9.3: A typical ROC curve.

The ROC convex hull can also be used as a robust method of identifying potentially optimal classifiers [Provost and Fawcett (2001)]. Given a family of ROC curves, the ROC convex hull can include points that are more towards the north-west frontier of the ROC space. If a line passes through a point on the convex hull, there is no other line with the same slope passing through another point with a larger true positive (TP) intercept.

9.1.6.2   *Hit Rate Curve*

The hit rate curve presents the hit ratio as a function of the quota size[An and Wang (2001)]. The *hit rate* is calculated by counting the actual positive labeled instances within a predetermined quota. More precisely, for a quota of size j and a ranked set of instances, *hit rate* is defined as:

$$\text{HitRate}(j) = \frac{\sum_{k=1}^{j} t^{[k]}}{j} \tag{9.10}$$

where $t^{[k]}$ represents the expected outcome of the instance located in the k'th position when the instances are sorted according to their conditional probability for "positive" in descending order. Note that if the k'th position can be uniquely defined (i.e., there is exactly one instance that can be located in this position), $t^{[k]}$ is either zero or one, depending on the actual outcome of this specific instance. Nevertheless, if the k'th position is not uniquely defined, and there are $m_{k,1}$ instances that can be located in this position, $m_{k,2}$ of which are truly positive, then:

$$t^{[k]} = m_{k,2}/m_{k,1} \tag{9.11}$$

The sum of $t^{[k]}$ over the entire test set is equal to the number of instances that are labeled "positive." Moreover, $Hit - Rate(j) \approx Precision(p^{[j]})$ where $p^{[j]}$ denotes the j'th order of $\hat{P}_I(pos\,|x_1),\cdot,\hat{P}_I(pos\,|x_m)$. The values are strictly equal when the value of j'th is uniquely defined.

9.1.6.3   *Qrecall (Quota Recall)*

The hit rate measure presented above is the "precision" equivalent for quota-limited problems. Similarly, we suggest the qrecall (for quota recall) to be the "recall" equivalent for quota-limited problems. The qrecall for a certain position in a ranked list is calculated by dividing the number of positive instances (from the beginning of the list until that position) by the total positive instances in the entire dataset. Thus, the qrecall for a quota of j is defined as:

$$\text{Qrecall}(j) = \frac{\sum_{k=1}^{j} t^{[k]}}{n^+} \tag{9.12}$$

The denominator stands for the total number of instances that are classified as positive in the entire dataset. Formally, it can be calculated as:

$$n^+ = |\{< x_i, y_i >: y_i = pos\}| \tag{9.13}$$

9.1.6.4 *Lift Curve*

A popular method of evaluating probabilistic models is *lift* [Coppock (2002)]. After a ranked test set has been divided into several portions (usually deciles), lift is calculated as follows: the ratio of positive instances in a specific decile is divided by the average ratio of positive instances in the population. Regardless of how the test set is divided, a good model is achieved if the lift decreases when proceeding to the end of the scoring list. A good model should demonstrate a lift greater than one in the top deciles and a lift smaller than one in the last deciles. Figure 9.4 illustrates a lift chart for a typical model prediction. A comparison between models can be made by comparing the lift of the top portions, depending on the resources available and cost/benefit considerations.

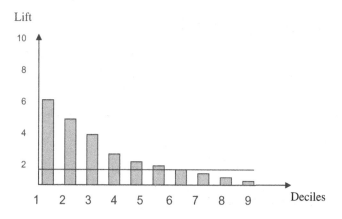

Fig. 9.4: A typical lift chart.

9.1.6.5   *Pearson Correlation Coefficient*

There are also some statistical measures that may be used to evaluate models' performance. These measures are well-known and can be found in many introductory statistics books. In this section, we examine the Pearson correlation coefficient. This measure can be used to determine the correlation between the ordered estimated conditional probability ($p^{[k]}$) and the ordered actual expected outcome ($t^{[k]}$). A Pearson correlation coefficient can have any value between -1 and 1, where the value 1 represents the strongest positive correlation. It should be noted that this measure takes into account not only the ordinal place of an instance but also its value (i.e., the estimated probability attached to it). The *Pearson* correlation coefficient for two random variables is calculated by dividing the co-variance by the product of both standard deviations. In this case, the standard deviations of the two variables assuming a quota size of j are:

$$\sigma_p(j) = \sqrt{\frac{1}{j}\sum_{i=1}^{j}\left(p^{[i]} - \bar{p}(j)\right)} \; ; \; \sigma_t(j) = \sqrt{\frac{1}{j}\sum_{i=1}^{j}\left(t^{[i]} - \bar{t}(j)\right)} \qquad (9.14)$$

where $\bar{p}(j), \bar{t}(j)$ represents the average of $p^{[i]}$'s and $t^{[i]}$'s respectively:

$$\bar{p}(j) = \frac{\sum_{i=1}^{j} p^{[i]}}{j} \quad ; \quad \bar{t}(j) = \frac{\sum_{i=1}^{j} t^{[i]}}{j} = HitRate(j) \qquad (9.15)$$

The co-variance is calculated as follows:

$$Cov_{p,t}(j) = \frac{1}{j}\sum_{i-1}^{j}\left(p^{[i]} - \bar{p}(j)\right)\left(t^{[i]} - \bar{t}(j)\right) \qquad (9.16)$$

Thus, the Pearson correlation coefficient for a quota j is:

$$\rho_{p,t}(j) = \frac{Cov_{p,t}(j)}{\sigma_p(j) \cdot \sigma_t(j)} \qquad (9.17)$$

9.1.6.6   *Area Under Curve (AUC)*

Evaluating a probabilistic model without using a specific fixed quota is not a trivial task. Using continuous measures like hit curves, ROC curves, and lift charts, mentioned previously, is problematic. Such measures can give a definite answer to the question "Which is the best model?" only if one model dominates in the curve space, meaning that the curves of all of the other models are beneath it or equal to it over the entire chart space. If a dominating model does not exist, then there is no answer to that question when using just the continuous measures mentioned above. Perfect order demands no intersections of the curves. Of course, in practice there is almost never one dominating model. In such cases we can divide the x-axis into intervals such that in each interval one model clearly outperforms the others.

As shown in Figure 9.5, every model obtains different values in different areas. If a perfect order of model performance is needed, another measure should be used.

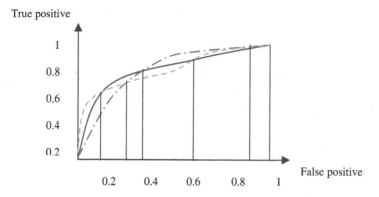

Fig. 9.5: Areas of dominancy. A ROC curve is an example of a measure that gives areas of dominancy and not a perfect order of the models. In this example, the equally dashed line model is the best for f.p (false positive) < 0.2. The solid line model is the best for 0.2 < f.p <0.4. The dotted line model is best for 0.4 < f.p < 0.9, and from 0.9 to 1 the dashed line model is again the best.

The area under the ROC curve (AUC) is a useful metric for classifier performance, since it is independent of the decision criterion selected and prior probabilities. The AUC comparison can establish a dominance relationship between classifiers. If the ROC curves intersect, the total AUC is an average comparison between models [Lee (2000)]. The larger it is, the better the model is. As opposed to other measures, the area under the ROC curve (AUC) does not depend on the imbalance of the training set

[Kolcz (2003)]. Thus, a comparison of the AUC of two classifiers is fairer and more informative than comparing their misclassification rates.

9.1.6.7 *Average Hit Rate*

The average hit rate is a weighted average of all of the hit rate values. If the model is optimal, all of the actual positive instances are located at the beginning of the ranked list, and the value of the average hit rate is one. The use of this measure is appropriate for an organization that needs to minimize type II statistical error (namely, to include a certain object in the quota, although the object will be labeled as "negative"). Formally, the average hit rate for a binary classification problems is defined as:

$$AverageHitRate = \frac{\sum_{j=1}^{n} t^{[j]} \cdot HitRate(j)}{n^+} \quad (9.18)$$

where $t^{[j]}$ is defined as in Equation 4 and is used as a weighting factor. Note that the average hit rate ignores all hit rate values on unique positions that are actually labeled as the "negative" class (because $t^{[j]}=0$ in these cases).

9.1.6.8 *Average Qrecall*

Average qrecall is the average of all the qrecalls that extend from the position that is equal to the number of positive instances in the test set to the bottom of the list. Average qrecall is suitable for an organization that needs to minimize type I statistical error (namely, not including a certain object in the quota although the object will be labeled as "positive"). Formally, the average Qrecall is defined as:

$$\frac{\sum_{j=n^+}^{n} Qrecall(j)}{n - (n^+ - 1)} \quad (9.19)$$

where n is the total number of instances, and n^+ is defined in Equation (9.13).

Table 9.2 illustrates the calculation of the average qrecall and average hit rate for a dataset of ten instances. The table presents a list of instances in descending order according to their estimated conditional probability to be classified as "positive."

Because all probabilities are unique, the third column $(t^{[k]})$ indicates the actual class ("1" represents "positive" and "0" represents "negative"). The average values are simple algebraic averages of the highlighted cells.

Table 9.2: An example for calculating average Qrecall and average hit rate.

Place in list (j)	Positive proba-bility	$t^{[k]}$	Qrecall	Hit rate
1	0.45	1	0.25	1
2	0.34	0	0.25	0.5
3	0.32	1	0.5	0.667
4	0.26	1	0.75	0.75
5	0.15	0	0.75	0.6
6	0.14	0	0.75	0.5
7	0.09	1	1	0.571
8	0.07	0	1	0.5
9	0.06	0	1	0.444
10	0.03	0	1	0.4
		Average:	0.893	0.747

Note that both *average qrecall* and *average hit rate* obtain a value of one in an optimum classification, where all of the positive instances are located at the beginning of the list. This case is illustrated in Table 9.3. A summary of the key differences is provided in Table 9.4.

Table 9.3: Qrecall and hit rate in an optimum prediction.

Place in list (j)	Positive proba-bility	$t^{[k]}$	Qrecall	Hit rate
1	0.45	1	0.25	1
2	0.34	1	0. 5	1
3	0.32	1	0.75	1
4	0.26	1	1	1
5	0.15	0	1	0.8
6	0.14	0	1	0.667
7	0.09	0	1	0.571
8	0.07	0	1	0.5
9	0.06	0	1	0.444
10	0.03	0	1	0.4
		Average:	1	1

Table 9.4: Characteristics of Qrecall and hit rate.

Parameter	Hit-rate	Qrecall
Function increasing/decreasing	Non-monotonic	Monotonically increasing
End point	Proportion of positive samples in the set	1
Sensitivity of the measure's value to positive instances	Very sensitive to positive instances at the beginning of the list. Less sensitive to the instances at the bottom of the list.	Same sensitivity to positive instances in all places on the list.
Effect of negative class on the measure	A negative instance affects the measure and causes its value to decrease.	A negative instance does not affect the measure.
Range	0≤ Hit rate ≤1	0≤ Qrecall ≤1

9.1.6.9 *Potential Extract Measure (PEM)*

To better understand the behavior of qrecall curves, consider the cases of random prediction and optimum prediction.

Suppose no learning process was applied on the data, and the list produced as a prediction is the test set in its original (random) order. On the assumption that positive instances are distributed uniformly in the population, a random size quota contains a number of positive instances that are proportional to the a priori proportion of positive instances in the population. Thus, a qrecall curve that describes a uniform distribution (which can be considered as a model that predicts as well as a random guess, without any learning) is a linear line (or semilinear because values are discrete) which starts at zero (for a zero quota size) and ends in one.

Suppose now that a model gave an optimal prediction, meaning that all of the positive instances are located at the beginning of the list, and all negative instances are located at the end of the list. In this case, the qrecall curve climbs linearly until a value of one is achieved at point n^+ (n^+ = number of positive samples).

Note that a "good model" which outperforms random classification, though not an optimal one, will fall, on average,' between these two curves.

Occasionally it may drop below the random curve, but generally, more area is delineated between the "good model" curve and the random curve. If the opposite is true, the model is a "bad model" which performs worse than a random guess.

The last observation leads us to consider a measure that evaluates the performance of a model by summing the areas delineated between the qrecall curve of the examined model and the qrecall curve of a random model (which is linear). Areas above the linear curve are added to the total sum, and areas below the linear curve are subtracted from the total sum. The areas themselves are calculated by subtracting the qrecall of a random classification from the qrecall of the model's classification at every point, as shown in Figure 9.6. The areas where the model performed better than a random guess increase the measure's value, while the areas where the model performed worse than a random guess decrease it. If the last total computed area is divided within the area delineated between the optimal model's qrecall curve and the random model's (linear) qrecall curve, it reaches the extent to which the potential is extracted, independently of the number of instances in the dataset.

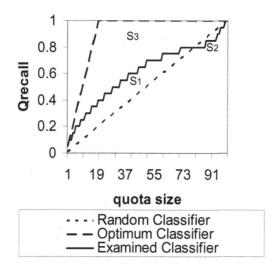

Fig. 9.6: A qualitative representation of PEM.

Formally, the PEM measure is calculated as:

$$PEM = \frac{S_1 - S_2}{S_3} \qquad (9.20)$$

where S_1 is the area bounded between the qrecall curve of the examined model above the qrecall curve of a random model; S_2 is the area bounded between the qrecall curve of the examined model under the qrecall curve of a random model; and S_3 is the area bounded between the optimal qrecall curve and the curve of the random model. The division by S_3 is required in order to normalize the measure, thus datasets of different sizes can be compared. In this way, if the model is optimal, the PEM obtains a value of one. If the model is as good as a random choice, the PEM obtains the value zero. If it obtains the worst possible result (that is to say, it puts the positive samples at the end of the list), then its PEM is -1. Based on the notations defined above, the PEM can be formulated as:

$$PEM = \frac{S_1 - S_2}{S_3} = \frac{\sum_{j=1}^{n} \left(qrecall(j) - \frac{j}{n} \right)}{\sum_{j=1}^{n^+} \left(\frac{j}{n^+} \right) + n^- - \sum_{j=1}^{n} \left(\frac{j}{n} \right)} \qquad (9.21)$$

$$= \frac{\sum_{j=1}^{n} \left(qrecall(j) \right) - \frac{(n+1)}{2}}{\frac{(n^++1)}{2} + n^- - \frac{(n+1)}{2}} = \frac{\sum_{j=1}^{n} \left(qrecall(j) \right) - \frac{(n+1)}{2}}{\frac{n^-}{2}} \qquad (9.22)$$

where n^- denotes the number of instances that are actually classified as "negative." Table 9.5 illustrates the calculation of the PEM for the instances in Table 9.2. Note that the random qrecall does not represent a certain realization but rather represents the expected values. The optimal qrecall is calculated as if the "positive" instances were located at the beginning of the list.

Note that the PEM somewhat resembles the Gini index produced from Lorentz curves which are used in economics when dealing with the distribution of income. Indeed, this measure represents the difference between the distribution of positive samples in a prediction and the uniform distribution. Note also that this measure provides an indication of the total lift of the model at every point. In every quota size, the difference between the qrecall of the model and the qrecall of a random model estimates the the potential gain in accuracy due to the use in the model (for good or for bad).

Table 9.5: An example for calculating PEM for instances of Table 9.2.

Place in list	Success probability	$t^{[k]}$	Model Qrecall	Random Qrecall	Optimal Qrecall	S1	S2	S3
1	0.45	1	0.25	0.1	0.25	0.15	0	0.15
2	0.34	0	0.25	0.2	0.5	0.05	0	0.3
3	0.32	1	0.5	0.3	0.75	0.2	0	0.45
4	0.26	1	0.75	0.4	1	0.35	0	0.6
5	0.15	0	0.75	0.5	1	0.25	0	0.5
6	0.14	0	0.75	0.6	1	0.15	0	0.4
7	0.09	1	1	0.7	1	0.3	0	0.3
8	0.07	0	1	0.8	1	0.2	0	0.2
9	0.06	0	1	0.9	1	0.1	0	0.1
10	0.03	0	1	1	1	0	0	0
					Total	1.75	0	3

9.1.7 Statistical Tests for Comparing Ensembles

In this section, we discuss some of the most common statistical methods proposed [Dietterich (1998)] for answering the following question: *Given two inducers A and B and a dataset S, which inducer will produce more accurate classifiers when trained on datasets of the same size?*

9.1.7.1 McNemar's Test

Let S be the available set of data, which is divided into a training set R and a test set T. Then we consider two inducers A and B trained on the training set. The result is two classifiers which are tested on T, and for each example $x \in T$, we record its classification. Thus, the contingency table presented in Table 9.6 is constructed.

Table 9.6: McNemar's test: contingency table.

Number of examples misclassified by both classifiers (n_{00})	Number of examples misclassified by $\hat{f}_A$ but not by $\hat{f}_B$(n_{01})
Number of examples misclassified by $\hat{f}_B$ but not by $\hat{f}_A$(n_{10})	Number of examples misclassified neither by $\hat{f}_A$ nor by $\hat{f}_B$(n_{11})

The two inducers should have the same error rate under the null hypothesis H_0. The McNemar's test is based on a χ^2 test for goodness of fit that compares the expected counts under the null hypothesis to the observed counts. The expected counts under H_0 are presented in Table 9.7.

Table 9.7: Expected counts under H_0.

n_{00}	$(n_{01} + n_{10})/2$
$(n_{01} + n_{10})/2$	$n_{11})$

The statistic s is distributed as χ^2 with one degree of freedom. It incorporates a "continuity correction" term (of -1 in the numerator) to account for the fact that the statistic is discrete while the χ^2 distribution is continuous:

$$s = \frac{(|n_{10} - n_{01}| - 1)^2}{n_{10} + n_{01}} \qquad (9.23)$$

According to the probabilistic theory [Athanasopoulos (1991)], if the null hypothesis is correct, the probability that the value of the statistic, s, is greater than $\chi^2_{1,0.95}$ is less than 0.05, i.e. $P(|s| > \chi^2_{1,0.95}) < 0.05$. Then, to compare the inducers A and B, the induced classifiers $\hat{f}_A$ and $\hat{f}_B$ are tested on T, and the value of s is estimated as described above. Then, if $|s| > \chi^2_{1,0.95}$, the null hypothesis could be rejected in favor of the hypothesis that the two inducers have different performance when trained on the particular training set R.

The shortcomings of this test are:

(1) It does not directly measure variability due to the choice of the training set or the internal randomness of the inducer. The inducers are compared using a single training set R. Thus, the McNemar's test should be only applied if we consider that the sources of variability are small.

(2) It compares the performance of the inducers on training sets, which are substantially smaller than the size of the whole dataset. Hence, we must assume that the relative difference observed on training sets will still hold for training sets of a size equal to the whole dataset.

9.1.7.2   *A Test for the Difference of Two Proportions*

This statistical test is based on measuring the difference between the error rates of algorithms A and B [Snedecor and Cochran (1989)]. More specifically, let $p_A = (n_{00} + n_{01})/n$ be the proportion of test examples incorrectly classified by algorithm A and let $p_B = (n_{00} + n_{10})/n$ be the proportion of test examples incorrectly classified by algorithm B. The assumption underlying this statistical test is that when algorithm A classifies an example x from the test set T, the probability of misclassification is p_A. Then, the number of misclassifications of n test examples is a binomial random variable with a mean of np_A and variance of $p_A(1 - p_A)n$.

The binomial distribution can be well approximated by a normal distribution for reasonable values of n. The difference between two independent normally distributed random variables is itself normally distributed. Thus, the quantity $p_A - p_B$ can be viewed as normally distributed, if we assume that the measured error rates p_A and p_B are independent. Under the null hypothesis, Ho, the quantity $p_A - p_B$ has a mean of zero and a standard deviation error of:

$$se = \sqrt{2p \cdot \left(1 - \frac{p_A + p_B}{2}\right) / n} \qquad (9.24)$$

where n is the number of test examples. Based on the analysis above, we obtain the statistic:

$$z = \frac{p_A - p_B}{\sqrt{2p(1 - p)/n}} \qquad (9.25)$$

which has a standard normal distribution. According to the probabilistic theory, if the z value is greater than $Z_{0.975}$, the probability of incorrectly rejecting the null hypothesis is less than 0.05. Thus, if $|z| > Z_{0.975} = 1.96$, the null hypothesis could be rejected in favor of the hypothesis that the two algorithms have different performance. Two of the most important problems with this statistic are:

(1) The probabilities p_A and p_B are measured on the same test set, and thus they are not independent.
(2) The test does not measure variation due to the choice of the training set or the internal variation of the learning algorithm. In addition, it measures the performance of the algorithms on training sets of a size significantly smaller than the whole dataset.

9.1.7.3   *The Resampled Paired t Test*

The resampled paired t test is frequently used in machine learning. Usually, there is a series of 30 trials in the test. In each trial, the available sample

S is randomly divided into a training set R (which is typically two-thirds of the data) and a test set T. Algorithms A and B are both trained on R, and the resulting classifiers are tested on T. Let $p_A^{(i)}$ and $p_B^{(i)}$ be the observed proportions of test examples misclassified by algorithm A and B, respectively during the i-th trial. If we assume that the 30 differences $p^{(i)} = p_A^{(i)} - p_B^{(i)}$ were drawn independently from a normal distribution, we can apply Student's t-test by computing the statistic:

$$t = \frac{\bar{p} \cdot \sqrt{n}}{\sqrt{\frac{\sum_{i=1}^{n}(p^{(i)} - \bar{p})^2}{n-1}}} \tag{9.26}$$

where $\bar{p} = \frac{1}{n} \cdot \sum_{i=1}^{n} p^{(i)}$. Under the null hypothesis, this statistic has a t distribution with $n-1$ degrees of freedom. Then, for 30 trials the null hypothesis could be rejected if $|t| > t_{29,0.975} = 2.045$. The main drawbacks of this approach are:

(1) Since $p_A^{(i)}$ and $p_B^{(i)}$ are not independent, the difference $p^{(i)}$ will not have a normal distribution.
(2) The $p^{(i)}$'s are not independent, because the test and training sets in the trials overlap.

9.1.7.4   *The k-Fold Cross-validated Pairedt Test*

This approach is similar to the resampled paired t test, except that instead of constructing each pair of training and test sets by randomly dividing S, the dataset is randomly divided into k disjoint sets of equal size, $T_1, T_2, \ldots, T_k$. Then, k trials are conducted. In each trial, the test set is T_i, and the training set is the union of all of the others T_j, $j \neq i$. The t statistic is computed as described in Section 9.1.7.3. The advantage of this approach is that each test set is independent of the others. However, there is the problem that the training sets overlap. This overlap may prevent this statistical test from obtaining a good estimation of the amount of variation that would be observed if each training set were completely independent of the other training sets.

9.2   Computational Complexity

Another useful criterion for comparing inducers and classifiers is their computational complexity. Strictly speaking, computational complexity is the amount of CPU consumed by each inducer. It is convenient to differentiate between three metrics of computational complexity:

- Computational complexity for generating a new classifier: This is the most important metric, especially when there is a need to scale the data mining algorithm to massive datasets. Because most of the algorithms have computational complexity that is worse than linear in the numbers of tuples, mining massive datasets might be prohibitively expensive.
- Computational complexity for updating a classifier: Given new data, what is the computational complexity required for updating the current classifier such that the new classifier reflects the new data?
- Computational complexity for classifying a new instance: Generally, this type of metric is neglected, because it is relatively small. However, in certain methods (like k-nearest neighbors) or some real-time applications (like anti-missile applications), this type of metric can be critical.

A smaller ensemble requires less memory in order to store its members. Moreover, smaller ensembles have a higher classification speed. This is particularly crucial in several near real-time applications, such as worm detection. In addition to pursuing the highest possible accuracy, these applications require that classification time be kept to a minimum.

9.3 Interpretability of the resulting ensemble

Interpretability (also known as comprehensibility) indicates the ability of user X to understand the ensemble results. While the generalization error measures how the classifier fits the data, comprehensibility measures the "mental fit" of that classifier. This is especially important in applications in which the user is required to understand the system behavior or explain its classification. For example, the revised version of AdaBoost presented in [Friedman *et al.* (2000)] is considered to provide interpretable descriptions of the aggregate decision rule.

Interpretability is usually a subjective criterion. Nevertheless, there are several quantitative measures and indicators that can help us in evaluating this criterion. For example:

- Compactness - This measures the complexity of the model. Obviously, smaller models are easier to understand. In ensemble methods, compactness can be measured by the ensemble size (number of classifiers) and the complexity of each classifier (e.g. the number of nodes in a classification tree). According to Freund and Mason [Freund and Mason (1999)] even for modest values of ensemble size, boosting of decision trees could result in a final combined classifier with thousands (or millions) of nodes which it is difficult to visualize.

- Base Inducer Used - The base inducer used by the ensemble can determine its interpretability. Many techniques, like neural networks or support vector machines (SVM), are designed solely to achieve accuracy. However, as their classifiers are represented using large assemblages of real valued parameters, they are also difficult to understand and are referred to as black-box models. On the other hand, decision trees are easier to understand than black-box methods.

However, it is often important for the researcher to be able to inspect an induced classifier. For domains like medical diagnosis, users must understand how the system makes its decisions in order to be confident of the outcome. Since machine learning can also play an important role in the process of scientific discovery, a system may discover salient features in the input data whose importance was not previously recognized [Hunter and Klein (1993)].

Most recently the term Explainable AI (XAI) was coined to refer to machine learning models whose outputs can be easily explained to humans in contrast to black box models that are hardly understood by humans.

9.4   Scalability to Large Datasets

Scalability refers to the ability of the method to construct the classification model efficiently given large amounts of data. Classical induction algorithms have been applied with practical success in many relatively simple and small-scale problems. However, trying to discover knowledge in real life and large databases introduces time and memory problems.

There are ensemble methods (such as partitioning methods) that are more suitable for scaling to large datasets than other methods. Moreover, independent methods are considered more scalable than dependent methods, because in the former case, classifiers can be trained in parallel.

As large databases have become the norm in many fields (including astronomy, molecular biology, finance, marketing, and healthcare), the use of machine learning to discover patterns within the data has become a common way to improve productivity. Many companies are staking their future on machine learning applications and are looking to the research community for solutions to the fundamental problems they encounter.

While a very large amount of data used to be the dream of every data analyst, today the synonym for "very large" has become a "terabyte," a volume of information that is difficult to imagine. Information intensive organizations (like telecom companies and banks) accumulate several terabytes of raw data every one to two years.

However, the availability of an electronic data repository (in its enhanced form known as a "data warehouse") has caused a number of previously unknown problems, which, if ignored, may transform the task of efficient data mining into mission impossible. Managing and analyzing huge data warehouses requires very expensive specialized hardware and software, a restriction which often causes a company to exploit just a small portion of the stored data.

According to [Fayyad *et al.* (1996)], the explicit challenge for the data mining research community is to develop methods that facilitate the use of data mining algorithms for real-world databases which are often characterized by a high volume of data.

Huge databases pose several challenges:

- Computional complexity: Since most induction algorithms have a computational complexity that is greater than linear in the number of attributes or tuples, the execution time needed to process such databases might become an important issue.
- Poor classification accuracy due to difficulties in finding the correct classifier: Large databases (also known as big data) increase the size of the search space, and thus having large training set increases the chance that the inducer will select an overfitted classifier that is generally invalid.
- Storage problems: In most machine learning algorithms, the entire training set should be read from the secondary storage (such as magnetic storage) into the computer's primary storage (main memory) before the induction process begins. This causes problems, since the main memory's capability is much smaller than the capability of magnetic disks.

The difficulties in implementing classification algorithms as is on high volume databases derives from the increase in the number of records/instances in the database and the increase in the number of attributes/features in each instance (high-dimensionality).

Approaches for dealing with a large number of records include:

- Sampling methods — statisticians select records from a population using different sampling techniques.
- Aggregation — reduces the number of records by treating a group of records as one or by ignoring subsets of "unimportant" records.
- Massively parallel processing — exploiting parallel technology to simultaneously solve various aspects of the problem.
- Efficient storage methods — enabling the algorithm to handle many records.
- Reducing the algorithm's search space.

9.5   Robustness

The ability of the model to handle noise or data with missing values and make correct predictions is called robustness. Different ensemble algorithms have different robustness levels. In order to estimate the robustness of an ensemble, it is common to train the ensemble on a clean training set and train a different ensemble on a noisy training set. The noisy training set is usually the clean training set to which some artificial noisy instances have been added. The robustness level is measured as the difference in the accuracy of these two training situations.

9.6   Stability

Formally, the stability of a classification algorithm is defined as the degree to which an algorithm generates repeatable results given different batches of data from the same process. In mathematical terms, the stability is the expected agreement between two models on a random sample of the original data, where agreement on a specific example means that both models assign it to the same class. The users view the learning algorithm as an oracle. Obviously, it is difficult to trust an oracle that says something radically different each time you make a slight change to the data.

9.7   Flexibility

Flexibility indicates the ability to use any inducer (inducer-independent) or combiner (combiner-independent), provide a solution to a variety of classification tasks (for example, the ensemble learning algorithm should not be limited to just a binary classification task), and a set of controlling parameters which enable the user to examine several variations of the ensemble techniques.

9.8 Usability

Machine learning is a highly iterative process. Practitioners typically adjust an algorithm's parameters to generate better classifiers. A good ensemble method should provide a set of controlling parameters that are comprehensive and can be easily tuned.

9.9 Software Availability

The software availability of an ensemble method indicates the number of off-the-shelf software packages that support the ensemble method. High software availability implies that the practitioner can move from one software to another, without the need to select a different ensemble method.

9.10 Which Ensemble Method Should be Used?

Given the vast repertoire of ensemble methods to choose from and the various potentially contradicting criteria, it is not surprising that choosing an ensemble method is not a simple task. It is widely acceptable that random forest is the method of choice if the user has limited time for tuning the hyperparameters of the learning algorithm. Moreover, it is widely acceptable that gradient boosted trees usually can yield a better predictive performance (comparing to random forest) once its hyperparameters are carefully tuned. Nevertheless, there is no guarantee that a certain ensemble learning algorithm will constantly outperforms other ensemble learning algorithms.

In fact, empirical comparison of the predictive performance of different approaches and their variants in a wide range of application domains has shown that each performs best in some, but not all, domains. This has been termed the selective superiority problem [Brodley (1995a)].

As indicated in Chapter 3, no induction algorithm can be the best in all possible domains; each algorithm contains an explicit or implicit bias [Mitchell (1980)] that leads it to prefer certain generalizations over others. The algorithm will be successful only insofar as this bias matches the characteristics of the application domain [Brazdil *et al.* (1994)]. Furthermore, other results have demonstrated the existence and correctness of the "conservation law" [Schaffer (1994)] and "no-free-lunch theorem" [Wolpert (1996)]: if one inducer is better than another in some domains, then there are necessarily other domains in which this relationship is reversed.

The "no-free-lunch theorem" implies that for a given problem, a certain approach can yield more information from the same data than other approaches.

A distinction should be made between all of the mathematically possible domains, which are simply a product of the representation languages used, and the domains that occur in the real world and are therefore the domains of primary interest [Rao *et al.* (1995)]. Without a doubt there are many domains in the former set that are not in the latter, and average accuracy in the real-world domains can be increased at the expense of accuracy in the domains that never occur in practice. Indeed, achieving this is the goal of inductive learning research. It is still true that some algorithms will match certain classes of naturally occurring domains better than other algorithms and so achieve higher accuracy than those algorithms. While this may be reversed in other real-world domains, it does not preclude an improved algorithm from being as accurate as the best in each of the domain classes.

Indeed, in many application domains, the generalization error of even the best methods is far above 0%, and the question of whether a method can be improved, and if so how, is an open and important one. One aspect in answering this question is determining the minimum error achievable by any classifier in the application domain (known as the optimal Bayes error). If existing classifiers do not reach this level, new approaches are needed. Although this problem has received considerable attention (see, for instance, [Tumer and Ghosh (1996)]), no generally reliable method has been demonstrated thus far.

Recall that the "no free lunch" concept presents a dilemma to the analyst approaching a new task: Which inducer should be used?

If the analyst is looking for accuracy only, one solution is to try each one in turn, and by estimating the generalization error, choose the one that appears to perform best [Schaffer (1994)]. Another approach, known as *multistrategy learning* [Michalski and Tecuci (1994)], attempts to combine two or more different paradigms in a single algorithm. Most research in this area has been concerned with combining empirical approaches with analytical methods (see, for instance, [Towell and Shavlik (1994)]. Ideally, a multistrategy learning algorithm would always perform as well as the best of its base paradigms that make up the multistrategy learning algorithm. Even more ambitiously, there is hope that this combination of paradigms might produce synergistic effects (for instance, by allowing different types of frontiers between classes in different regions of the example space), leading to levels of accuracy that neither atomic approach would be able to achieve on its own.

Unfortunately, this approach often has just limited success. Although it is true that in some industrial applications (e.g., demand planning) this strategy proved to boost the error performance, in many other cases the resulting algorithms are cumbersome, and often achieve predictive performance that does not match to the best performance achieved by base paradigms. The dilemma of what method to choose becomes even more challenging, if many criteria must be considered.

The difficulty in choosing the ensemble methods results from the fact that this is a MCDM (Multiple Criteria Decision Making) problem. There are tradeoff relationships among the criteria, and some criteria ca not be measured in commensurate units. Thus, in order to systematically choose the right method, the practitioner is encouraged to implement one of the MCDM solving techniques such as the AHP (analytic hierarchy process).

Moreover, the context of the specific classification problem to be solved has a tremendous effect on the results. In general, all comparative studies in the literature that aim to compare the predictive performance, show that the no-free-lunch theorem holds [Brown *et al.* (2005); Sohna (2007)], i.e., the best ensemble technique depends greatly on the particular training dataset used. The next challenge, then, is how to automate the process of selecting the best ensemble technique in a given situation. There are two common techniques that can be used to achieve this goal:

- The wrapper approach – Given a certain dataset, use each ensemble method and select the one that performs the best on a validation set. The main advantage of this approach is its ability to accurately predict the performance of each method examined. The main disadvantage of this method is its prolonged processing time; for some inducers, the induction times may be very long, particularly in large real-life datasets. Several researchers have implemented this approach for selecting induction algorithms or dimension reduction algorithms and showed that it produces superior results [Schaffer (1993)].
- The metalearning approach [Vilalta *et al.* (2005)] – Based on a dataset's characteristics, the metaclassifier decides whether to use an ensemble

method or not and what technique to use. If a specific ensemble method outperforms other methods with a particular dataset, one should expect that this method will be preferable when other problems with similar characteristics are presented. For this purpose, one can employ metalearning. Metalearning is concerned with accumulating experience about the performance of multiple applications of a learning system. One possible output of the metalearning process is a metaclassifier which is capable of indicating which learning method is most appropriate for a given problem. This goal can be accomplished by performing the following steps: In the first step, one should examine the performance of all of the investigated ensemble methods on various datasets. Upon examination of each dataset, the characteristics of the dataset are extracted. The dataset's characteristics, together with the indication of the most preferable ensemble method for this dataset are stored in a metadataset which reflects the experience accumulated across different datasets. In the second step, an inducer is applied to the metadataset in order to induce a metaclassifier that can map the dataset to the most appropriate ensemble method (based on the characteristics of the dataset). In the last step, the metaclassifier is used to match a new unseen dataset to the most appropriate ensemble method. Several researchers have implemented this approach for selecting an ensemble method and showed that it produces superior results [Rokach (2006)]

The task of selecting the best learning algorithm is part of a greater process known as AutoML (Automated machine learning). AutoML is the process of automating the end-to-end process of applying machine learning to a given and previously unseen dataset. AutoML is considered to be outstanding research issue.

Bibliography

Abeel Thomas, Yves Van de Peer, Yvan Saeys, Java-ML: A Machine Learning Library, Journal of Machine Learning Research 10 (2009) 931-934.

Adem, J., Gochet, W., 2004. Aggregating classifiers with mathematical programming. Comput. Statist. Data Anal. 47 (4), 791-807.

Aha, D. W.; Kibler, D.; and Albert, M. K., Instancebased learning algorithms. Machine Learning 6(1):37-66, 1991.

Ahmad, A. and Brown, G., Random Projection Random Discretization EnsemblesEnsembles of Linear Multivariate Decision Trees. IEEE Transactions on Knowledge and data Engineering, 26(5), pp.1225-1239, 2014.

Ahn H., Moon H., Fazzari M. J., Noha Lim,James J. Chen, Ralph L. Kodell, Classification by ensembles from random partitions of high-dimensional data, Computational Statistics and Data Analysis 51 (2007) 6166-6179

Al-Sultan K. S. , Khan M. M. : Computational experience on four algorithms for the hard clustering problem. Pattern Recognition Letters 17(3): 295-308, 1996.

A1-Sultan K. S., A tabu search approach to the clustering problem, Pattern Recognition, 28:1443-1451,1995.

Alba, E., Chicano, J.F., (2004), Solving the error correcting code problem with parallel hybrid heuristics. In: Proceedings of 2004 ACM Symposium on Applied Computing. Volume 2. 985–989.

Alba, E., Cotta, C., Chicano, F., Nebro, A.J., (2002), Parallel evolutionary algorithms in telecommunications: two case studies. In: Proceedings of Congresso Argentino de Ciencias de la Computacion.

Ali K. M., Pazzani M. J., Error Reduction through Learning Multiple Descriptions, Machine Learning, 24: 3, 173-202, 1996.

Allwein, E.L., Shapire, R.E., Singer, Y., (2000), Reducing multiclass to binary: a unifying approach for magin classifiers. In: Proceedings of the 17th International Conference on Machine Learning, Morgan Kaufmann 9–16.

Almuallim H,. and Dietterich T.G., Learning Boolean concepts in the presence of many irrelevant features. Artificial Intelligence, 69: 1-2, 279-306, 1994.

Almuallim H., An Efficient Algorithm for Optimal Pruning of Decision Trees. Artificial Intelligence 83(2): 347-362, 1996.

Alpaydin, E., Mayoraz, E., (1999), Learning error-correcting output codes from data. In: Proceedings of the 9th International Conference on Neural Networks. 743–748.

Alsabti K., Ranka S. and Singh V., CLOUDS: A Decision Tree Classifier for Large Datasets, Conference on Knowledge Discovery and Data Mining (KDD-98), August 1998.

Altincay H., Decision trees using model ensemble-based nodesPattern Recognition 40 (2007) 3540 - 3551.

An A. and Wang Y., Comparisons of classification methods for screening potential compounds. In IEEE International Conference on Data Mining, 2001.

Anand R, Methrotra K, Mohan CK, Ranka S. Efficient classification for multiclass problems using modular neural networks. IEEE Trans Neural Networks, 6(1): 117-125, 1995.

Anderson, J.A. and Rosenfeld, E. Talking Nets: An Oral History of Neural Network Research. Cambridge, MA: MIT Press, 2000.

L. Antwarg, L. Rokach, B. Shapira, Attribute-driven hidden markov model trees for intention prediction, IEEE Trans. Syst. Man Cybernet. Part C, 42 (6) (2012), pp. 1103-1119

Arbel, R. and Rokach, L., Classifier evaluation under limited resources, Pattern Recognition Letters, 27(14): 1619–1631, 2006, Elsevier.

Archer K. J., Kimes R. V., Empirical characterization of random forest variable importance measures, Computational Statistics and Data Analysis 52 (2008) 2249-2260

Ashenhurst, R. L., The decomposition of switching functions, Technical report, Bell Laboratories BL-1(11), pp. 541-602, 1952.

Athanasopoulos, D. (1991). *Probabilistic Theory*. Stamoulis, Piraeus.

Attneave F., Applications of Information Theory to Psychology. Holt, Rinehart and Winston, 1959.

Averbuch, M. and Karson, T. and Ben-Ami, B. and Maimon, O. and Rokach, L., Context-sensitive medical information retrieval, The 11th World Congress on Medical Informatics (MEDINFO 2004), San Francisco, CA, September 2004, IOS Press, pp. 282-286

Averbuch M., Maimon O., Rokach L., and Ezer E., Free-Text Information Retrieval System for a Rapid Enrollment of Patients into Clinical Trials, Clinical Pharmacology and Therapeutics, 77(2): 13-14, 2005.

Avnimelech R. and Intrator N., Boosted Mixture of Experts: an ensemble learning scheme, Neural Computations, 11(2):483-497, 1999.

Bäck, T., Fogel, D.B., Michalewicz, T., (2000), Evolutionary Computation 1: Basic Algorithms and Operators. Institute of Physics Publishing.

Baker E., and Jain A. K., On feature ordering in practice and some finite sample effects. In Proceedings of the Third International Joint Conference on Pattern Recognition, pages 45-49, San Diego, CA, 1976.

Bala J., Huang J., Vafaie H., De Jong K., Wechsler H., Hybrid Learning Using Genetic Algorithms and Decision Trees for Pattern Classification, IJCAI conference, 1995.

Banfield R., OpenDT, http://opendt.sourceforge.net/, 2005.

Banfield J. D. and Raftery A. E. . Model-based Gaussian and non-Gaussian clustering. Biometrics, 49:803-821, 1993.

Robert E. Banfield, Lawrence O. Hall, Kevin W. Bowyer, W.P. Kegelmeyer, A Comparison of Decision Tree Ensemble Creation Techniques, IEEE Transactions on Pattern Analysis and Machine Intelligence, vol. 29, no. 1, pp. 173-180, Jan., 2007

Bao Y., Ishii N., Combining multiple K-nearest neighbor classifiers for text classification by reducts. In: Proceedings of 5th international conference on discovery science, LNCS 2534, Springer, 2002, pp 340-347

Barros, Rodrigo C and De Carvalho, Andre CPLF and Freitas, Alex A and others, Automatic design of decision-tree induction algorithms, Springer, 2015

Bartlett P. and Shawe-Taylor J., Generalization Performance of Support Vector Machines and Other Pattern Classifiers, In "Advances in Kernel Methods, Support Vector Learning", Bernhard Scholkopf, Christopher J. C. Burges, and Alexander J. Smola (eds.), MIT Press, Cambridge, USA, 1998.

Bartlett, P., Traskin, M., 2007. Adaboost is consistent. Journal of Machine Learning Research 8, 2347-2368.

Basak J., Online adaptive decision trees, Neural Computations, 16(9):1959-1981, 2004.

Basak J., Online Adaptive Decision Trees: Pattern Classification and Function Approximation, Neural Computations, 18(9):2062-2101, 2006.

Bauer, E. and Kohavi, R., "An Empirical Comparison of Voting Classification Algorithms: Bagging, Boosting, and Variants". Machine Learning, 35: 1-38, 1999.

Baxt, W. G., Use of an artificial neural network for data analysis in clinical decision making: The diagnosis of acute coronary occlusion. Neural Computation, 2(4):480-489, 1990.

Bay, S., Nearest neighbor classification from multiple feature subsets. Intelligent Data Analysis, 3(3): 191-209, 1999.

Beasley, D. (2000), Bäck, T., Fogel, D.B., Michalewicz, T., (2000), Evolutionary Computation 1: Basic Algorithms and Operators. Institute of Physics Publishing, 4–18

Bellman, R., Adaptive Control Processes: A Guided Tour, Princeton University Press, 1961.

Bennett X. and Mangasarian O.L., Multicategory discrimination via linear programming. Optimization Methods and Software, 3:29-39, 1994.

Kristin P. Bennett and Ayhan Demiriz and Richard Maclin, Exploiting unlabeled data in ensemble methods, Proceedings of the eighth ACM SIGKDD international conference on Knowledge discovery and data mining, pp. 289–296, ACM Press, New York, NY, USA, 2002.

Bensusan H. and Kalousis A., Estimating the Predictive Accuracy of a Classifier, In Proc. Proceedings of the 12th European Conference on Machine Learning, pages 25-36, 2001.

Bentley J. L. and Friedman J. H., Fast algorithms for constructing minimal spanning trees in coordinate spaces. IEEE Transactions on Computers, C-27(2):97-105, February 1978. 275

Berger, A., (1999), Error-correcting output coding for text classification.

Bernard M.E., Decision trees and diagrams. Computing Surveys, 14(4):593-623, 1982.

Berry M., and Linoff G., Mastering Data Mining, John Wiley & Sons, 2000.

Bhargava H. K., Data Mining by Decomposition: Adaptive Search for Hypothesis Generation, INFORMS Journal on Computing Vol. 11, Iss. 3, pp. 239-47, 1999.

Biermann, A. W., Faireld, J., and Beres, T. (1982). Signature table systems and learning. IEEE Trans. Syst. Man Cybern., 12(5):635-648.

Black, M. and Hickey, R.J., Maintaining the Performance of a Learned Classifier under Concept Drift, Intelligent Data Analysis 3(1),pp. 453474, 1999.

Blake, C.L., Merz, C.J., (1998), UCI repository of machine learning databases.

H. Blockeel, L. De Raedt, J. Ramon, Top-down induction of clustering trees, Proceedings of the 15th International Conference on Machine Learning, Morgan Kaufmann (1998), pp. 55-63

Blum, A. L. and Langley, P., 1997, Selection of relevant features and examples in machine learning, Artificial Intelligence, 97, pp.245-271.

Blum A., and Mitchell T., Combining Labeled and Unlabeled Data with CoTraining. In Proc. of the 11th Annual Conference on Computational Learning Theory, pages 92-100, 1998.

Bonner, R., On Some Clustering Techniques. IBM journal of research and development, 8:22-32, 1964.

Booker L., Goldberg D. E., and Holland J. H., Classifier systems and genetic algorithms. Artificial Intelligence, 40(1-3):235-282, 1989.

Boser, R.C., Ray-Chaudhuri, D.K., (1960), On a class of error-correcting binary group codes. Information and Control **3** 68–79.

I. Bou-Hamad, D. Larocque, H. Ben-Ameur, A review of survival trees, Stat. Surv., 5 (2011), pp. 44-71

Brachman, R. and Anand, T., 1994, The process of knowledge discovery in databases, in: Advances in Knowledge Discovery and Data Mining, AAAI/MIT Press, pp. 37-58.

Bratko I., and Bohanec M., Trading accuracy for simplicity in decision trees, Machine Learning 15: 223-250, 1994.

Brazdil P., Gama J., Henery R., Characterizing the Applicability of Classification Algorithms using Meta Level Learning, in Machine Learning: ECML-94, F.Bergadano e L. de Raedt (eds.), LNAI No. 784: pp. 83-102, Springer-Verlag, 1994.

Breiman, L., Random forests. Machine Learn-ing, 45, 532, 2001.

Breiman L., Friedman J., Olshen R., and Stone C.. Classification and Regression Trees. Wadsworth Int. Group, 1984.

Breiman L. (1996a), Bagging predictors, Machine Learning, 24(2):123-140, 1996.

Breiman L. (1996b), Stacked regressions, Machine Learning, 24(2):4964, 1996.

Breiman L., Arcing classifiers, Annals of Statistics, vol. 26,no. 3, pp. 801-849, 1998.

Breiman, L., Pasting small votes for classification in large databases and on-line.Machine Learning, 36, 85-103.

Breiman, L., Randomizing outputs to increase prediction accuracy, Mach. Learn. 40 (3) (2000) 229-242.

Brodley C. E. and Utgoff. P. E., Multivariate decision trees. Machine Learning, 19:45-77, 1995.

Brodley, C. E., Automatic selection of split criterion during tree growing based on node selection. In Proceedings of the Twelth International Conference on Machine Learning, 73-80 Taho City, Ca. Morgan Kaufmann, 1995a.

Brodley C.E., Recursive automatic bias selection for classifier construction, Machine Learning 20 (1995b) 63-94.

Brown G., Wyatt J. L., Negative Correlation Learning and the Ambiguity Family of Ensemble Methods. Multiple Classifier Systems 2003: 266–275

Brown G., Wyatt J., Harris R., Yao X., Diversity creation methods: a survey and categorisation, Information Fusion, 6(1):5–20.

Bruzzone L., Cossu R., Vernazza G., Detection of land-cover transitions by combining multidate classifiers, Pattern Recognition Letters, 25(13): 1491–1500, 2004.

R. Bryll, Gutierrez-Osuna R., Quek F., Attribute bagging: improving accuracy of classifier ensembles by using random feature subsets, Pattern Recognition Volume 36 (2003): 1291-1302

Buchanan, B.G. and Shortliffe, E.H., Rule Based Expert Systems, 272-292, Addison-Wesley, 1984.

Bucilua, C., Caruana, R., Niculescu-Mizil, A. (2006). Model compression. In Proceedings of the 12th ACM SIGKDD international conference on knowledge discovery and data mining (p. 535). New York, NY, 541: ACM.

Buczak A. L. and Ziarko W., "Neural and Rough Set Based Data Mining Methods in Engineering", Klosgen W. and Zytkow J. M. (Eds.), Handbook of Data Mining and Knowledge Discovery, pages 788-797. Oxford University Press, 2002.

Buja, A. and Lee, Y.S., Data mining criteria for tree based regression and classification, Proceedings of the 7th International Conference on Knowledge Discovery and Data Mining, (pp 27-36), San Diego, USA, 2001.

Buntine W., Niblett T., A Further Comparison of Splitting Rules for Decision-Tree Induction. Machine Learning, 8: 75-85, 1992.

Buntine, W., A Theory of Learning Classification Rules. Doctoral dissertation. School of Computing Science, University of Technology. Sydney. Australia, 1990.

Buntine, W. (1992), "Learning Classification Trees", Statistics and Computing, 2, 63–73.

Buntine, W., "Graphical Models for Discovering Knowledge", in U. Fayyad, G. Piatetsky-Shapiro, P. Smyth, and R. Uthurusamy, editors, Advances in Knowledge Discovery and Data Mining, pp 59-82. AAAI/MIT Press, 1996.

Buttrey, S.E., Karo, C., 2002. Using k-nearest-neighbor classification in the leaves of a tree. Comput. Statist. Data Anal. 40, 27-37.

Buhlmann, P. and Yu, B., Boosting with L_2 loss: Regression and classification, Journal of the American Statistical Association, 98, 324338. 2003.

Califf M.E. and Mooney R.J., Relational learning of pattern-match rules for information extraction. Proceedings of the Sixteenth National Conf. on Artificial Intelligence, page 328-334, 1999.

Can F. , Incremental clustering for dynamic information processing, in ACM Transactions on Information Systems, no. 11, pp 143-164, 1993.

Cantu-Paz E., Kamath C., Inducing oblique decision trees with evolutionary algorithms, IEEE Trans. on Evol. Computation 7(1), pp. 54-68, 2003.

Cardie, C. (1995). Using decision trees to improve cased- based learning. In *Proceedings of the First International Conference on Knowledge Discovery and Data Mining*. AAAI Press.

Caropreso M., Matwin S., and Sebastiani F., A learner-independent evaluation of the useful-ness of statistical phrases for automated text categorization, Text Databases and Document Management: Theory and Practice. Idea Group Publishing , page 78-102, 2001.

Caruana R., Niculescu-Mizil A. , Crew G. , Ksikes A., Ensemble selection from libraries of models, Twenty-first international conference on Machine learning, July 04-08, 2004, Banff, Alberta, Canada.

Carvalho D.R., Freitas A.A., A hybrid decision-tree - genetic algorithm method for data mining, Information Science 163, 13-35, 2004.

Catlett J., Mega induction: Machine Learning on Vary Large Databases, PhD, University of Sydney, 1991.

Chai B., Huang T., Zhuang X., Zhao Y., Sklansky J., Piecewise-linear classifiers using binary tree structure and genetic algorithm, Pattern Recognition 29(11), pp. 1905-1917, 1996.

Chan P. K. and Stolfo, S. J., Toward parallel and distributed learning by meta-learning, In AAAI Workshop in Knowledge Discovery in Databases, pp. 227-240, 1993.

Chan P.K. and Stolfo, S.J., A Comparative Evaluation of Voting and Meta-learning on Partitioned Data, Proc. 12th Intl. Conf. On Machine Learning ICML-95, 1995.

Chan P.K. and Stolfo S.J, On the Accuracy of Meta-learning for Scalable Data Mining, J. Intelligent Information Systems, 8:5-28, 1997.

Charnes, A., Cooper, W. W., and Rhodes, E., Measuring the efficiency of decision making units, European Journal of Operational Research, 2(6):429-444, 1978.

Chawla N. V., Moore T. E., Hall L. O., Bowyer K. W., Springer C., and Kegelmeyer W. P.. Distributed learning with bagging-like performance. Pattern Recognition Letters, 24(1-3):455-471, 2002.

Chawla N. V., Hall L. O., Bowyer K. W., Kegelmeyer W. P., Learning Ensembles from Bites: A Scalable and Accurate Approach, The Journal of Machine Learning Research archive, 5:421–451, 2004.

Cheeseman P., Stutz J.: Bayesian Classification (AutoClass): Theory and Results. Advances in Knowledge Discovery and Data Mining 1996: 153-180

Chen, T. and Guestrin, C., Xgboost: A scalable tree boosting system, Proceedings of the 22nd acm sigkdd international conference on knowledge discovery and data mining, 785–794, 2016.

Chen K., Wang L. and Chi H., Methods of Combining Multiple Classifiers with

Different Features and Their Applications to Text-Independent Speaker Identification, International Journal of Pattern Recognition and Artificial Intelligence, 11(3): 417-445, 1997.

Cherkauer, K. J. and Shavlik, J. W., Growing simpler decision trees to facilitate knowledge discovery. In *Proceedings of the Second International Conference on Knowledge Discovery and Data Mining*. AAAI Press, 1996.

Cherkauer, K.J., Human Expert-Level Performance on a Scientific Image Analysis Task by a System Using Combined Artificial Neural Networks. In Working Notes, Integrating Multiple Learned Models for Improving and Scaling Machine Learning Algorithms Workshop, Thirteenth National Conference on Artificial Intelligence. Portland, OR: AAAI Press, 1996.

Chizi, B., Maimon, O. and Smilovici A. On Dimensionality Reduction of High Dimensional Data Sets, Frontiers in Artificial Intelligence and Applications, IOS press, pp. 230-236, 2002.

Christensen S. W. , Sinclair I., Reed P. A. S., Designing committees of models through deliberate weighting of data points, The Journal of Machine Learning Research, 4(1):39–66, 2004.

Christmann A., Steinwart I., Hubert M.,Robust learning from bites for data mining, Computational Statistics and Data Analysis 52 (2007) 347-361

Cieslak, D. A., Chawla, N. V, Learning decision trees for unbalanced data. In Machine learning and knowledge discovery in databases. Springer Berlin Heidelberg, 2008, pp. 241-256.

Cios K. J. and Sztandera L. M., Continuous ID3 algorithm with fuzzy entropy measures, Proc. IEEE lnternat. Con/i on Fuzz)' Systems, 1992, pp. 469-476.

Clark, P. and Boswell, R., "Rule induction with CN2: Some recent improvements." In Proceedings of the European Working Session on Learning, pp. 151-163, Pitman, 1991.

Clark P., and Niblett T., The CN2 rule induction algorithm. Machine Learning, 3:261-284, 1989.

Clearwater, S., T. Cheng, H. Hirsh, and B. Buchanan. Incremental batch learning. In Proceedings of the Sixth International Workshop on Machine Learning, San Mateo CA:, pp. 366-370. Morgan Kaufmann, 1989.

Clemen R., Combining forecasts: A review and annotated bibliography. International Journal of Forecasting, 5:559–583, 1989

Cohen S., Rokach L., Maimon O., Decision Tree Instance Space Decomposition with Grouped Gain-Ratio, Information Science, Volume 177, Issue 17, pp. 3592-3612, 2007.

Collins, M., Shapire, R.E., Singer, Y., (2002), Logistic regression, adaboost and bregman distances. Machine Learning **47**(2/3) 253–285.

Coppock D. S., Data Modeling and Mining: Why Lift?, Published in DM Review online, June 2002.

Crammer, K., Singer, Y., (2002), On the learnability and design of output codes for multiclass problems. Machine Learning **47**(2-3) 201–233.

Crawford S. L., Extensions to the CART algorithm. Int. J. of ManMachine Studies, 31(2):197-217, August 1989.

Criminisi, A., Shotton, J. (2013). Decision forests for computer vision and medical image analysis. Springer Science and Business Media.

Cristianini, N., Shawe-Taylor, J., (2000), An introduction to Support Vector Machines and other kernel-based learning methods. Cambridge University Press.

Croux C., Joossens K., Lemmens A., Trimmed bagging, Computational Statistics and Data Analysis 52 (2007) 362-368

Cunningham P., and Carney J., Diversity Versus Quality in Classification Ensembles Based on Feature Selection, In: R. L. de Mntaras and E. Plaza (eds.), Proc. ECML 2000, 11th European Conf. On Machine Learning,Barcelona, Spain, LNCS 1810, Springer, 2000, pp. 109-116.

Curtis, H. A., A New Approach to the Design of Switching Functions, Van Nostrand, Princeton, 1962.

Cutzu F., Polychotomous classification with pairwise classifiers: A new voting principle. In Proc. 4th International Workshop on Multiple Classifier Systems (MCS 2003), Lecture Notes in Computer Science, Guildford, UK, 2003, Vol. 2709, pp. 115-124.

Džeroski S., Ženko B., Is Combining Classifiers with Stacking Better than Selecting the Best One?, Machine Learning, 54(3): 255–273, 2004.

Darwin, C., (1859), On the origin of species by means of natural selection. John Murray, London.

Dasarathy B.V. and Sheela B.V., Composite classifier system design: Concepts and methodology, Proceedings of the IEEE, vol. 67, no. 5, pp. 708-713, 1979.

Deb, K., (2000), An efficient constraint handling method for genetic algorithms. Computer Methods in Applied Mechanics and Engineering **186** 311–338.

Dekel, O., Singer, Y., (2003), Multiclass learning by probabilistic embeddings. In: Advances in Neural Information Processing Systems. Volume 15., MIT Press 945–952.

Del Rio S., Lopez V., Benitez J.M., Herrera F., On the use of MapReduce for imbalanced big data using Random Forest Inform. Sci., 285, pp. 112–137, 2014

Dempster A.P., Laird N.M., and Rubin D.B., Maximum likelihood from incomplete data using the EM algorithm. Journal of the Royal Statistical Society, 39(B), 1977.

Demsar J., Zupan B., Leban G. (2004) Orange: From ExperimentalMachine Learning to Interactive Data Mining, White Paper(www.ailab.si/orange), Faculty of Computer and InformationScience, University of Ljubljana.

Deng, H. (2014). Interpreting tree ensembles with intrees. arXiv preprint arXiv:14085456.

Deng, L., Platt, J. (2014). Ensemble deep learning for speech recognition. In Proceedings of the 15th Annual Conference of the International Speech Communication Association, Singapore, September 1418, 2014.

Denison D.G.T., Adams N.M., Holmes C.C., Hand D.J., Bayesian partition modelling, Computational Statistics and Data Analysis 38 (2002) 475-485

Derbeko P. , El-Yaniv R. and Meir R., Variance optimized bagging, European Conference on Machine Learning, 2002.

Dhillon I. and Modha D., Concept Decomposition for Large Sparse Text Data Using Clustering. Machine Learning. 42, pp.143-175. (2001).

Dietterich, T. G., and Ghulum Bakiri. Solving multiclass learning problems via error-correcting output codes. Journal of Artificial Intelligence Research, 2:263-286, 1995.

Dietterich, T. G., and Kong, E. B., Machine learning bias, statistical bias, and statistical variance of decision tree algorithms. Tech. rep., Oregon State University, 1995.

Dietterich, T. G., and Michalski, R. S., A comparative review of selected methods for learning from examples, Machine Learning, an Artificial Intelligence approach, 1: 41-81, 1983.

Dietterich, T. G., Kearns, M., and Mansour, Y., Applying the weak learning framework to understand and improve C4.5. Proceedings of the Thirteenth International Conference on Machine Learning, pp. 96-104, San Francisco: Morgan Kaufmann, 1996.

Dietterich, T. G., "Approximate statistical tests for comparing supervised classi-fication learning algorithms". Neural Computation, 10(7): 1895-1924, 1998.

Dietterich, T. G., An Experimental Comparison of Three Methods for Construct-ing Ensembles of Decision Trees: Bagging, Boosting and Randomization. 40(2):139-157, 2000.

Dietterich T., Ensemble methods in machine learning. In J. Kittler and F. Roll, editors, First International Workshop on Multiple Classifier Systems, Lec-ture Notes in Computer Science, pages 1-15. Springer-Verlag, 2000

Dimitrakakis C., Bengio S., Online adaptive policies for ensemble classi-fiers,Neurocomputing 64:211-221, 2005.

Dimitriadou E., Weingessel A., Hornik K., A cluster ensembles framework, Design and application of hybrid intelligent systems, IOS Press, Amsterdam, The Netherlands, 2003.

Domingo, C., and Watanabe, O. (2000). Madaboost: A modification of adaboost. colt2000 pp. 180-189.

Domingos, P. and Hulten, G., Mining Time-Changing Data Streams, Proc. of KDD-2001, ACM Press, 2001.

Domingos, P., & Pazzani, M., On the Optimality of the Naive Bayes Classifier under Zero-One Loss, Machine Learning, 29: 2, 103-130, 1997.

Domingos, P., Using Partitioning to Speed Up Specific-to-General Rule Induction. In Proceedings of the AAAI-96 Workshop on Integrating Multiple Learned Models, pp. 29-34, AAAI Press, 1996.

Dominigos P. (1999): *MetaCost: A general method for making classifiers cost sen-sitive.* In proceedings of the Fifth International Conference on Knowledge Discovery and Data Mining, pp. 155-164. ACM Press.

Domingos, P., The master algorithm: How the quest for the ultimate learning machine will remake our world. 2015.

Dontas, K., Jong, K.D., (1990), Discovery of maximal distance codes using genetic algorithms. In: Proceedings of the 2nd International IEEE Conference on Tools for Artificial Intelligence, IEEE Computer Society Press 905–811.

Dougherty, J., Kohavi, R, Sahami, M., Supervised and unsupervised discretization of continuous attributes. Machine Learning: Proceedings of the twelfth International Conference, Morgan Kaufman pp. 194-202, 1995.

M. Dror, A. Shabtai, L. Rokach, Y. Elovici, OCCT: a one-class clustering tree for implementing one-to-many data linkage, IEEE Trans. Knowl. Data Eng., 26 (3) (2014), pp. 682-697

Drucker H., Effect of pruning and early stopping on performance of a boosting ensemble, Computational Statistics and Data Analysis 38 (2002) 393-406

Duda, R., and Hart, P., Pattern Classification and Scene Analysis, New-York, Wiley, 1973.

Duda, P. E. Hart and D. G. Stork, Pattern Classification, Wiley, New York, 2001.

Duin, R. P. W., The combining classifier: to train or not to train? In Proc. 16th International Conference on Pattern Recognition, ICPR02, Canada, 2002, pp. 765-770.

Dunteman, G.H., Principal Components Analysis, Sage Publications, 1989.

Eiben, A.E., Smith, J.E., (2003), Introduction to Evolutionary Computing. Springer.

Eibl, G., Pfeiffer, K. P., Multiclass boosting for weak classifiers. Journal of Machine Learning Research, 6(Feb), 189-210, 2005.

Elder I. and Pregibon, D., "A Statistical Perspective on Knowledge Discovery in Databases", In U. Fayyad, G. Piatetsky-Shapiro, P. Smyth, and R. Uthurusamy editors., Advances in Knowledge Discovery and Data Mining, pp. 83-113, AAAI/MIT Press, 1996.

Escalera, S., Pujol, O., Radeva, R., (2006), Decoding of ternary error correcting output codes. In: Proceedings of the 11th Iberoamerican Congress on Pattern Recognition. Volume 4225 of Lecture Notes in Computer Science., Springer-Verlag 753–763.

Esmeir, S., and Markovitch, S. 2004. Lookahead-basedalgorithms for anytime induction of decision trees. InICML04, 257264.

Esposito F., Malerba D. and Semeraro G., A Comparative Analysis of Methods for Pruning Decision Trees. EEE Transactions on Pattern Analysis and Machine Intelligence, 19(5):476-492, 1997.

Ester M., Kriegel H.P., Sander S., and Xu X., A density-based algorithm for discovering clusters in large spatial databases with noise. In E. Simoudis, J. Han, and U. Fayyad, editors, Proceedings of the 2nd International Conference on Knowledge Discovery and Data Mining (KDD-96), pages 226-231, Menlo Park, CA, 1996. AAAI, AAAI Press.

Estivill-Castro, V. and Yang, J. A Fast and robust general purpose clustering algorithm. Pacific Rim International Conference on Artificial Intelligence, pp. 208-218, 2000.

A. Eyal, L. Rokach, M. Kalech, O. Amir, R. Chougule, R. Vaidyanathan, K. Pattada, Survival analysis of automobile components using mutually exclusive forests, IEEE Trans. Syst. Man Cybernet.: Syst., 44 (2) (2014), pp. 246-253

Fürnkranz, J., (2002), Round robin classification. Journal of Machine Learning Research **2** 721–747.

Fan, W. and Stolfo, S.J. and Zhang, J. and Chan, P.K. (1999), AdaCost: Misclassication Cost-sensitive Boosting, ICML 1999, pp. 97-105.

Fraley C. and Raftery A.E., "How Many Clusters? Which Clustering Method? Answers Via Model-Based Cluster Analysis", Technical Report No. 329. Department of Statistics University of Washington, 1998.

Fayyad U., and Irani K. B., The attribute selection problem in decision tree generation. In proceedings of Tenth National Conference on Artificial Intelligence, pp. 104–110, Cambridge, MA: AAAI Press/MIT Press, 1992.

Fayyad, U., Piatesky-Shapiro, G. & Smyth P., From Data Mining to Knowledge Discovery: An Overview. In U. Fayyad, G. Piatetsky-Shapiro, P. Smyth, & R. Uthurusamy (Eds), Advances in Knowledge Discovery and Data Mining, pp 1-30, AAAI/MIT Press, 1996.

Fayyad, U., Grinstein, G. and Wierse, A., Information Visualization in Data Mining and Knowledge Discovery, Morgan Kaufmann, 2001.

Feigenbaum E. (1988): *Knowledge Processing – From File Servers to Knowledge Servers. In J.R. Queinlan ed., "Applications of Expert Systems". Vol. 2, Turing Institute Press, Chpater 1, pp. 3-11*

M. Fernandez-Delgado, E. Cernadas, S. Barro, D. Amorim, Do we need hundreds of classifiers to solve real world classification problems? J. Mach. Learn. Res., 15 (1) (2014), pp. 3133-3181

Ferri C., Flach P., and Hernández-Orallo J., Learning Decision Trees Using the Area Under the ROC Curve. In Claude Sammut and Achim Hoffmann, editors, Proceedings of the 19th International Conference on Machine Learning, pp. 139-146. Morgan Kaufmann, July 2002

Fifield D. J., Distributed Tree Construction From Large Datasets, Bachelor's Honor Thesis, Australian National University, 1992.

Fisher,R.A., 1936, The use of multiple measurements in taxonomic problems" Annual Eugenics, 7, Part II, pp. 179-188.

Fisher, D., 1987, Knowledge acquisition via incremental conceptual clustering, in machine learning 2, pp. 139-172.

Fischer, B., "Decomposition of Time Series - Comparing Different Methods in Theory and Practice", Eurostat Working Paper, 1995.

Fix, E., and Hodges, J.L., Discriminatory analysis. Nonparametric discrimination. Consistency properties. Technical Report 4, US Air Force School of Aviation Medicine. Randolph Field, TX, 1957.

Fortier, J.J. and Solomon, H. 1996. Clustering procedures. In proceedings of the Multivariate Analysis, '66, P.R. Krishnaiah (Ed.), pp. 493-506.

Fountain, T. Dietterich T., Sudyka B., "Mining IC Test Data to Optimize VLSI Testing", ACM SIGKDD Conference, 2000, pp. 18-25, 2000.

Frank E., Hall M., Holmes G., Kirkby R., Pfahringer B., WEKA - A Machine Learning Workbench for Data Mining, in O. Maimon, L. Rokach, editors The Data Mining and Knowledge Discovery Handbook, Springer, pp. 1305-1314, 2005.

Frawley W. J., Piatetsky-Shapiro G., and Matheus C. J., "Knowledge Discovery in Databases: An Overview," G. Piatetsky-Shapiro and W. J. Frawley, editors, Knowledge Discovery in Databases, 1-27, AAAI Press, Menlo Park, California, 1991.

Freitas A. (2005), "Evolutionary Algorithms for Data Mining", in Oded Maimon and Lior Rokach (Eds.), The Data Mining and Knowledge Discovery Handbook, Springer, pp. 435-467.

Freitas X., and Lavington S. H., Mining Very Large Databases With Parallel Processing, Kluwer Academic Publishers, 1998.

Frelicot C. and Mascarilla L., Reject Strategies Driver Combination of Pattern Classifiers, 2001.

Freund S. (1995), Boosting a weak learning algorithm by majority. Information and Computation, 121(2):256-285, 1995

Freund S. (2001), An adaptive version of the boost by majority algorithm, Machine Learning 43(3): 293-318.

Freund S., A more robust boosting algorithm, arXiv:0905.2138, 2009.

Yoav Freund and Llew Mason. The Alternating Decision Tree Algorithm. Proceedings of the 16th International Conference on Machine Learning, pages 124-133 (1999)

Freund, Y., Schapire, R.E., (1997), A decision-theoretic generalization of on-line learning and an application to boosting. Journal of Computer and System Sciences 1(55) 119–139.

Freund Y. and Schapire R. E., Experiments with a new boosting algorithm. In Machine Learning: Proceedings of the Thirteenth International Conference, pages 325-332, 1996.

Y. Freund, R. Iyer, R.E. Schapire, Y. Singer, An efficient boosting algorithm for combining preferences, J. Mach. Learn. Res., 4 (2003), pp. 933-96

Friedman, J.H. & Tukey, J.W., A Projection Pursuit Algorithm for Exploratory Data Analysis, IEEE Transactions on Computers, 23: 9, 881-889, 1973.

Friedman, J., Kohavi, R., Yun, Y. 1996. Lazy decision trees. Proceedings of the Thirteenth National Conference on Artificial Intelligence. (pp. 717-724). Cambridge, MA: AAAI Press/MIT Press.

Friedman N., Geiger D., and Goldszmidt M., Bayesian Network Classifiers, Machine Learning 29: 2-3, 131-163, 1997.

Friedman, J., T. Hastie and R. Tibshirani (2000) Additive Logistic Regression: a Statistical View of Boosting, Annals of Statistics, 28(2):337-407.

Friedman J. H., A recursive partitioning decision rule for nonparametric classifiers. IEEE Trans. on Comp., C26:404-408, 1977.

Friedman, J. H., "Multivariate Adaptive Regression Splines", The Annual Of Statistics, 19, 1-141, 1991.

Friedman, J.H. (1997a). Data Mining and Statistics: What is the connection? 1997.

Friedman, J.H. (1997b). On bias, variance, 0/1 - loss and the curse of dimensionality, Data Mining and Knowledge Discovery, 1: 1, 55-77, 1997.

Friedman, J.H., 2001. Greedy function approximation: a gradient boosting machine. Annals of statistics, pp.1189-1232.

Friedman, J.H., 2002. Stochastic gradient boosting. Comput. Statist. Data Anal. 38 (4), 367-378.

Fu Q., Hu S., and Zhao S. (2005), Clusterin-based selective neural network ensemble, Journal of Zhejiang University SCIENCE, 6A(5), 387-392.

Fukunaga, K., Introduction to Statistical Pattern Recognition. San Diego, CA:

Academic, 1990.

Fürnkranz, J., More efficient windowing, In Proceeding of The 14th national Conference on Artificial Intelegence (AAAI-97), pp. 509-514, Providence, RI. AAAI Press, 1997.

Gago, P. and Bentos, C. (1998). A metric for selection of the most promising rules. In Proceedings of the 2nd European Conference on The Pronciples of Data Mining and Knowledge Discovery.

Galar, M., Fernandez, A., Barrenechea, E., Bustince, H., Herrera, F., A review on ensembles for the class imbalance problem: bagging-, boosting-, and hybrid-based approaches. IEEE Transactions on Systems, Man, and Cybernetics, Part C: Applications and Reviews, 42(4), 463-484, 2012.

Galar, M., Fernndez, A., Barrenechea, E., Herrera, F., Eusboost: enhancing ensembles for highly imbalanced data-sets by evolutionary undersampling. Pattern Recognition, 46(12), 3460-3471, 2013.

Gallinari, P., Modular Neural Net Systems, Training of. In (Ed.) M.A. Arbib. The Handbook of Brain Theory and Neural Networks, Bradford Books/MIT Press, 1995.

Gama J., A Linear-Bayes Classifier. In C. Monard, editor, Advances on Artificial Intelligence – SBIA2000. LNAI 1952, pp 269-279, Springer Verlag, 2000

Gama, J., Fernandes, R., and Rocha, R., Decision trees for mining data streams. Intelligent Data Analysis, 10(1), 23-45, 2006.

Gams, M., New Measurements Highlight the Importance of Redundant Knowledge. In European Working Session on Learning, Montpeiller, France, Pitman, 1989.

Garcia-Pddrajas N., Garcia-Osorio C., Fyfe C., Nonlinear Boosting Projections for Ensemble Construction, Journal of Machine Learning Research 8 (2007) 1-33.

Gardner M., Bieker, J., Data mining solves tough semiconductor manufacturing problems. KDD 2000: pp. 376-383, 2000.

Gehrke J., Ganti V., Ramakrishnan R., Loh W., BOAT-Optimistic Decision Tree Construction. SIGMOD Conference 1999: pp. 169-180, 1999.

Gehrke J., Ramakrishnan R., Ganti V., RainForest - A Framework for Fast Decision Tree Construction of Large Datasets,Data Mining and Knowledge Discovery, 4 (2/3) 127-162, 2000.

Gelfand S. B., Ravishankar C. S., and Delp E. J., An iterative growing and pruning algorithm for classification tree design. IEEE Transaction on Pattern Analysis and Machine Intelligence, 13(2):163-174, 1991.

Galton F., Vox populi, Nature, 75(7): 450–45, 1907.

Geman S., Bienenstock, E., and Doursat, R., Neural networks and the bias/variance dilemma. Neural Computation, 4:1-58, 1995.

George, E. and Foster, D. (2000),Calibration and empirical Bayes variable selection, Biometrika, 87(4):731-747.

A. Gershman, A. Meisels, K.H. Lke, L. Rokach, A. Schclar, A. Sturm, A Decision Tree Based Recommender System, in: IICS, 2010, pp. 170179.

Geurts P., Ernst D., Wehenkel L., Extremely randomized trees, Mach. Learn., 63 (1), pp. 3–42, 2006.

Gey, S., Poggi, J.-M., 2006. Boosting and instability for regression trees Comput. Statist. Data Anal. 50, 533-550.

Ghani, R., (2000), Using error correcting output codes for text classification. In: Proceedings of the 17th International Conference on Machine Learning, Morgan Kaufmann 303–310.

Giacinto G., Roli F., and Fumera G., Design of effective multiple classifier systems by clustering of classifiers, in 15th International Conference on Pattern Recognition, ICPR 2000, pp. 160-163, September 2000.

Gilad-Bachrach, R., Navot, A. and Tisliby. (2004) N. Margin based feature selection - theory and algorithms. *Proceeding of the 21'st International Conferenc on Machine Learning*, 2004.

Gillo M. W., MAID: A Honeywell 600 program for an automatised survey analysis. Behavioral Science 17: 251-252, 1972.

Giraud–Carrier Ch., Vilalta R., Brazdil R., Introduction to the Special Issue of on Meta-Learning, Machine Learning, 54 (3), 197-194, 2004.

Gluck, M. and Corter, J. (1985). Information, uncertainty, and the utility of categories. Proceedings of the Seventh Annual Conference of the Cognitive Science Society (pp. 283-287). Irvine, California: Lawrence Erlbaum Associates.

Grossman R., Kasif S., Moore R., Rocke D., and Ullman J., Data mining research: Opportunities and challenges. Report of three NSF workshops on mining large, massive, and distributed data, 1999.

Grumbach S., Milo T., Towards Tractable Algebras for Bags. Journal of Computer and System Sciences 52(3): 570-588, 1996.

Guha, S., Rastogi, R. and Shim, K. CURE: An efficient clustering algorithm for large databases. In Proceedings of ACM SIGMOD International Conference on Management of Data, pages 73-84, New York, 1998.

Gunter S., Bunke H. , Feature Selection Algorithms for the generation of multiple classifier systems, Pattern Recognition Letters, 25(11):1323–1336, 2004.

Guo Y. and Sutiwaraphun J., Knowledge probing in distributed data mining, in Proc. 4h Int. Conf. Knowledge Discovery Data Mining, pp 61-69, 1998.

Guruswami, V., Sahai, A., Multiclass learning, boosting, and error-correcting codes. Proc. 12th Annual Conf. Computational Learning Theory, pp. 145155. Santa Cruz, California, 1999.

Guyon I. and Elisseeff A., An introduction to variable and feature selection, Journal of Machine Learning Research 3, pp. 1157-1182, 2003.

Hall, M. Correlation- based Feature Selection for Machine Learning. University of Waikato, 1999.

Hampshire, J. B., and Waibel, A. The meta-Pi network - building distributed knowledge representations for robust multisource pattern-recognition. Pattern Analyses and Machine Intelligence 14(7): 751-769, 1992.

Han, J. and Kamber, M. Data Mining: Concepts and Techniques. Morgan Kaufmann Publishers, 2001.

Hancock T. R., Jiang T., Li M., Tromp J., Lower Bounds on Learning Decision Lists and Trees. Information and Computation 126(2): 114-122, 1996.

Hand, D., Data Mining – reaching beyond statistics, Research in Official Stat.

1(2):5-17, 1998.

Hansen, L. K., and Salamon, P., Neural network ensembles. IEEE Transactions on Pattern Analysis and Machine Intelligence, 12(10), 993–1001, 1990.

Hansen J., Combining Predictors. Meta Machine Learning Methods and Bias/-Variance & Ambiguity Decompositions. PhD dissertation. Aurhus University. 2000.

Hartigan, J. A. Clustering algorithms. John Wiley and Sons., 1975.

Hastie, T., Tibshirani, R., (1998), Classification by pairwise coupling. The Annals of Statistics **2** 451–471.

Huang, Z., Extensions to the k-means algorithm for clustering large data sets with categorical values. Data Mining and Knowledge Discovery, 2(3), 1998.

Haykin, S., (1999), Neural Networks - A Compreensive Foundation. 2nd edn. Prentice-Hall, New Jersey.

He D. W., Strege B., Tolle H., and Kusiak A., Decomposition in Automatic Generation of Petri Nets for Manufacturing System Control and Scheduling, International Journal of Production Research, 38(6): 1437-1457, 2000.

He P., Chen L., Xu X.H., Fast C4.5, International Conference on IEEE Machine Learning and Cybernetics, vol. 5, 2007, pp. 28412846, 2007.

Hilderman, R. and Hamilton, H. (1999). Knowledge discovery and interestingness measures: A survey. In *Technical Report CS 99-04*. Department of Computer Science, University of Regina.

Ho T. K. , Hull J.J., Srihari S.N.,Decision Combination in Multiple Classifier Systems, PAMI 1994, 16(1):66–75.

Ho T. K., Nearest Neighbors in Random Subspaces, Proc. of the Second International Workshop on Statistical Techniques in Pattern Recognition, Sydney, Australia, August 11-13, 1998, 640–648.

Ho T. K., The Random Subspace Method for Constructing Decision Forests, IEEE Transactions on Pattern Analysis and Machine Intelligence, Vol. 20, No. 8, 1998, pp. 832-844.

Ho T. K., Multiple Classifier Combination: Lessons and Next Steps, in Kandel and Bunke, (eds.), Hybrid Methods in Pattern Recognition, World Scientific, 2002, 171–198.

Holland, J.H., (1975), Adaptation in Natural and Artificial Systems. University of Michigan Press.

Holmes, G. and Nevill-Manning, C. G. (1995) . Feature selection via the discovery of simple classification rules. In *Proceedings of the Symposium on Intelligent Data Analysis*, Baden- Baden, Germany.

Holmstrom, L., Koistinen, P., Laaksonen, J., and Oja, E., Neural and statistical classifiers - taxonomy and a case study. IEEE Trans. on Neural Networks, 8,:5–17, 1997.

Holte, R. C.; Acker, L. E.; and Porter, B. W., Concept learning and the problem of small disjuncts. In Proceedings of the 11th International Joint Conference on Artificial Intelligence, pp. 813-818, 1989.

Holte R. C., Very simple classification rules perform well on most commonly used datasets. Machine Learning, 11:63-90, 1993.

Hong S., Use of Contextual Information for Feature Ranking and Discretization, IEEE Transactions on Knowledge and Data Engineering, 9(5):718-730, 1997.

Hoppner F. , Klawonn F., Kruse R., Runkler T., Fuzzy Cluster Analysis, Wiley, 2000.

Hothorn T., Lausen B., Bundling classifiers by bagging trees, Computational Statistics and Data Analysis 49 (2005) 1068-1078

Hothorn T., Hornik K., and Zeileis A., Unbiased Recursive Partitioning: A Conditional Inference Framework, Journal of Computational and Graphical Statistics, 15(3):651–674, 2006.

Hrycej T., Modular Learning in Neural Networks. New York: Wiley, 1992.

Hsu, C.W., Lin, C.J., (2002), A comparison of methods for multi-class support vector machines. IEEE Transactions on Neural Networks **13**(2) 415–425.

Hu Q. H., Yu D. R., Wang M. Y., Constructing Rough Decision Forests, D. Slezak et al. (Eds.): RSFDGrC 2005, LNAI 3642, Springer, 2005, pp. 147-156

Hu Q., Yu D., Xie Z., Li X., EROS: Ensemble rough subspaces,Pattern Recognition 40 (2007) 3728 - 3739.

Hu, X., Using Rough Sets Theory and Database Operations to Construct a Good Ensemble of Classifiers for Data Mining Applications. ICDM01. pp 233-240, 2001.

Huang, J., Fang, H., Fan, X., Decision forest for classification of gene expression data. Computers in biology and medicine, 40(8), 698-704, 2010.

Huang Y. S. and Suen C. Y. , A method of combining multiple experts for the recognition of unconstrained handwritten numerals, IEEE Trans. Patt. Anal. Mach. Intell. 17 (1995) 90-94.

Hubert, L. and Arabie, P. (1985) Comparing partitions. Journal of Classification, 5. 193-218.

Hunter L., Klein T. E., Finding Relevant Biomolecular Features. ISMB 1993, pp. 190-197, 1993.

Hwang J., Lay S., and Lippman A., Nonparametric multivariate density estimation: A comparative study, IEEE Transaction on Signal Processing, 42(10): 2795-2810, 1994.

Hyafil L. and Rivest R.L., Constructing optimal binary decision trees is NP-complete. Information Processing Letters, 5(1):15-17, 1976.

Iqbal, M. (2012). Rule extraction from ensemble methods using aggregated decision trees. In Neural information processing (pp. 599607). Heidelberg: Springer.

Islam M. M., Yao X., Murase K., A constructive algorithm for training cooperative neuralnetwork ensembles, IEEE Transactions on Neural Networks 14 (4)(2003) 820-834.

Jackson, J., *A User's Guide to Principal Components*. New York: John Wiley and Sons, 1991.

Jacobs, R. A., Jordan, M. I., Nowlan, S. J., and Hinton, G. E. Adaptive mixtures of local experts. Neural Computation 3(1):79-87, 1991.

Jain, A. and Zonker, D., Feature Selection: Evaluation, Application, and Small Sample Performance. IEEE Trans. on Pattern Analysis and Machine Intelligence, 19, 153-158, 1997.

Jain, A.K. Murty, M.N. and Flynn, P.J. Data Clustering: A Survey. ACM Computing Surveys, Vol. 31, No. 3, September 1999.

Jang J., "Structure determination in fuzzy modeling: A fuzzy CART approach," in Proc. IEEE Conf. Fuzzy Systems, 1994, pp. 480485.

Janikow, C.Z., Fuzzy Decision Trees: Issues and Methods, IEEE Transactions on Systems, Man, and Cybernetics, Vol. 28, Issue 1, pp. 1-14. 1998.

Jenkins R. and Yuhas, B. P. A simplified neural network solution through problem decomposition: The case of Truck backer-upper, IEEE Transactions on Neural Networks 4(4):718-722, 1993.

Jimenez, L. O., & Landgrebe D. A., Supervised Classification in High- Dimensional Space: Geometrical, Statistical, and Asymptotical Properties of Multivariate Data. IEEE Transaction on Systems Man, and Cybernetics — Part C: Applications and Reviews, 28:39-54, 1998.

Johansen T. A. and Foss B. A., A narmax model representation for adaptive control based on local model -Modeling, Identification and Control, 13(1):25-39, 1992.

John G. H., and Langley P., Estimating Continuous Distributions in Bayesian Classifiers. Proceedings of the Eleventh Conference on Uncertainty in Artificial Intelligence. pp. 338-345. Morgan Kaufmann, San Mateo, 1995.

John G. H., Kohavi R., and Pfleger P., Irrelevant features and the subset selection problem. In Machine Learning: Proceedings of the Eleventh International Conference. Morgan Kaufmann, 1994.

John G. H., Robust linear discriminant trees. In D. Fisher and H. Lenz, editors, Learning From Data: Artificial Intelligence and Statistics V, Lecture Notes in Statistics, Chapter 36, pp. 375-385. Springer-Verlag, New York, 1996.

Jordan, M. I., and Jacobs, R. A. Hierarchies of adaptive experts. In Advances in Neural Information Processing Systems, J. E. Moody, S. J. Hanson, and R. P. Lippmann, Eds., vol. 4, Morgan Kaufmann Publishers, Inc., pp. 985-992, 1992.

Jordan, M. I., and Jacobs, R. A., Hierarchical mixtures of experts and the EM algorithm. Neural Computation, 6, 181-214, 1994.

Joshi, V. M., "On Evaluating Performance of Classifiers for Rare Classes", Second IEEE International Conference on Data Mining, IEEE Computer Society Press, pp. 641-644, 2002.

Kamath, C., and E. Cantu-Paz, Creating ensembles of decision trees through sampling, Proceedings, 33-rd Symposium on the Interface of Computing Science and Statistics, Costa Mesa, CA, June 2001.

Kamath, C., Cant-Paz, E. and Littau, D. (2002). Approximate splitting for ensembles of trees using histograms. In Second SIAM International Conference on Data Mining (SDM-2002).

Kanal, L. N., "Patterns in Pattern Recognition: 1968-1974". IEEE Transactions on Information Theory IT-20, 6: 697-722, 1974.

Kang H., Lee S., Combination Of Multiple Classifiers By Minimizing The Upper Bound Of Bayes Error Rate For Unconstrained Handwritten Numeral Recognition, International Journal of Pattern Recognition and Artificial Intelligence, 19(3):395 - 413, 2005.

Kargupta, H. and Chan P., eds, Advances in Distributed and Parallel Knowledge Discovery , pp. 185-210, AAAI/MIT Press, 2000.

Kass G. V., An exploratory technique for investigating large quantities of categorical data. Applied Statistics, 29(2):119-127, 1980.

Kaufman, L. and Rousseeuw, P.J., 1987, Clustering by Means of Medoids, In Y. Dodge, editor, Statistical Data Analysis, based on the L1 Norm, pp. 405-416, Elsevier/North Holland, Amsterdam.

Kaufmann, L. and Rousseeuw, P.J. Finding groups in data. New-York: Wiley, 1990.

Guolin Ke, Qi Meng, Thomas Finley, Taifeng Wang, Wei Chen, Weidong Ma, Qiwei Ye, and Tie-Yan Liu. LightGBM: A Highly Efficient Gradient Boosting Decision Tree. In Advances in Neural Information Processing Systems (NIPS), pp. 3149-3157. 2017.

Kearns M. and Mansour Y., A fast, bottom-up decision tree pruning algorithm with near-optimal generalization, in J. Shavlik, ed., 'Machine Learning: Proceedings of the Fifteenth International Conference', Morgan Kaufmann Publishers, Inc., pp. 269-277, 1998.

Kearns M. and Mansour Y., On the boosting ability of top-down decision tree learning algorithms. Journal of Computer and Systems Sciences, 58(1): 109-128, 1999.

Kenney, J. F. and Keeping, E. S. "Moment-Generating and Characteristic Functions," "Some Examples of Moment-Generating Functions," and "Uniqueness Theorem for Characteristic Functions." §4.6-4.8 in Mathematics of Statistics, Pt. 2, 2nd ed. Princeton, NJ: Van Nostrand, pp. 72-77, 1951.

Kerber, R., 1992, ChiMerge: Discretization of numeric attributes, in AAAI-92, Proceedings Ninth National Conference on Artificial Intelligence, pp. 123-128, AAAI Press/MIT Press.

Kim J.O. & Mueller C.W., Factor Analysis: Statistical Methods and Practical Issues. Sage Publications, 1978.

Kim, D.J., Park, Y.W. and Park,. A novel validity index for determination of the optimal number of clusters. IEICE Trans. Inf., Vol. E84-D, no.2 (2001), 281-285.

King, B. Step-wise Clustering Procedures, J. Am. Stat. Assoc. 69, pp. 86-101, 1967.

Kira, K. and Rendell, L. A., A practical approach to feature selection. In *Machine Learning: Proceedings of the Ninth International Conference.*, 1992.

Klautau, A., Jevtić, N., Orlistky, A., (2003), On nearest-neighbor error-correcting output codes with application to all-pairs multiclass support vector machines. Journal of Machine Learning Research 4 1–15.

Klosgen W. and Zytkow J. M., "KDD: The Purpose, Necessity and Chalanges", Klosgen W. and Zytkow J. M. (Eds.), Handbook of Data Mining and Knowledge Discovery, pp. 1-9. Oxford University Press, 2002.

Knerr, S., Personnaz, L., Dreyfus, G., (1992), Handwritten digit recognition by neural networks with single-layer training. IEEE Transactions on Neural Networks 3(6) 962–968.

Knerr, S., Personnaz, L., Dreyfus, G., (1990), In: Single-layer learning revisited:

a stepwise procedure for building and training a neural network. Springer-Verlag, pp. 41–50

Kohavi R. and John G., The Wrapper Approach, In Feature Extraction, Construction and Selection: A Data Mining Perspective, H. Liu and H. Motoda (eds.), Kluwer Academic Publishers, 1998.

Kohavi, R. and Kunz, C. (1997), Option decision trees with majority votes, in D. Fisher, ed., 'Machine Learning: Proceedings of the Fourteenth International Conference', Morgan Kaufmann Publishers, Inc., pp. 161–169.

Kohavi R., and Provost F., Glossary of Terms, Machine Learning 30(2/3): 271-274, 1998.

Kohavi R. and Quinlan J. R., Decision-tree discovery. In Klosgen W. and Zytkow J. M., editors, Handbook of Data Mining and Knowledge Discovery, chapter 16.1.3, pages 267-276. Oxford University Press, 2002.

Kohavi R. and Sommerfield D., Targeting business users with decision table classifiers, in R. Agrawal, P. Stolorz & G. Piatetsky-Shapiro, eds, 'Proceedings of the Fourth International Conference on Knowledge Discovery and Data Mining', AAAI Press, pp. 249-253, 1998.

Kohavi R. and Wolpert, D. H., Bias Plus Variance Decomposition for Zero-One Loss Functions, Machine Learning: Proceedings of the 13th International Conference. Morgan Kaufman, 1996.

Kohavi R., Becker B., and Sommerfield D., Improving simple Bayes. In Proceedings of the European Conference on Machine Learning, 1997.

Kohavi, R., Bottom-up induction of oblivious read-once decision graphs, in F. Bergadano and L. De Raedt, editors, Proc. European Conference on Machine Learning, pp. 154-169, Springer-Verlag, 1994.

Kohavi R., Scaling up the accuracy of naive-bayes classifiers: a decision-tree hybrid. In Proceedings of the Second International Conference on Knowledge Discovery and Data Mining, pages 114–119, 1996.

Kolcz, A. Chowdhury, and J. Alspector, Data duplication: An imbalance problem "In Workshop on Learning from Imbalanced Data Sets" (ICML), 2003.

Kolen, J. F., and Pollack, J. B., Back propagation is sesitive to initial conditions. In Advances in Neural Information Processing Systems, Vol. 3, pp. 860-867 San Francisco, CA. Morgan Kaufmann, 1991.

Koller, D. and Sahami, M. (1996). Towards optimal feature selection. In *Machine Learning: Proceedings of the Thirteenth International Conference on machine Learning*. Morgan Kaufmann, 1996.

Kolter, J. Z., Maloof, M., Dynamic weighted majority: A new ensemble method for tracking concept drift. In Third IEEE International Conference on Data Mining, 2003. ICDM 2003, pp. 123-130.

Kolter, Z. J., Maloof, M. A. (2007). Dynamic Weighted Majority: An Ensemble Method. Journal of Machine Learning Research , 2756-2790.

Kong E. B. and Dietterich T. G., Error-correcting output coding corrects bias and variance. In Proc. 12th International Conference on Machine Learning, Morgan Kaufmann, CA, USA, 1995, pp. 313321.

Kononenko, I., Comparison of inductive and Naive Bayes learning approaches to automatic knowledge acquisition. In B. Wielinga (Ed.), Current Trends in

Knowledge Acquisition, Amsterdam, The Netherlands IOS Press, 1990.

Kononenko, I., SemiNaive Bayes classifier, Proceedings of the Sixth European Working Session on Learning, pp. 206-219, Porto, Portugal: SpringerVerlag, 1991.

Kontschieder, P., Fiterau, M., Criminisi, A., Rota Bulo, S. (2015). Deep neural decision forests. In Proceedings of the IEEE international conference on computer vision, Santiago, Chile (pp. 14671475).

Kreßel, U., (1999), Pairwise classification and support vector machines. In Schölkopf, B., Burges, C.J.C., Smola, A.J., (Eds.), Advances in Kernel Methods - Support Vector Learning, MIT Press 185–208.

Krogh, A., and Vedelsby, J., Neural network ensembles, cross validation and active learning. In Advances in Neural Information Processing Systems 7, pp. 231-238 1995.

Krtowski M., Grze M., Global learning of decision trees by an evolutionary algorithm (Khalid Saeed and Jerzy Peja), Information Processing and Security Systems, Springer, pp. 401-410, 2005.

Krtowski M., An evolutionary algorithm for oblique decision tree induction, Proc. of ICAISC'04, Springer, LNCS 3070, pp.432-437, 2004.

Kuhn H. W., The Hungarian method for the assignment problem. Naval Research Logistics Quarterly, 2:83–97, 1955.

Kulkarni, V. Y., Sinha, P. K. (2013). Random Forest Classifiers: A Survey and Future Research Directions. International Journal of Advanced Computing,36(1), 1144-1153.

Kuncheva, L.I., (2005a), Using diversity measures for generating error-correcting output codes in classifier ensembles. Pattern Recognition Letters **26** 83–90.

Kuncheva L., Combining Pattern Classifiers, Wiley Press 2005.

Kuncheva, L., & Whitaker, C., Measures of diversity in classifier ensembles and their relationship with ensemble accuracy. Machine Learning, pp. 181–207, 2003.

Kuncheva L.I. (2005b) Diversity in multiple classifier systems (Editorial), Information Fusion, 6 (1), 2005, 3-4.

Kuncheva L.I. (2014), Combining Pattern Classifiers Methods and Algorithms, Second Edition Hoboken, NJ: Wiley; 2014;

Kusiak A., Kurasek C., Data Mining of Printed-Circuit Board Defects, IEEE Transactions on Robotics and Automation, 17(2): 191-196, 2001.

Kusiak, E. Szczerbicki, and K. Park, A Novel Approach to Decomposition of Design Specifications and Search for Solutions, International Journal of Production Research, 29(7): 1391-1406, 1991.

Kusiak, A., Decomposition in Data Mining: An Industrial Case Study, IEEE Transactions on Electronics Packaging Manufacturing, Vol. 23, No. 4, pp. 345-353, 2000.

Kusiak, A., Rough Set Theory: A Data Mining Tool for Semiconductor Manufacturing, IEEE Transactions on Electronics Packaging Manufacturing, 24(1): 44-50, 2001A.

Kusiak, A., 2001, Feature Transformation Methods in Data Mining, IEEE Transactions on Elctronics Packaging Manufacturing, Vol. 24, No. 3, pp. 214–221,

2001B.

Lam L., Classifier combinations: implementations and theoretical issues. In J. Kittlerand F. Roli, editors, Multiple Classifier Systems, Vol. 1857 of Lecture Notes in ComputerScience, Cagliari, Italy, 2000, Springer, pp. 78-86.

Langdon W. B., Barrett S. J., Buxton B. F., Combining decision trees and neural networks for drug discovery, in: Genetic Programming, Proceedings of the 5th European Conference, EuroGP 2002, Kinsale, Ireland, 2002, pp. 60–70.

Langley, P. and Sage, S., Oblivious decision trees and abstract cases. in Working Notes of the AAAI-94 Workshop on Case-Based Reasoning, pp. 113-117, Seattle, WA: AAAI Press, 1994.

Langley, P. and Sage, S., Induction of selective Bayesian classifiers. in Proceedings of the Tenth Conference on Uncertainty in Artificial Intelligence, pp. 399-406. Seattle, WA: Morgan Kaufmann, 1994.

Langley, P., Selection of relevant features in machine learning, in Proceedings of the AAAI Fall Symposium on Relevance, pp. 140-144, AAAI Press, 1994.

Larsen, B. and Aone, C. 1999. Fast and effective text mining using linear-time document clustering. In Proceedings of the 5th ACM SIGKDD, 16-22, San Diego, CA.

Lazarevic A. and Obradovic Z., Effective pruning of neural network classifiers, in 2001 IEEE/INNS International Conference on Neural Networks, IJCNN 2001, pp. 796-801, July 2001.

Ball, Philip. (2013), Counting Google searches predicts market movements. Nature 12879 (2013).

LeCun, Y., Bengio, Y., Hinton, G. (2015). Deep learning. Nature, 521(7553), 436444.

Lee, S., Noisy Replication in Skewed Binary Classification, Computational Statistics and Data Analysis, 34, 2000.

Leigh W., Purvis R., Ragusa J. M., Forecasting the NYSE composite index with technical analysis, pattern recognizer, neural networks, and genetic algorithm: a case study in romantic decision support, Decision Support Systems 32(4): 361–377, 2002.

Lewis D., and Catlett J., Heterogeneous uncertainty sampling for supervised learning. In Machine Learning: Proceedings of the Eleventh Annual Conference, pp. 148-156 , New Brunswick, New Jersey, Morgan Kaufmann, 1994.

Lewis, D., and Gale, W., Training text classifiers by uncertainty sampling, In seventeenth annual international ACM SIGIR conference on research and development in information retrieval, pp. 3-12, 1994.

Jing Li, Nigel Allinson, Dacheng Tao, and Xuelong Li, Multitraining Support Vector Machine for Image Retrieval, IEEE Transactions on Image Processing, vol. 15, no. 11, pp. 3597-3601, November 2006.

Li X. and Dubes R. C., Tree classifier design with a Permutation statistic, Pattern Recognition 19:229-235, 1986.

Liao Y., and Moody J., Constructing Heterogeneous Committees via Input Feature Grouping, in Advances in Neural Information Processing Systems, Vol.12, S.A. Solla, T.K. Leen and K.-R. Muller (Eds.),MIT Press, 2000.

Liaw, Andy and Wiener, Matthew, Classification and Regression by randomForest, R news, 2(3):18–22, 2002.

Lim X., Loh W.Y., and Shih X., A comparison of prediction accuracy, complexity, and training time of thirty-three old and new classification algorithms . Machine Learning 40:203-228, 2000.

Lin Y. K. and Fu K., Automatic classification of cervical cells using a binary tree classifier. Pattern Recognition, 16(1):69-80, 1983.

Lin L., Wang X., Yeung D., Combining Multiple Classifiers Based On A Statistical Method For Handwritten Chinese Character Recognition, International Journal of Pattern Recognition and Artificial Intelligence, 19(8):1027 - 1040, 2005.

Lin H., Kao Y., Yang F., Wang P., Content-Based Image Retrieval Trained By Adaboost For Mobile Application, International Journal of Pattern Recognition and Artificial Intelligence, 20(4):525-541, 2006.

Lindbergh D.A.B. and Humphreys B.L., The Unified Medical Language System. In: van Bemmel JH and McCray AT, 1993 Yearbook of Medical Informatics. IMIA, the Nether-lands, page 41-51, 1993.

Ling C. X., Sheng V. S., Yang Q., Test Strategies for Cost-Sensitive Decision Trees IEEE Transactions on Knowledge and Data Engineering,18(8):1055-1067, 2006.

Liu C., Classifier combination based on confidence transformation, Pattern Recognition 38 (2005) 11 - 28

Liu H. & Motoda H., Feature Selection for Knowledge Discovery and Data Mining, Kluwer Academic Publishers, 1998.

Liu, H. and Setiono, R. (1996) A probabilistic approach to feature selection: A filter solution. In Machine Learning: *Proceedings of the Thirteenth International Conference on Machine Learning*. Morgan Kaufmann.

Liu, H., Hsu, W., and Chen, S. (1997). Using general impressions to analyze discovered classification rules. In *Proceedings of the Third International Conference on Knowledge Discovery and Data Mining (KDD'97)*. Newport Beach, California.

Liu H., Mandvikar A., Mody J., An Empirical Study of Building Compact Ensembles. WAIM 2004: pp. 622-627.

Liu Y.: Generate Different Neural Networks by Negative Correlation Learning. ICNC (1) 2005: 149-156

Loh W.Y., and Shih X., Split selection methods for classification trees. Statistica Sinica, 7: 815-840, 1997.

Loh W.Y. and Shih X., Families of splitting criteria for classification trees. Statistics and Computing 9:309-315, 1999.

Loh W.Y. and Vanichsetakul N., Tree-structured classification via generalized discriminant Analysis. Journal of the American Statistical Association, 83:715-728, 1988.

Long C., Bi-Decomposition of Function Sets Using Multi-Valued Logic, Eng.Doc. Dissertation, Technischen Universitat Bergakademie Freiberg 2003.

Lopez de Mantras R., A distance-based attribute selection measure for decision tree induction, Machine Learning 6:81-92, 1991.

Lorena, A.C., (2006),Investigação de estratégias para a geração de máquinas de vetores de suporte multiclasses [in portuguese], Ph.D. thesis, Departamento de Ciências de Computação, Instituto de Ciências Matemáticas e de Computação, Universidade de São Paulo, São Carlos, Brazil.

Lorena, A.C., Carvalho, A.C.P.L.F., Evolutionary design of multiclass support vector machines. Journal of Intelligent and Fuzzy Systems, 18(5): 445-454 (2007)

Lorena A. and de Carvalho A. C. P. L. F. : Evolutionary Design of Code-matrices for Multiclass Problems, in Oded Maimon and Lior Rokach (Eds.), Soft Computing for Knowledge Discovery and Data Mining, Springer, pp. 153-184, 2008.

Lu B.L., Ito M., Task Decomposition and Module Combination Based on Class Relations: A Modular Neural Network for Pattern Classification, IEEE Trans. on Neural Networks, 10(5):1244-1256, 1999.

Lu H., Setiono R., and Liu H., Effective Data Mining Using Neural Networks. IEEE Transactions on Knowledge and Data Engineering, 8 (6): 957-961, 1996.

Luba, T., Decomposition of multiple-valued functions, in Intl. Symposium on Multiple-Valued Logic', Bloomigton, Indiana, pp. 256-261, 1995.

Lubinsky D., Algorithmic speedups in growing classification trees by using an additive split criterion. Proc. AI&Statistics93, pp. 435-444, 1993.

Maher P. E. and Clair D. C,, Uncertain reasoning in an ID3 machine learning framework, in Proc. 2nd IEEE Int. Conf. Fuzzy Systems, 1993, pp. 712.

Maimon O., and Rokach, L. Data Mining by Attribute Decomposition with semi-conductors manufacturing case study, in Data Mining for Design and Manufacturing: Methods and Applications, D. Braha (ed.), Kluwer Academic Publishers, pp. 311-336, 2001.

Maimon O. and Rokach L., "Improving supervised learning by feature decomposition", Proceedings of the Second International Symposium on Foundations of Information and Knowledge Systems, Lecture Notes in Computer Science, Springer, pp. 178-196, 2002.

Maimon O., Rokach L., Ensemble of Decision Trees for Mining Manufacturing Data Sets, Machine Engineering, vol. 4 No1-2, 2004.

Maimon, O. and Rokach, L., Decomposition Methodology for Knowledge Discovery and Data Mining: Theory and Applications, Series in Machine Perception and Artificial Intelligence - Vol. 61, World Scientific Publishing, ISBN:981-256-079-3, 2005.

Mallows, C. L., Some comments on Cp . *Technometrics* 15, 661- 676, 1973.

Mangiameli P., West D., Rampal R., Model selection for medical diagnosis decision support systems, Decision Support Systems, 36(3): 247–259, 2004.

Mansour, Y. and McAllester, D., Generalization Bounds for Decision Trees, in Proceedings of the 13th Annual Conference on Computer Learning Theory, pp. 69-80, San Francisco, Morgan Kaufmann, 2000.

Marcotorchino, J.F. and Michaud, P. Optimisation en Analyse Ordinale des Donns. Masson, Paris.

Margineantu, D. (2001). Methods for Cost-Sensitive Learning. Doctoral Dissertation, Oregon State University.

Margineantu D. and Dietterich T., Pruning adaptive boosting. In Proc. Fourteenth Intl. Conf. Machine Learning, pages 211–218, 1997.

Martí, R., Laguna, M., Campos, V., (2005), Scatter search vs. genetic algorithms: An experimental evaluation with permutation problems. In Rego, C., Alidaee, B., eds.: Metaheuristic Optimization Via Adaptive Memory and Evolution: Tabu Search and Scatter Search. Kluwer Academic Publishers 263–282.

Martin J. K., An exact probability metric for decision tree splitting and stopping. An Exact Probability Metric for Decision Tree Splitting and Stopping, Machine Learning, 28 (2-3):257-291, 1997.

Martinez-Munoz G., Suarez A., Switching class labels to generate classification ensembles, Pattern Recognition, 38 (2005): 1483–1494.

Martinez-Munoz G., Suarez A., Using all data to generate decision tree ensembles. IEEE Transactions on Systems, Man, and Cybernetics, Part C (Applications and Reviews), 34(4), 393-397, 2004.

Masulli, F., Valentini, G., (2000), Effectiveness of error correcting output codes in multiclass learning problems. In: Proceedings of the 1st International Workshop on Multiple Classifier Systems. Volume 1857 of Lecture Notes in Computer Science., Springer-Verlag 107–116.

Mayoraz, E., Alpaydim, E., (1998), Support vector machines for multi-class classification. Research Report IDIAP-RR-98-06, Dalle Molle Institute for Perceptual Artificial Intelligence, Martigny, Switzerland.

Mayoraz, E., Moreira, M., (1996), On the decomposition of polychotomies into dichotomies. Research Report 96-08, IDIAP, Dalle Molle Institute for Perceptive Artificial Intelligence, Martigny, Valais, Switzerland.

Mease D., Wyner W., Evidence Contrary to the Statistical View of Boosting, Journal of Machine Learning Research 9 (2008) 131-156

Mehta M., Rissanen J., Agrawal R., MDL-Based Decision Tree Pruning. KDD 1995: pp. 216-221, 1995.

Mehta M., Agrawal R. and Rissanen J., SLIQ: A fast scalable classifier for data mining: In Proc. If the fifth Int'l Conference on Extending Database Technology (EDBT), Avignon, France, March 1996.

Meir R., Ratsch G., An introduction to boosting and leveraging, In Advanced Lectures on Machine Learning, LNCS (2003), pp. 119-184.

Melville P., Mooney R. J., Constructing Diverse Classifier Ensembles using Artificial Training Examples. IJCAI 2003: 505-512

Menahem, E., Rokach, L., Elovici, Y., Troika - An Improved Stacking Schema for Classification Tasks, Information Sciences (to appear).

Menahem, E., Shabtai, A., Rokach, L., Elovici, Y., Improving malware detection by applying multi-inducer ensemble. Computational Statistics and Data Analysis, 53(4):1483–1494, 2009.

Qi Meng, Guolin Ke, Taifeng Wang, Wei Chen, Qiwei Ye, Zhi-Ming Ma, Tieyan Liu. A Communication-Efficient Parallel Algorithm for Decision Tree. Advances in Neural Information Processing Systems, pp. 1279-1287. 2016

Meretakis, D. and Wthrich, B., Extending Nave Bayes Classifiers Using Long

Itemsets, in Proceedings of the Fifth International Conference on Knowledge Discovery and Data Mining, pp. 165-174, San Diego, USA, 1999.

Merkwirth C., Mauser H., Schulz-Gasch T., Roche O., Stahl M., Lengauer T., Ensemble methods for classification in cheminformatics, Journal of Chemical Information and Modeling, 44(6):1971–1978, 2004.

Merler S., Caprile B., Furlanello C., Parallelizing AdaBoost by weights dynamics, Computational Statistics and Data Analysis 51 (2007) 2487-2498

Merz, C. J. and Murphy. P.M., UCI Repository of machine learning databases. Irvine, CA: University of California, Department of Information and Computer Science, 1998.

Merz, C. J., Using Correspondence Analysis to Combine Classifier, Machine Learning, 36(1-2):33-58, 1999.

Michalewicz, Z., Fogel, D.B., (2004), How to solve it: modern heuristics. Springer.

Michalski R. S., and Tecuci G.. Machine Learning, A Multistrategy Approach, Vol. J. Morgan Kaufmann, 1994.

Michalski R. S., A theory and methodology of inductive learning. Artificial Intelligence, 20:111- 161, 1983.

Michalski R. S., Understanding the nature of learning: issues and research directions, in R. Michalski, J. Carbonnel and T. Mitchell,eds, Machine Learning: An Artificial Intelligence Approach, Kaufmann, Paolo Alto, CA, pp. 3–25, 1986.

Michie D., Spiegelhalter D.J., Taylor C .C., Machine Learning, Neural and Statistical Classification, Prentice Hall, 1994.

Michie, D., Problem decomposition and the learning of skills, in Proceedings of the European Conference on Machine Learning, pp. 17-31, Springer-Verlag, 1995.

Mierswa I., Wurst M., Klinkenberg R., Scholz M., and Euler T.: YALE: Rapid Prototyping forComplex Data Mining Tasks, in Proceedings of the 12th ACM SIGKDD, International Conference on Knowledge Discovery and Data Mining(KDD-06), 2006.

Mingers J., An empirical comparison of pruning methods for decision tree induction. Machine Learning, 4(2):227-243, 1989.

Minku, L. L., White, A. P., and Yao, X., The impact of diversity on online ensemble learning in the presence of concept drift. IEEE Transactions on Knowledge and Data Engineering, , 22(5), 730-742, 2010.

Minku, L. L., and Yao, X., DDD: A new ensemble approach for dealing with concept drift. Knowledge and Data Engineering, IEEE Transactions on, 24(4), 619-633, 2012.

Minsky M., Logical vs. Analogical or Symbolic vs. Connectionist or Neat vs. Scruffy, in Artificial Intelligence at MIT., Expanding Frontiers, Patrick H. Winston (Ed.), Vol 1, MIT Press, 1990. Reprinted in AI Magazine, 1991.

Mishra, S. K. and Raghavan, V. V., An empirical study of the performance of heuristic methods for clustering. In Pattern Recognition in Practice, E. S. Gelsema and L. N. Kanal, Eds. 425436, 1994.

Mitchell, M., (1999), An introduction to Genetic Algorithms. MIT Press.

Mitchell, T., The need for biases in learning generalizations. Technical Report

CBM-TR-117, Rutgers University, Department of Computer Science, New Brunswick, NJ, 1980.

Mitchell, T., Machine Learning, McGraw-Hill, 1997.

Montgomery D.C. (1997) Design and analysis, 4th edn. Wiley, New York.

Moody, J. and Darken, C., Fast learning in networks of locally tuned units. Neural Computations, 1(2):281-294, 1989.

Moore S. A., Daddario D. M., Kurinskas J. and Weiss G. M., Are decision trees always greener on the open (source) side of the fence?, Proceedings of DMIN,pp. 185188, 2009.

F. Moosmann, E. Nowak, F. Jurie, Randomized clustering forests for image classification, IEEE Trans. Pattern Anal. Mach. Intell., 30 (9) (2008), pp. 1632-1646

Francisco Moreno-Seco, Jose M. Inesta, Pedro J. Ponce de Leon, and Luisa Mic, Comparison of Classifier Fusion Methods for Classification in Pattern Recognition Tasks, D. Y. Yeung et al. (Eds.): SSPR-SPR 2006, LNCS 4109, pp. 705–713, 2006.

Morgan J. N. and Messenger R. C., THAID: a sequential search program for the analysis of nominal scale dependent variables. Technical report, Institute for Social Research, Univ. of Michigan, Ann Arbor, MI, 1973.

Moskovitch R, Elovici Y, Rokach L, Detection of unknown computer worms based on behavioral classification of the host, Computational Statistics and Data Analysis, 52(9):4544–4566, 2008.

Muller W., and Wysotzki F., Automatic construction of decision trees for classification. Annals of Operations Research, 52:231-247, 1994.

Murphy, O. J., and McCraw, R. L. 1991. Designing storage efficient decision trees. IEEE-TC 40(3):315320.

Murtagh, F. A survey of recent advances in hierarchical clustering algorithms which use cluster centers. Comput. J. 26 354-359, 1984.

Murthy S. K., Kasif S., and Salzberg S.. A system for induction of oblique decision trees. Journal of Artificial Intelligence Research, 2:1-33, August 1994.

Murthy, S. and Salzberg, S. (1995), Lookahead and pathology in decision tree induction, in C. S. Mellish, ed., 'Proceedings of the 14th International Joint Con- ference on Articial Intelligence', Morgan Kaufmann, pp. 1025-1031.

Murthy S. K., Automatic Construction of Decision Trees from Data: A Multi-Disciplinary Survey. Data Mining and Knowledge Discovery, 2(4):345-389, 1998.

Myers E.W., An O(ND) Difference Algorithm and Its Variations, Algorithmica, 1(1): page 251-266, 1986.

Naumov G.E., NP-completeness of problems of construction of optimal decision trees. Soviet Physics: Doklady, 36(4):270-271, 1991.

Neal R., Probabilistic inference using Markov Chain Monte Carlo methods. Tech. Rep. CRG-TR-93-1, Department of Computer Science, University of Toronto, Toronto, CA, 1993.

Ng, R. and Han, J. 1994. Very large data bases. In Proceedings of the 20th International Conference on Very Large Data Bases (VLDB94, Santiago, Chile, Sept.), VLDB Endowment, Berkeley, CA, 144–155.

Niblett T., Constructing decision trees in noisy domains. In Proceedings of the Second European Working Session on Learning, pages 67-78, 1987.

Nikulin V, McLachlan G, Ng S, Ensemble Approach for Classification of Imbalanced Data, Proceedings of the 22nd Australian Joint Conference on Advances in Artificial Intelligence, Springer-Verlag, 2009.

Nowlan S. J., and Hinton G. E. Evaluation of adaptive mixtures of competing experts. In Advances in Neural Information Processing Systems, R. P. Lippmann, J. E. Moody, and D. S. Touretzky, Eds., vol. 3, pp. 774-780, Morgan Kaufmann Publishers Inc., 1991.

Nunez, M. (1988): *Economic induction: A case study.* In D. Sleeman (Ed.), Proceeding of the Third European Working Session on Learning. London: Pitman Publishing

Nunez, M. (1991): *The use of Background Knowledge in Decision Tree Induction.* Machine Learning, 6(1), pp. 231-250.

Oates, T., Jensen D., 1998, Large Datasets Lead to Overly Complex Models: An Explanation and a Solution, KDD 1998, pp. 294-298.

Ohno-Machado, L., and Musen, M. A. Modular neural networks for medical prognosis: Quantifying the benefits of combining neural networks for survival prediction. Connection Science 9, 1 (1997), 71-86.

Olaru C., Wehenkel L., A complete fuzzy decision tree technique, Fuzzy Sets and Systems, 138(2):221–254, 2003.

Oliveira L.S., Sabourin R., Bortolozzi F., and Suen C. Y. (2003) A Methodology for Feature Selection using Multi-Objective Genetic Algorithms for Handwritten Digit String Recognition, *International Journal of Pattern Recognition and Artificial Intelligence*, 17(6):903-930.

Opitz, D., Feature Selection for Ensembles, In: Proc. 16th National Conf. on Artificial Intelligence, AAAI,1999, pp. 379-384.

Opitz, D. and Maclin, R., Popular Ensemble Methods: An Empirical Study, Journal of Artificial Research, 11: 169-198, 1999.

Opitz D. and Shavlik J., Generating accurate and diverse members of a neural-network ensemble. In David S. Touretzky, Michael C. Mozer, and Michael E. Hasselmo, editors, Advances in Neural Information Processing Systems, volume 8, pages 535–541. The MIT Press, 1996.

Pérez-Cruz, F., Artés-Rodríguez, A., (2002), Puncturing multi-class support vector machines. In: Proceedings of the 12th International Conference on Neural Networks (ICANN). Volume 2415 of Lecture Notes in Computer Science., Springer-Verlag 751–756.

Pagallo, G. and Huassler, D., Boolean feature discovery in empirical learning, Machine Learning, 5(1): 71-99, 1990.

Palit I., Reddy C.K., Scalable and parallel boosting with mapreduce IEEE Trans. Knowl. Data Eng., 24 (10), pp. 1904-1916, 2012.

Panda B., Herbach J.S., Basu S., Bayardo R.J., Planet: massively parallel learning of tree ensembles with mapreduce Proc. VLDB Endowment, 2 (2) (2009), pp. 1426–1437, 2009.

S. Pang, D. Kim, S. Y. Bang, Membership authentication in the dynamic group by face classification using SVM ensemble. Pattern Recognition Letters, 24:

215–225, 2003.

Park C., Cho S., Evolutionary Computation for Optimal Ensemble Classifier in Lymphoma Cancer Classification. 521-530. Ning Zhong, Zbigniew W. Ras, Shusaku Tsumoto, Einoshin Suzuki (Eds.): Foundations of Intelligent Systems, 14th International Symposium, ISMIS 2003, Maebashi City, Japan, October 28-31, 2003, Proceedings. Lecture Notes in Computer Science, pp. 521-530, 2003.

Parmanto, B., Munro, P. W., and Doyle, H. R., Improving committee diagnosis with resampling techinques. In Touretzky, D. S., Mozer, M. C., and Hesselmo, M. E. (Eds). Advances in Neural Information Processing Systems, Vol. 8, pp. 882-888 Cambridge, MA. MIT Press, 1996.

Terence Parr and Jeremy Howard, How to explain gradient boosting, http://explained.ai/gradient-boosting/, 2018

Partridge D. , Yates W. B. (1996), Engineering multiversion neural-net systems, Neural Computation, 8(4):869-893.

Passerini, A., Pontil, M., Frasconi, P., (2004), New results on error correcting output codes of kernel machines. IEEE Transactions on Neural Networks **15** 45–54.

Pazzani M., Merz C., Murphy P., Ali K., Hume T., and Brunk C. (1994): *Reducing Misclassification costs*. In Proc. 11th International conference on Machine Learning, 217-25. Morgan Kaufmann.

Pearl, J., Probabilistic Reasoning in Intelligent Systems: Networks of Plausible Inference. Morgan-Kaufmann, 1988.

Peng, F. and Jacobs R. A., and Tanner M. A., Bayesian Inference in Mixtures-of-Experts and Hierarchical Mixtures-of-Experts Models With an Application to Speech Recognition, Journal of the American Statistical Association 91, 953-960, 1996.

Peng Y., Intelligent condition monitoring using fuzzy inductive learning, Journal of Intelligent Manufacturing, 15 (3): 373-380, June 2004.

Perkowski, M.A., Luba, T., Grygiel, S., Kolsteren, M., Lisanke, R., Iliev, N., Burkey, P., Burns, M., Malvi, R., Stanley, C., Wang, Z., Wu, H., Yang, F., Zhou, S. and Zhang, J. S., Unified approach to functional decompositions of switching functions, Technical report, Warsaw University of Technology and Eindhoven University of Technology, 1995.

Perkowski, M., Jozwiak, L. and Mohamed, S., New approach to learning noisy Boolean functions, Proceedings of the Second International Conference on Computational Intelligence and Multimedia Applications, pp. 693–706, World Scientific, Australia, 1998.

Perkowski, M. A., A survey of literature on function decomposition, Technical report, GSRP Wright Laboratories, Ohio OH, 1995.

Perner P., Improving the Accuracy of Decision Tree Induction by Feature Pre-Selection, Applied Artificial Intelligence 2001, vol. 15, No. 8, p. 747-760.

Peterson W. W,, Weldon E. J., Error-correcting codes, The MIT Press; 2 edition, March 15, 1972.

Pfahringer, B., Bensusan H., and Giraud-Carrier C., Tell Me Who Can Learn You and I Can Tell You Who You are: Landmarking Various Learning Algorithms, In Proc. of the Seventeenth International Conference on Machine Learning (ICML2000), pages 743-750, 2000.

Pfahringer, B., Controlling constructive induction in CiPF, In Bergadano, F. and De Raedt, L. (Eds.), Proceedings of the seventh European Conference on Machine Learning, pp. 242-256, Springer-Verlag, 1994.

Pfahringer, B., Compression- based feature subset selection. In *Proceeding of the IJCAI- 95 Workshop on Data Engineering for Inductive Learning*, pp. 109-119, 1995.

Phama T., Smeuldersb A., Quadratic boosting, Pattern Recognition 41(2008): 331 - 341.

Piatetsky-Shapiro, G. (1991). *Discovery analysis and presentation of strong rules.* Knowledge Discovery in Databases, AAAI/MIT Press.

Pimenta, E., Gama, J., (2005), A study on error correcting output codes. In: Proceedings of the 2005 Portuguese Conference on Artificial Intelligence, IEEE Computer Society Press 218–223.

Poggio T., Girosi, F., Networks for Approximation and Learning, Proc. IEER, Vol 78(9): 1481-1496, Sept. 1990.

Polikar R., "Ensemble Based Systems in Decision Making," IEEECircuits and Systems Magazine, vol.6, no. 3, pp. 21-45, 2006.

Pratt, L. Y., Mostow, J., and Kamm C. A., Direct Transfer of Learned Information Among Neural Networks, in: Proceedings of the Ninth National Conference on Artificial Intelligence, Anaheim, CA, 584-589, 1991.

Prodromidis, A. L., Stolfo, S. J. and Chan, P. K., Effective and efficient pruning of metaclassifiers in a distributed data mining system. Technical report CUCS-017-99, Columbia Univ., 1999.

Provan, G. M. and Singh, M. (1996). Learning Bayesian networks using feature selection. In D. Fisher and H. Lenz, (Eds.), *Learning from Data, Lecture Notes in Statistics*, pages 291– 300. Springer- Verlag, New York.

Provost, F. (1994): *Goal-Directed Inductive learning: Trading off accuracy for reduced error cost.* AAAI Spring Symposium on Goal-Driven Learning.

Provost F. and Fawcett T. (1997): *Analysis and visualization of Classifier Performance Comparison under Imprecise Class and Cost Distribution.* In Proceedings of KDD-97, pages 43-48. AAAI Press.

Provost F. and Fawcett T. (1998): *The case against accuracy estimation for comparing induction algorithms.* Proc. 15th Intl. Conf. On Machine Learning, pp. 445-453, Madison, WI.

Provost, F. and Fawcett, T. (2001), Robust {C}lassification for {I}mprecise {E}nvironments, Machine Learning, 42/3:203-231.

Provost, F.J. and Kolluri, V., A Survey of Methods for Scaling Up Inductive Learning Algorithms, Proc. 3rd International Conference on Knowledge Discovery and Data Mining, 1997.

Provost, F., Jensen, D. and Oates, T., 1999, Efficient Progressive Sampling, In Proceedings of the Fifth International Conference on Knowledge Discovery and Data Mining, pp.23-32.

Pujol, O., Tadeva, P., Vitrià, J., (2006), Discriminant ECOC: a heuristic method for application dependetn design of error correcting output codes. IEEE

Transactions on Pattern Analysis and Machine Intelligence **28**(6) 1007–1012.

Qiu, X., Zhang, L., Ren, Y., Suganthan, P. N., and Amaratunga, G. (2014). Ensemble deep learning for regression and time series forecasting. In 2014 I.E. symposium on computational intelligence in ensemble learning (CIEL) (pp. 16). Orlando, FL: IEEE.

Quinlan, J. R. and Rivest, R. L., Inferring Decision Trees Using The Minimum Description Length Principle. Information and Computation, 80:227-248, 1989.

Quinlan, J.R. *Learning efficient classification procedures and their application to chess endgames*. R. Michalski, J. Carbonell, T. Mitchel. Machine learning: an AI approach. Los Altos, CA. Morgan Kaufman , 1983.

Quinlan, J.R., Induction of decision trees, Machine Learning 1, 81-106, 1986.

Quinlan, J.R., Simplifying decision trees, International Journal of Man-Machine Studies, 27, 221-234, 1987.

Quinlan, J.R., Decision Trees and Multivalued Attributes, J. Richards, ed., Machine Intelligence, V. 11, Oxford, England, Oxford Univ. Press, pp. 305-318, 1988.

Quinlan, J. R., Unknown attribute values in induction. In Segre, A. (Ed.), Proceedings of the Sixth International Machine Learning Workshop Cornell, New York. Morgan Kaufmann, 1989.

Quinlan, J. R., Unknown attribute values in induction. In Segre, A. (Ed.), Proceedings of the Sixth International Machine Learning Workshop Cornell, New York. Morgan Kaufmann, 1989.

Quinlan, J. R., C4.5: Programs for Machine Learning, Morgan Kaufmann, Los Altos, 1993.

Quinlan, J. R., Bagging, Boosting, and C4.5. In Proceedings of the Thirteenth National Conference on Artificial Intelligence, pages 725-730, 1996.

R Development Core Team (2004), R: A language and environment for statistical computing. R Foundation for Statistical Computing, Vienna, Austria. ISBN 3-900051-00-3, http://cran.r-project.org/, 2004

R'enyi A., Probability Theory, North-Holland, Amsterdam, 1970

Rätsch, G., Smola, A.J., Mika, S., (2003), Adapting codes and embeddings for polychotomies. In: Advances in Neural Information Processing Systems. Volume 15., MIT Press 513–520.

Ragavan, H. and Rendell, L., Look ahead feature construction for learning hard concepts. In Proceedings of the Tenth International Machine Learning Conference: pp. 252-259, Morgan Kaufman, 1993.

Rahman, A. F. R., and Fairhurst, M. C. A new hybrid approach in combining multiple experts to recognize handwritten numerals. Pattern Recognition Letters, 18: 781-790,1997.

Rakotomalala R., "TANAGRA: a free software for research andacademic purposes", in Proceedings of EGC'2005, RNTI-E-3, vol. 2,pp.697-702, 2005

Ramamurti, V., and Ghosh, J., Structurally Adaptive Modular Networks for Non-Stationary Environments, IEEE Transactions on Neural Networks, 10 (1):152-160, 1999.

Rand, W. M., Objective criteria for the evaluation of clustering methods. Journal of the American Statistical Association, 66: 846–850, 1971.

Rao, R., Gordon, D., and Spears, W., For every generalization action, is there really an equal or opposite reaction? Analysis of conservation law. In Proc. of the Twelveth International Conference on Machine Learning, pp. 471-479. Morgan Kaufmann, 1995.

Rastogi, R., and Shim, K., PUBLIC: A Decision Tree Classifier that Integrates Building and Pruning,Data Mining and Knowledge Discovery, 4(4):315-344, 2000.

Ratsch G., Onoda T., and Muller K. R., Soft Margins for Adaboost, Machine Learning 42(3):287-320, 2001.

Ray, S., and Turi, R.H. Determination of Number of Clusters in K-Means Clustering and Application in Color Image Segmentation. Monash university, 1999.

Buczak A. L. and Ziarko W., "Stages of The Discovery Process", Klosgen W. and Zytkow J. M. (Eds.), Handbook of Data Mining and Knowledge Discovery, pages 185-192. Oxford University Press, 2002.

Ridgeway, G., Madigan, D., Richardson, T. and O'Kane, J. (1998), "Interpretable Boosted Naive Bayes Classification", Proceedings of the Fourth International Conference on Knowledge Discovery and Data Mining, pp 101-104.

Rifkin, R., Klautau, A., (2004), In defense of one-vs-all classification. Journal of Machine Learning Research 5 1533–7928.

Rigoutsos I. and Floratos A., Combinatorial pattern discovery in biological sequences: The TEIRESIAS algorithm., Bioinformatics, 14(2): page 229, 1998.

Rissanen, J., Stochastic complexity and statistical inquiry. World Scientific, 1989.

Rodriguez J. J. (2006). Rotation Forest: A New Classifier Ensemble Method. IEEE Transactions on Pattern Analysis and Machine Intelligence, 20(10): 1619-1630

Rokach, L., 2016. Decision forest: Twenty years of research. Information Fusion, 27, pp.111-125.

Rokach L., Ensemble Methods for Classifiers, in Oded Maimon and Lior Rokach (Eds.), The Data Mining and Knowledge Discovery Handbook, Springer, pp. 957-980, 2005.

Rokach L., Decomposition Methodology for Classification Tasks - A Meta Decomposer Framework, Pattern Analysis and Applications, 9(2006):257-271.

Rokach L., Genetic algorithm-based feature set partitioning for classification problems,Pattern Recognition, 41(5):1676–1700, 2008.

Rokach L., Mining manufacturing data using genetic algorithm-based feature set decomposition, Int. J. Intelligent Systems Technologies and Applications, 4(1):57-78, 2008.

Rokach, L., Collective-agreement-based pruning of ensembles. Computational Statistics and Data Analysis, 53(4):1015–1026, 2009.

Rokach L., Taxonomy for characterizing ensemble methods in classification tasks: A review and annotated bibliography, Computational Statistics and Data Analysis, 53(12):4046-4072, 2009.

Rokach L., Maimon O. and Lavi I., Space Decomposition In Data Mining: A Clustering Approach, Proceedings of the 14th International Symposium On Methodologies For Intelligent Systems, Maebashi, Japan, Lecture Notes in Computer Science, Springer-Verlag, 2003, pp. 24–31.

Rokach L., Averbuch M. and Maimon O., Information Retrieval System for Medical Narrative Reports, Lecture Notes in Artificial intelligence 3055, page 217-228 Springer-Verlag, 2004.

Rokach L., Maimon O., Arad O., "Improving Supervised Learning by Sample Decomposition", International Journal of Computational Intelligence and Applications, 5(1):37-54, 2005.

Rokach L., R. Arbel, O. Maimon, "Selective Voting - Getting More For Less in Sensor Fusion", International Journal of PatternRecognition and Artificial Intelligence, 20(3):329-350, 2006.

Rokach L., Chizi B., Maimon O., A Methodology for Improving the Performance of Non-ranker Feature Selection Filters, International Journal of Pattern Recognition and Artificial Intelligence, 21(5): 809-830, 2007.

Rokach L., Romano R., Maimon O., Negation Recognition in Medical Narrative Reports, Information Retrieval, 11(6): 499-538, 2008

L. Rokach, S. Kisilevich, Initial profile generation in recommender systems using pairwise comparison, IEEE Trans. Syst. Man Cybernet. Part C: Appl. Rev., 42 (6) (2012), pp. 1854-1859

Rokach L. and Maimon O., "Theory and Application of Attribute Decomposition", Proceedings of the First IEEE International Conference on Data Mining, IEEE Computer Society Press, pp. 473-480, 2001

Rokach L. and Maimon O., Top Down Induction of Decision Trees Classifiers: A Survey, IEEE SMC Transactions Part C. Volume 35, Number 3, 2005a.

Rokach L. and Maimon O., Feature Set Decomposition for Decision Trees, Journal of Intelligent Data Analysis, Volume 9, Number 2, 2005b, pp 131-158.

Rokach, L. and Maimon, O., Clustering methods, Data Mining and Knowledge Discovery Handbook, pp. 321–352, 2005, Springer.

Rokach, L. and Maimon, O., Data mining for improving the quality of manufacturing: a feature set decomposition approach, Journal of Intelligent Manufacturing, 17(3):285–299, 2006, Springer.

Rokach, L., Maimon, O., Data Mining with Decision Trees: Theory and Applications, World Scientific Publishing, 2008.

Ronco, E., Gollee, H., and Gawthrop, P. J., Modular neural network and self-decomposition. CSC Research Report CSC-96012, Centre for Systems and Control, University of Glasgow, 1996.

Rosen B. E., Ensemble Learning Using Decorrelated Neural Networks. Connect. Sci. 8(3): 373-384 (1996)

Rounds, E., A combined non-parametric approach to feature selection and binary decision tree design, Pattern Recognition 12, 313-317, 1980.

Rudin C., Daubechies I., and Schapire R. E., The Dynamics of Adaboost: Cyclic behavior and convergence of margins, Journal of Machine Learning Research Vol. 5, 1557-1595, 2004.

Rumelhart, D., G. Hinton and R. Williams, Learning internal representations through error propagation. In Parallel Distributed Processing: Explorations in the Microstructure of Cognition, Volume 1: Foundations, D. Rumelhart and J. McClelland (eds.) Cambridge, MA: MIT Press., pp 2540, 1986.

Saaty, X., The analytic hierarchy process: A 1993 overview. Central European Journal for Operations Research and Economics, Vol. 2, No. 2, p. 119-137, 1993.

Safavin S. R. and Landgrebe, D., A survey of decision tree classifier methodology. IEEE Trans. on Systems, Man and Cybernetics, 21(3):660-674, 1991.

Sakar A., Mammone R.J., Growing and pruning neural tree networks, IEEE Trans. on Computers 42, 291-299, 1993.

Salzberg. S. L., On Comparing Classifiers: Pitfalls to Avoid and a Recommended Approach. Data Mining and Knowledge Discovery, 1: 312-327, Kluwer Academic Publishers, Bosto, 1997.

Samuel, A., Some studies in machine learning using the game of checkers II: Recent progress. IBM J. Res. Develop., 11:601-617, 1967.

Schaffer, C., When does overfitting decrease prediction accuracy in induced decision trees and rule sets? In Proceedings of the European Working Session on Learning (EWSL-91), pp. 192-205, Berlin, 1991.

Schaffer, C., Selecting a classification method by cross-validation. Machine Learning 13(1):135-143, 1993.

Schaffer J., A Conservation Law for Generalization Performance. In Proceedings of the 11th International Conference on Machine Learning: pp. 259-265, 1993.

Schapire, R.E., *The Strength of Weak Learnability*. Machine learning 5(2), 197-227, 1990.

Schapire, R. E. (1997). Using output codes to boost multiclass learning problems. Proc. 14th Intl Conf. Machine Learning (pp. 313321). Nashville, TN, USA.

Schapire, R.E., Freund, Y., Bartlett, P. and Lee, W.S., 1998. Boosting the margin: A new explanation for the effectiveness of voting methods. The annals of statistics, 26(5), pp.1651-1686

Schclar A., Rokach L.: Random Projection Ensemble Classifiers. ICEIS 2009: 309–316.

Schclar A., Rokach L., A. Meisels, Ensemble Methods for Improving the Performance of Neighborhood-based Collaborative Filtering, Proc. ACM RecSys 2009 (to appear).

Schlimmer, J. C. , Efficiently inducing determinations: A complete and systematic search algorithm that uses optimal pruning. In Proceedings of the 1993 International Conference on Machine Learning: pp 284-290, San Mateo, CA, Morgan Kaufmann, 1993.

Schmitt , M., On the complexity of computing and learning with multiplicative neural networks, Neural Computation 14: 2, 241-301, 2002.

Seewald, A. K., Exploring the Parameter State Space of Stacking. In: Proc. of the 2002 IEEE Int. Conf. on Data Mining, pp. 685–688, 2002A.

Seewald A.K., How to Make Stacking Better and Faster While Also Taking Care of an Unknown Weakness. In: Nineteenth International Conference on Machine Learning, 554–561, 2002B.

Seewald A.K., Towards Understanding Stacking. PhD Thesis, Vienna University of Technology, 2003.

Seewald, A.K. and Fürnkranz, J., Grading classifiers, Austrian research institute for Artificial intelligence, 2001.

Selfridge, O. G. Pandemonium: a paradigm for learning. In Mechanization of Thought Processes: Proceedings of a Symposium Held at the National Physical Laboratory, November, 1958, 513-526. London: H.M.S.O., 1958.

Selim, S. Z. AND Al-Sultan, K. 1991. A simulated annealing algorithm for the clustering problem. Pattern Recogn. 24, 10 (1991), 10031008.

Selim, S.Z., and Ismail, M.A. K-means-type algorithms: a generalized convergence theorem and characterization of local optimality. In IEEE transactions on pattern analysis and machine learning, vol. PAMI-6, no. 1, January, 1984.

Servedio, R., On Learning Monotone DNF under Product Distributions. Information and Computation 193, pp. 57-74, 2004.

Sethi, K., and Yoo, J. H., Design of multicategory, multifeature split decision trees using perceptron learning. Pattern Recognition, 27(7):939-947, 1994.

Sexton J., Laake P., LogitBoost with errors-in-variables, Computational Statistics and Data Analysis 52 (2008) 2549-2559

Shafer, J. C., Agrawal, R. and Mehta, M. , SPRINT: A Scalable Parallel Classifier for Data Mining, Proc. 22nd Int. Conf. Very Large Databases, T. M. Vijayaraman and Alejandro P. Buchmann and C. Mohan and Nandlal L. Sarda (eds), 544-555, Morgan Kaufmann, 1996.

Shapiro, A. D. and Niblett, T., Automatic induction of classification rules for a chess endgame, in M. R. B. Clarke, ed., Advances in Computer Chess 3, Pergamon, Oxford, pp. 73-92, 1982.

Shapiro, A. D., Structured induction in expert systems, Turing Institute Press in association with Addison-Wesley Publishing Company, 1987.

Sharkey A., Sharkey N., Combining diverse neural networks, The Knowledge Engineering Review 12(3): 231–247, 1997.

Sharkey, A., On combining artificial neural nets, Connection Science, Vol. 8, pp.299-313, 1996.

Sharkey, A., Multi-Net Iystems, In Sharkey A. (Ed.) Combining Artificial Neural Networks: Ensemble and Modular Multi-Net Systems. pp. 1-30, Springer-Verlag, 1999.

Shen, L., Tan, E.C., (2005), Seeking better output-codes with genetic algorithm for multiclass cancer classification. Submitted to Bioinformatics.

Shilen, S., Multiple binary tree classifiers. Pattern Recognition 23(7): 757-763, 1990.

Shilen, S., Nonparametric classification using matched binary decision trees. Pattern Recognition Letters 13: 83-87, 1992.

Simn, M.D.J., Pulido, J.A.G., Rodrguez, M.A.V., (2006), Prez, J.M.S., Criado, J.M.G., A genetic algorithm to design error correcting codes. In: Proceedings of the 13th IEEE Mediterranean Eletrotechnical Conference 2006, IEEE Computer Society Press 807–810.

Sivalingam D., Pandian N., Ben-Arie J., Minimal Classification Method With

Error-Correcting Codes For Multiclass Recognition, International Journal of Pattern Recognition and Artificial Intelligence 19(5): 663 - 680, 2005.

Sklansky, J. and Wassel, G. N., Pattern classifiers and trainable machines. SpringerVerlag, New York, 1981.

Skurichina M. and Duin R.P.W., Bagging, boosting and the random subspace method for linear classifiers. Pattern Analysis and Applications, 5(2):121–135, 2002

Sloane N.J.A. (2007) A library of orthogonal arrays.

Smyth, P. and Goodman, R. (1991). *Rule induction using information theory.* Knowledge Discovery in Databases, AAAI/MIT Press.

Sneath, P., and Sokal, R. Numerical Taxonomy. W.H. Freeman Co., San Francisco, CA, 1973.

Snedecor, G. and Cochran, W. (1989). *Statistical Methods.* owa State University Press, Ames, IA, 8th Edition.

Sohn S. Y., Choi, H., Ensemble based on Data Envelopment Analysis, ECML Meta Learning workshop, Sep. 4, 2001.

Sohna S.Y., Shinb H.W., Experimental study for thecomparison of classifier combination methods, Pattern Recognition40 (2007) 33–40.

van Someren M.,Torres C. and Verdenius F. (1997): *A systematic Description of Greedy Optimisation Algorithms for Cost Sensitive Generalization.* X. Liu, P.Cohen, M. Berthold (Eds.): "Advance in Intelligent Data Analysis" (IDA-97) LNCS 1280, pp. 247-257.

Sonquist, J. A., Baker E. L., and Morgan, J. N., Searching for Structure. Institute for Social Research, Univ. of Michigan, Ann Arbor, MI, 1971.

Spirtes, P., Glymour C., and Scheines, R., Causation, Prediction, and Search. Springer Verlag, 1993.

Srivastava, N., Hinton, G. E., Krizhevsky, A., Sutskever, I., Salakhutdinov, R. (2014). Dropout: A simple way to prevent neural networks from overfitting. Journal of Machine Learning Research, 15(1), 19291958.

Statnikov, A., Aliferis, C.F., Tsamardinos, I., (2005), Hardin, D., Levy, S., A comprehensive evaluation of multicategory methods for microarray gene expression cancer diagnosis. Bioinformatics **21**(5) 631–643.

Steuer R.E.,Multiple Criteria Optimization: Theory, Computation and Application. John Wiley, New York, 1986.

Strehl A. and Ghosh J., Clustering Guidance and Quality Evaluation Using Relationship-based Visualization, Proceedings of Intelligent Engineering Systems Through Artificial Neural Networks, 5-8 November 2000, St. Louis, Missouri, USA, pp 483-488.

Strehl, A., Ghosh, J., Mooney, R.: Impact of similarity measures on web-page clustering. In Proc. AAAI Workshop on AI for Web Search, pp 58–64, 2000.

Sun Y., Todorovic S., Li J., Wu D., Unifying the Error-Correcting and Output-Code AdaBoost within the Margin Framework, Proceedings of the 22nd international conference on Machine learning (2005), pp. 872-879.

Sun Y., Todorovic S., Li L. Reducing The Overfitting Of Adaboost By Controlling Its Data Distribution Skewness, International Journal of Pattern Recognition and Artificial Intelligence, 20(7):1093-1116, 2006.

K.M. Svore, C.J. Burges, Large-scale learning to rank using boosted decision trees, Scaling Up Machine Learning, Cambridge U. Press (2011)

Tadepalli, P. and Russell, S., Learning from examples and membership queries with structured determinations, Machine Learning, 32(3), pp. 245-295, 1998.

Tan A. C., Gilbert D., Deville Y., Multi-class Protein Fold Classification using a New Ensemble Machine Learning Approach. Genome Informatics, 14:206–217, 2003.

Tang E. K., Suganthan P. N., Yao X., An analysis of diversity measures, Machine Learning (2006) 65:247271

Tani T. and Sakoda M., Fuzzy modeling by ID3 algorithm and its application to prediction of heater outlet temperature, Proc. IEEE Internat. Conf. on Fuzzy Systems, March 1992, pp. 923-930.

Dacheng Tao and Xiaoou Tang, SVM-based Relevance Feedback Using Random Subspace Method, IEEE International Conference on Multimedia and Expo, pp. 647-652, 2004

Dacheng Tao, Xiaoou Tang, Xuelong Li, and Xindong Wu, Asymmetric Bagging and Random Subspace for Support Vector Machines-based Relevance Feedback in Image Retrieval, IEEE Transactions on Pattern Analysis and Machine Intelligence, vol. 28, no.7, pp. 1088-1099, July 2006

Dacheng Tao, Xuelong Li, and Stephen J. Maybank, Negative Samples Analysis in Relevance Feedback, IEEE Transactions on Knowledge and Data Engineering, vol. 19, no. 4, pp. 568-580, April 2007.

Tapia, E., González, J.C., García-Villalba, J., Villena, J., (2001), Recursive adaptive ECOC models. In: Proceedings of the 10th Portuguese Conference on Artificial Intelligence. Volume 2258 of Lecture Notes in Artificial Intelligence., Springer-Verlag 96–103.

Tapia, E., González, J.C., García-Villalba, J., (2003), Good error correcting output codes for adaptive multiclass learning. In: Proceedings of the 4th International Workshop on Multiple Classifier Systems 2003. Volume 2709 of Lecture Notes in Computer Science., Springer-Verlag 156–165.

Taylor P. C., and Silverman, B. W., Block diagrams and splitting criteria for classification trees. Statistics and Computing, 3(4):147-161, 1993.

Therneau, T. M., and Atkinson, E. J., An Introduction to Recursive Partitioning Using the RPart Routine, Technical Report 61, Section of Biostatistics, Mayo Clinic, Rochester, 1997.

Tibshirani, R., Walther, G. and Hastie, T. (2000). Estimating the number of clusters in a dataset via the gap statistic. Tech. Rep. 208, Dept. of Statistics, Stanford University.

Ting K.M. and Witten I.H. (1999), Issues in stacked generalization, J. Artif. Intell. Res. 10: 271289, 1999.

Towell, G. Shavlik, J., Knowledge-based artificial neural networks, Artificial Intelligence, 70: 119-165, 1994.

Tresp, V. and Taniguchi, M. Combining estimators using non-constant weighting functions. In Tesauro, G., Touretzky, D., & Leen, T. (Eds.), Advances in Neural Information Processing Systems, volume 7: pp. 419-426, The MIT

Press, 1995.

Tsallis C., Possible Generalization of Boltzmann-Gibbs Statistics, J. Stat.Phys., 52, 479-487, 1988.

Tsao, C.A., Chang, Y.I., 2007. A stochastic approximation view of boosting. Comput. Stat. Data Anal. 52 (1), 325-344.

Tsoumakas G., Partalas I., Vlahavas I., A Taxonomy and Short Review of Ensemble Selection, Proc. Workshop on Supervised and Unsupervised Ensemble Methods, ECAI, Patras, Greece, 2008.

Tsymbal A., and Puuronen S., Ensemble Feature Selection with the Simple Bayesian Classification in Medical Diagnostics, In: Proc. 15thIEEE Symp. on Computer-Based Medical Systems CBMS2002, Maribor, Slovenia,IEEE CS Press, 2002, pp. 225-230.

Tsymbal A., and Puuronen S., and D. Patterson, Feature Selection for Ensembles of Simple Bayesian Classifiers,In: Foundations of Intelligent Systems: ISMIS2002, LNAI, Vol. 2366, Springer, 2002, pp. 592-600

Tsymbal A., Pechenizkiy M., Cunningham P., Diversity in search strategies for ensemble feature selection. Information Fusion 6(1): 83-98, 2005.

Tukey J.W., Exploratory data analysis, Addison-Wesley, Reading, Mass, 1977.

Tumer, K. and Ghosh J., Error Correlation and Error Reduction in Ensemble Classifiers, Connection Science, Special issue on combining artificial neural networks: ensemble approaches, 8 (3-4): 385-404, 1996.

Tumer, K., and Ghosh J., Linear and Order Statistics Combiners for Pattern Classification, in Combining Articial Neural Nets, A. Sharkey (Ed.), pp. 127-162, Springer-Verlag, 1999.

Tumer, K., and Ghosh J., Robust Order Statistics based Ensembles for Distributed Data Mining. In Kargupta, H. and Chan P., eds, Advances in Distributed and Parallel Knowledge Discovery , pp. 185-210, AAAI/MIT Press, 2000.

K. Tumer, C. N. Oza, Input decimated ensembles. Pattern Analysis and Application 6 (2003) 65-77.

Turney P. (1995): *Cost-Sensitive Classification: Empirical Evaluation of Hybrid Genetic Decision Tree Induction Algorithm.* Journal of Artificial Intelligence Research 2, pp. 369-409.

Turney P. (2000): *Types of Cost in Inductive Concept Learning.* Workshop on Cost Sensitive Learning at the 17th ICML, Stanford, CA.

Tutz, G., Binder, H., 2006. Boosting ridge regression. Computational Statistics and Data Analysis. Corrected Proof, Available online 22 December 2006, in press.

Tuv, E. and Torkkola, K., Feature filtering with ensembles using artificial contrasts. In *Proceedings of the SIAM 2005 Int. Workshop on Feature Selection for Data Mining*, Newport Beach, CA, 69-71, 2005.

Tyron R. C. and Bailey D.E. Cluster Analysis. McGraw-Hill, 1970.

Urquhart, R. Graph-theoretical clustering, based on limited neighborhood sets. Pattern recognition, vol. 15, pp. 173-187, 1982.

Utgoff, P. E., and Clouse, J. A., A Kolmogorov-Smirnoff Metric for Decision Tree Induction, Technical Report 96-3, University of Massachusetts, Department of Computer Science, Amherst, MA, 1996.

Utgoff, P. E., Perceptron trees: A case study in hybrid concept representations. Connection Science, 1(4):377-391, 1989.

Utgoff, P. E., Incremental induction of decision trees. Machine Learning, 4:161-186, 1989.

Utgoff, P. E., Decision tree induction based on efficient tree restructuring, Machine Learning 29 (1):5-44, 1997.

Vafaie, H. and De Jong, K. (1995). Genetic algorithms as a tool for restructuring feature space representations. In *Proceedings of the International Conference on Tools with A. I.* IEEE Computer Society Press.

Valentini G. and Masulli F., Ensembles of learning machines. In R. Tagliaferri andM. Marinaro, editors, Neural Nets, WIRN, Vol. 2486 of Lecture Notes in ComputerScience, Springer, 2002, pp. 3-19.

Valiant, L. G. (1984). A theory of the learnable. Communications of the ACM 1984, pp. 1134-1142.

Van Assche, A., Blockeel, H. (2007). Seeing the forest through the trees: Learning a comprehensible model from an ensemble. In ECML (Vol. 7, pp. 418429). Heidelberg: Springer.

Van Rijsbergen, C. J., Information Retrieval. Butterworth, ISBN 0-408-70929-4, 1979.

Van Zant, P., Microchip fabrication: a practical guide to semiconductor processing, New York: McGraw-Hill, 1997.

Vandewiele, G., Janssens, O., Ongenae, F., De Turck, F. and Van Hoecke, S., 2016. GENESIM: genetic extraction of a single, interpretable model. In NIPS2016, the 30th Conference on Neural Information Processing Systems, pp. 1-6. 2016.

Vapnik, V.N., The Nature of Statistical Learning Theory. Springer-Verlag, New York, 1995.

Verikas A., Gelzinis A., Bacauskiene M. (2011), Mining data with random forests: A survey and results of new tests, Pattern Recognition 44 , 330 - 349.

Veyssieres, M.P. and Plant, R.E. Identification of vegetation state-and-transition domains in California's hardwood rangelands. University of California, 1998.

Vilalta R., Giraud–Carrier C., Brazdil P., "Meta-Learning", in O. Maimon and L. Rokach (Eds.), Handbook of Data Mining and Knowledge Discovery in Databases, pp. 731-748, Springer, 2005.

Villalba Santiago D., Rodrguez Juan J., Alonso Carlos J., An Empirical Comparison of Boosting Methods via OAIDTB, an Extensible Java Class Library, In II International Workshop on Practical Applications of Agents and Multiagent Systems - IWPAAMS'2003.

Wallace C. S. and Dowe D. L., Intrinsic classification by mml – the snob program. In Proceedings of the 7th Australian Joint Conference on Artificial Intelligence, pages 37-44, 1994.

Wallace, C. S., and Patrick J., Coding decision trees, Machine Learning 11: 7-22, 1993.

Wallace, C. S., MML Inference of Predictive Trees, Graphs and Nets. In A. Gammerman (ed), Computational Learning and Probabilistic Reasoning, pp 43-66, Wiley, 1996.

Wallet, B.C., Marchette, D.J., Solka, J.L., (1996), A matrix representation for genetic algorithms. In: Automatic object recognition VI, Proceedings of the International Society for Optical Engineering. 206–214.

Wallis, J.L., Houghten, S.K., (2002), A comparative study of search techniques applied to the minimum distance problem of BCH codes. Technical Report CS-02-08, Department of Computer Science, Brock University.

Walsh P., Cunningham P., Rothenberg S., O'Doherty S., Hoey H., Healy R., An artificial neural network ensemble to predict disposition and length of stay in children presenting with bronchiolitis. European Journal of Emergency Medicine. 11(5):259-264, 2004.

Wan, W. and Perkowski, M. A., A new approach to the decomposition of incompletely specified functions based on graph-coloring and local transformations and its application to FPGAmapping, In Proc. of the IEEE EURO-DAC '92, pp. 230-235, 1992.

Wanas Nayer M., Dara Rozita A. , Kamel Mohamed S., Adaptivefusion and cooperative training for classifier ensembles, PatternRecognition 39 (2006) 1781 - 1794

Wang, X. and Yu, Q. Estimate the number of clusters in web documents via gap statistic. May 2001.

Wang W., Jones P., Partridge D., Diversity between neural networks and decision trees for building multiple classifier systems, in: Proc. Int. Workshop on Multiple Classifier Systems (LNCS 1857), Springer, Calgiari, Italy, 2000, pp. 240–249.

Ward, J. H. Hierarchical grouping to optimize an objective function. Journal of the American Statistical Association, 58:236-244, 1963.

Warshall S., A theorem on Boolean matrices, Journal of the ACM 9, 1112, 1962.

Webb G., and Zheng Z., Multistrategy Ensemble Learning: Reducing Error by Combining Ensemble Learning Techniques. IEEE Transactions on Knowledge and Data Engineering, 16 No. 8:980-991, 2004.

Webb G., MultiBoosting: A technique for combining boosting and wagging. Machine Learning, 40(2): 159-196, 2000.

Weigend, A. S., Mangeas, M., and Srivastava, A. N. Nonlinear gated experts for time-series - discovering regimes and avoiding overfitting. International Journal of Neural Systems 6(5):373-399, 1995.

Wen, G., Hou, Z., Li, H., Li, D., Jiang, L., and Xun, E. (2017). Ensemble of deep neural networks with probability-based fusion for facial expression recognition. Cognitive Computation, 9, 114.

J. Weston and C. Watkins. Support vector machines for multi-class pattern recognition. In M. Verleysen (ed.) Proceedings of the 7th European Symposium on Artificial Neural Networks (ESANN-99), pp. 219224, Bruges, Belgium, 1999.

Widmer, G. and Kubat, M., 1996, Learning in the Presence of Concept Drift and Hidden Contexts, Machine Learning 23(1), pp. 69101.

Windeatt T. and Ardeshir G., An Empirical Comparison of Pruning Methods for

Ensemble Classifiers, IDA2001, LNCS 2189, pp. 208-217, 2001.

Windeatt, T., Ghaderi, R., (2003), Coding and decoding strategies for multi-class learning problems. Information Fusion 4(1) 11–21.

Wolf L., Shashua A., Feature Selection for Unsupervised and Supervised Inference: The Emergence of Sparsity in a Weight-Based Approach, Journal of Machine Learning Research, Vol 6, pp. 1855-1887, 2005.

Wolpert, D., Macready, W. 1996. Combining Stacking with Bagging to Improve a Learning Algorithm. Santa Fe Institute Technical Report 96-03-123.

Wolpert, D.H., Stacked Generalization, Neural Networks, Vol. 5, pp. 241-259, Pergamon Press, 1992.

Wolpert, D. H., The relationship between PAC, the statistical physics framework, the Bayesian framework, and the VC framework. In D. H. Wolpert, editor, The Mathematics of Generalization, The SFI Studies in the Sciences of Complexity, pages 117-214. AddisonWesley, 1995.

Wolpert, D. H., "The lack of a priori distinctions between learning algorithms," Neural Computation 8: 1341–1390, 1996.

Wolpert, D. H., "The supervised learning no-free-lunch theorems", Proceedings of the 6th Online World Conference on Soft Computing in Industrial Applications, 2001.

Woods K., Kegelmeyer W., Bowyer K., Combination of multiple classifiers using local accuracy estimates, IEEE Transactions on Pattern Analysis and Machine Intelligence 19:405–410, 1997.

Wozniak, M., Grana, M., Corchado, E. (2014). A survey of multiple classifier systems as hybrid systems. Information Fusion, 16, 3-17.

Q. X. Wu , D. Bell and M. McGinnity, Multi-knowledge for decision making, Knowledge and Information Systems, 7(2005): 246-266

Wyse, N., Dubes, R. and Jain, A.K., A critical evaluation of intrinsic dimensionality algorithms, Pattern Recognition in Practice, E.S. Gelsema and L.N. Kanal (eds.), North-Holland, pp. 415–425, 1980.

F. Xia, W. Zhang, F. Li, Y. Yang, Ranking with decision tree, Knowl. Inform. Syst., 17 (3) (2008), pp. 381-395

Xu L., Krzyzak A., Suen C.Y., Methods of combining multiple classifiers and their application to handwriting recognition, IEEE Trans. SMC 22, 418-435, 1992

Yanim S., Kamel Mohamad S., Wong Andrew K.C., Wang Yang (2007). Cost-sensitive boosting for classification of imbalanced data. Pattern Recognition (40): 3358-3378

Yates W., Partridge D., Use of methodological diversity to improve neural network generalization,Neural Computing and Applications 4 (2) (1996) 114-128.

Ye J., Chow J.H., Chen J., Zheng Z., Stochastic gradient boosted distributed decision trees, in: Proceedings of the 18th ACM Conference on Information and Knowledge Management, 2009, pp. 20612064.

Yuan Y., Shaw M., Induction of fuzzy decision trees, Fuzzy Sets and Systems 69(1995):125-139.

Zadrozny B. and Elkan C. (2001): *Learning and Making Decisions When Costs and Probabilities are Both Unknown.* In Proceedings of the Seventh International Conference on Knowledge Discovery and Data Mining (KDD'01).

Zahn, C. T., Graph-theoretical methods for detecting and describing gestalt clusters. IEEE trans. Comput. C-20 (Apr.), 68-86, 1971.

Zaki, M. J., Ho C. T., Eds., Large- Scale Parallel Data Mining. New York: Springer- Verlag, 2000.

Zaki, M. J., Ho C. T., and Agrawal, R., Scalable parallel classification for data mining on shared- memory multiprocessors, in Proc. IEEE Int. Conf. Data Eng., Sydney, Australia, WKDD99, pp. 198– 205, 1999.

Zantema, H., and Bodlaender H. L., Finding Small Equivalent Decision Trees is Hard, International Journal of Foundations of Computer Science, 11(2):343-354, 2000.

Zeileis, A. Hothorn, T. and Hornik, K., Model-Based Recursive Partitioning, Journal of Computational and Graphical Statistics, 17(2):492–514, 2008.

Zeira, G., Maimon, O., Last, M. and Rokach, L,, Change detection in classification models of data mining, Data Mining in Time Series Databases. World Scientific Publishing, 2003.

Zenobi, G., and Cunningham, P. Using diversity in preparing ensembles of classifiers based on different feature subsets to minimize generalization error. In Proceedings of the European Conference on Machine Learning, 2001.

Zhang, C.X., Zhang, J.S. (2008), RotBoost: A technique for combining Rotation Forest and AdaBoost, Pattern Recognition Letters, Volume 29, pages 1524-1536.

Zhang, C.X., Zhang, J.S., 2008. A local boosting algorithm for solving classification problems. Comput. Stat. Data Anal. 52 (4), 1928-1941.

Zhang, A., Wu, Z.L., Li, C.H., Fang, K.T., (2003), On hadamard-type output coding in multiclass learning. In: Proceedings of IDEAL. Volume 2690 of Lecture Notes in Computer Science., Springer-Verlag 397–404.

Zhang, C.X., Zhang, J.S., Zhang G. Y., An efficient modified boosting method for solving classification problems , Journal of Computational and Applied Mathematics 214 (2008) 381 - 392

Zhang, C.X., Zhang, J.S., Zhang G. Y., Using Boosting to prune Double-Bagging ensembles. Computational Statistics and Data Analysis, 53(4):1218-1231

Zhou Z., Chen C., Hybrid decision tree, Knowledge-Based Systems 15, 515-528, 2002.

Zhou, Z. H., Feng, J. (2017). Deep forest: Towards an alternative to deep neural networks. arXiv preprint arXiv:170208835.

Zhou Z., Jiang Y., NeC4.5: Neural Ensemble Based C4.5, IEEE Transactions on Knowledge and Data Engineering, vol. 16, no. 6, pp. 770-773, Jun., 2004.

Zhou Z. H., and Tang, W., Selective Ensemble of Decision Trees, in Guoyin Wang, Qing Liu, Yiyu Yao, Andrzej Skowron (Eds.): Rough Sets, Fuzzy Sets, Data Mining, and Granular Computing, 9th International Conference, RSFDGrC, Chongqing, China, Proceedings. Lecture Notes in Computer Science 2639, pp.476-483, 2003.

Zhou, Z. H., Wu J., Tang W., Ensembling neural networks: many could be better than all. Artificial Intelligence 137: 239-263, 2002.

Zhoua J., Pengb H., Suenc C., Data-driven decomposition formulti-class classification, Pattern Recognition 41: 67 - 76, 2008.

Zimmermann H. J., Fuzzy Set Theory and its Applications, Springer, 4th edition, 2005.

Zitzler, E., Laumanns, M., Thiele, L., (2002), SPEA2: Improving the strength pareto evolutionary algorithm. In: Evolutionary Methods for Design, Optimisation, and Control, CIMNE, Barcelona, Spain. 95–100.

Zitzler, E., Laumanns, M., Bleuler, S., (2004), A tutorial on evolutionary multiobjective optimization. In Gandibleux, X., Sevaux, M., Srensen, K., T'kindt, V., eds.: Metaheuristics for Multiobjective Optimisation. Volume 535 of Lecture Notes in Economics and Mathematical Systems., Springer-Verlag 3–37.

Zupan, B., Bohanec, M., Demsar J., and Bratko, I., Feature transformation by function decomposition, IEEE intelligent systems & their applications, 13: 38-43, 1998.

Index

Printed in the United States
By Bookmasters